WOMEN
MBAS

A Foot in the Door

G. K. Hall

WOMEN'S STUDIES

Publications

Barbara Haber
Editor

WOMEN MBAs

A Foot in the Door

MARY DINGEE FILLMORE

G.K. Hall & Co.

Boston
1987

Library of Congress Cataloging-in-Publication Data

Fillmore, Mary Dingee.
  Women MBAs.

  Bibliography: p. 217
  1. Women executives—United States.   2. Women in
business—United States.   3. Sex discrimination in
employment—United States.   I. Title.
HD6054.4.U6F54   1987   331.4′816584′00973   86–32002
ISBN 0–8161–8728–2

This publication is printed on permanent/durable acid-free paper
MANUFACTURED IN THE UNITED STATES OF AMERICA

Contents

The Author

Mary Dingee Fillmore has helped hundreds of women in the United States and England evaluate their careers and make plans to change them. Through her consulting practice in organizational development and training, Ms. Fillmore has conducted workshops on many aspects of career development—including "Preparing to Manage" for women just below the management level, and "Should I Get an MBA?" for undergraduate women and career changers. She has facilitated the development of networks and mentoring systems for top women in organizations, as well as for secretaries and other professional employees. Prior to establishing her own business, Ms. Fillmore recruited and counselled women managers as director of the affirmative action program for the 6,000 women employed by the U.S. Environmental Protection Agency.

Preface

The MBA gives you a chance to play Cinderella, to change who you are.

A male manager

I don't know if anybody should get an MBA at this point in a shrinking market. I would advise them to be a plumber instead of going to business school.

A black woman MBA, now a high school teacher

It is as close as you can come to the MBA success story: she attended a top school, then slid comfortably into the career she had always wanted in publishing. Her job is demanding and rewarding; she loves it, and believes she has a good shot at moving up. It is easy to see why: she is funny, tough, smart. We are talking at her business school's club, complete with classic wooden panelling, leather chairs, and even the relics of big game hunts. After interviewing dozens of women, finally I think I have found someone who fits the popular image of Ms. MBA. Then she tells me. She was hired at $6,000 less than a classmate who was her twin in every qualification but one: sex. Several years later, the salary disparity between them is still there, and it still makes her angry.

What actually happened to the women who have been streaming out of business schools for the last ten years? Was it worth it? Were the claims for the MBA fulfilled? Did the degree turn schoolteachers and French literature majors into executives? Do male managers see an MBA graduate when they look at a woman, or is she still a female first?

A woman who is trying to decide whether to get an MBA or to plan her career once she has it has very little information to go on. On the one hand, she hears that there is a glut, that the degree has become so devalued that it is worthless. On the other, she knows how hard it is to find a well-paid job with good prospects, especially if she has other strikes against her, such as race, age, or disability. If she earns an MBA, she may at least have a chance at a better job, even if she never becomes an executive for a Fortune 500 company. At the same time, business school consumes an inordinate amount of time, energy (especially if the student is employed), and money. Those resources might well be devoted more constructively in a completely different direction: taking a short course in entrepreneurship, launching a job hunt or career move, or taking on a new project at work. What should she do?

Women who already have the degree also have important strategic decisions to make: about planning their careers to make the MBA work for them; choosing employers wisely; and establishing networks for support, action, and information. They also face contradictory signals: while they are told that women are moving up and it is only a matter of time before senior management is half female, the actual numbers of women at the top are tiny. Although it is claimed that they have equal opportunities, there is now little pressure to hire and promote women through affirmative action programs. Recent MBA graduates often like their entry-level jobs, but many feel stymied if they reach the middle level.

This book describes the experiences of a broad spectrum of women MBAs at different stages: deciding to get the degree, attending business school, looking for work, coping with the conventional workplace, and (for some) setting up a business of their own. By reading about the range of women's experiences, the reader will be able to decide for herself whether the MBA would be appropriate for her or, if she already has a degree, what she needs to know to make the best use of it in her career.

Some of the women who talked with me have achieved what they wanted with the MBA, but others saw little or no change in their careers. There are no formulas here to guarantee that a woman will make a "right" decision about the degree, devise a foolproof career strategy, or reach top management. What the reader can do is avoid some pitfalls and develop some creative tactics on the basis of women MBAs' experiences, and the broad trends affecting all women in the workplace.

Acknowledgments

Acknowledgments are a particular torture to an author. Better writers than I have already failed, time and again, to make them anything but formulaic and boring. Moreover, as a feminist I am acutely aware that what I think and write is not an individual woman's accomplishment but rather a complex product of many influences and collaborations. To talk about everyone who has been important to this book would be a volume in itself.

Nonetheless, many women and a few men had a direct hand in making *A Foot in the Door*. The most important of these was Barbara Haber, my editor, who first suggested, to my alternating horror and delight, that I write a book related to women in business. Her painstaking but never picky or tyrannical care for the manuscript was a model of friendship as well as craft. Although she once scrawled in the margin, "This sentence stinks. Fix it," on the whole she was most sensitive to an author's tenderest feelings.

My other major debt is to the women I interviewed, both MBAs and others, who were willing to talk with a complete stranger about their lives and work. They were thoughtful and generous; a number invited me home, and have kept in touch with me as this book has progressed. As I traveled around the country to talk with them, my friends put me up, fed me, drove me to buses in distant places at dawn, listened to my lamentations and triumphs, and found more women for me to interview. They made it tolerable to be on the road for months. My mother and my English friends made the writing process possible by providing space and peace when I needed it.

Almost everyone I know became involved in the book one way and another, reading a chapter here and there or taking me out for lunch to talk it over. The following did substantially more, providing invaluable criticism, ideas, and support:

Janet Stone disentangled one of the worst pieces of writing I have ever done, and made it make sense.

Roslyn Feldberg made me write ten pages a day when I didn't want to.

Marian Sandmaier convinced me that women would talk with me if I asked good questions and waited for the answers.

Tina Graf kept me honest, since she is a dear friend who went to business school, and I knew the book had to ring true to her.

Jane Baluss read it all when she was supposed to be on vacation.

Norma Swenson distracted me when I reached the inevitable point of needing to put the work down, as did Kyra Zola Norsigian and Sarah Berman Feldberg at critical moments when the manuscript might otherwise have perished.

Judy Norsigian told me she thought a chapter I liked was fine, even if all the other reviewers said it needed more work.

Irv Zola told me I had written a good book when I didn't know anymore.

All my work on women's employment is thanks to my mentor, Mae Morris-Chatman, who convinced me that I could do it and showed me how.

While I can't mention everyone here, my friends and colleagues know that they make my life and work possible, and often fun as well. Whatever use this book has for women generally, I hope the many people who contributed to it and me will feel that it reflects well on their efforts.

One

A Foot in the Door?

This book is the result of a tiny clipping tucked into the mounds of my in-basket in 1980. It said that women MBAs from one of the two top schools in the country made less money than men with the same degree—an image contrary to the one I had formed. At the time, I was sharing responsibility for a career-development program for about 6000 women employed by one organization. Once talented women were placed in the right spots, we expected the magic of upward mobility to take hold as the quality of their work was recognized.

The clipping suggested that credentials alone were not enough. It reported on Dr. Myra Strober's study of MBAs from the Stanford Graduate School of Business.[1] Although women and men might start at the same level, there was an ever-widening gap between them as the years passed. I read the full study, hoping to find an explanation other than gender, but Dr. Strober had eliminated all the other possibilities.

Her evidence ran counter to the picture I had of women MBAs, and, unfortunately, is in keeping with more recent research. On the basis of careerist women's magazines, self-help books, and the general business press, I thought of the MBA as the foot in the door, the extra edge that would allow women to compete with men as equals. From many sources I had formed an image of Ms. MBA as a young white woman who was already earning an enormous salary and who would make it to the top of the ladder if she only worked hard and played the right games. Before long, she and others like her would be moving steadily up into senior management, and the top floors of corporations would soon be as well integrated as hospital nurseries. In my mind, Ms. MBA always knew exactly what she wanted and she had a plan for achieving it; her personal life was harmonious and streamlined so as not to interfere with her job. She was admired as much for being a perfect wife and mother as for her success in the workplace.

I fantasized that her career was made over in just two years of study: a whole new world of opportunity was open to her and she had a chance to shoot for the top. No matter what Ms. MBA's background was, she could expect an egalitarian workplace where the past restraints on women—overt discrimination, sexual harassment, not being taken seriously—had all disappeared. She would be treated fairly and equally from initial interview to retirement. All she had to do was perform and wait for her rewards.

The Strober study said it was not that simple. Since then, other research on women MBA's has generally come to the same conclusion: there is a gap between the careers of equally qualified female and male MBAs. Important questions lingered in my mind, however, after I analyzed the additional data from the more recent studies. Not only did they usually pertain only to a small minority of women MBAs from elite schools, but they were restricted to responses to questions that can be asked on a form and returned by mail. I was interested in different kinds of data: what a broader range of women themselves thought about their experiences as they decided to go to business school, went through it, and entered the workplace. I especially wanted to know how or if the degree prepared them to cope with the workplace and what career strategies their experience could suggest to other women.

The Interviews

If reading studies of MBAs began to change my image of them, actually sitting down to talk with women across the country dispelled my fantasies completely! I realized that Ms. MBA was a mythical creature. In all, I conducted interviews lasting one to two hours with fifty women MBAs near Philadelphia, Washington, New York, Chicago, and San Francisco. They graduated between 1974 and 1984, about two-thirds of them in 1980 or later. Clearly, since there are half a million MBAs in the United States and increasingly substantial numbers are women, the conclusions drawn here reflect the reality of a diverse but limited sample, rather than a nationwide survey of thousands of women.

Even the settings in which I conducted the interviews belied my expectations. The women chose to talk to me in parks, bars, swanky apartments, modest rowhouses, posh rooftop restaurants, and delicatessens where waitresses yelled at the cook. Their offices were equally diverse: a few were in contemporary skyscrapers with rented modern art on the walls, but others were in open bays with only a few square feet to call their own.

What they all had in common was that they were willing to talk. Most wished that they had had a better idea of other women's experiences before they started on the MBA. In retrospect, many wished they had done something differently, and they all wanted to make it easier for other women to make informed choices.

Making the Decision

First we talked about how the women reached the point of choosing to earn an MBA. A few arrived at business school immediately after college, recognizing that their liberal arts degrees were not going to get them the jobs they wanted. Others, the majority, had experience in the workplace that pushed them to acquire an additional credential. Although one-third had business backgrounds of some kind, most were employed in traditional women's jobs before they went to business school: teacher, nurse, secretary, social worker, flight attendant, personnel officer, and so on. Their academic backgrounds were much more diverse: for example, an art historian eventually became an accountant; a comparative literature major turned to computers in the health care industry; and an anthropologist took up telecommunications. Most of them felt that they were at a dead end without the MBA.

As we talked, I learned more about the context in which each woman had made her decision. Because I wanted them to talk freely about their lives, I promised them that their names would not be used and that any identifying details would be eliminated or changed. (To give the readers the best contact with the women I interviewed, quotation is used extensively. Brackets indicate my own language.) More than half said they were married or living with men, and about half of these had children. Three were black and two were Asian-American. One had a physical disability affecting her mobility. Although there is no reason to expect a smaller percentage of lesbians among MBAs than in any other group, only one woman identified herself as such.

I asked each one about how she went about making the decision: for some, it was a careful process that drew on research and opinions from many sources; for most, it was less deliberate. One woman followed up on a less than auspicious moment:

> There were four of us, three art majors and an English major, sitting around one night lamenting our fate. We decided that what we really needed to do was go to business school. We were all not pleased with what we were doing, and somehow, without ever looking into it, those three letters were being billed out there as a key . . . . There was not a lot of reading catalogs and books and making a conscious decision.

Surviving Business School

Once they arrived at business school, women's experiences were as varied as their backgrounds. About two-thirds of all MBAs go part time, using a remarkable array of formats. I talked with women who spent literally years of evenings at graduate school while working forty to sixty hours a week. Others gave up their jobs, borrowed huge sums of money, and threw themselves into full-time programs. They juggled the many parts of their lives in countless ways, enlisting some help from others but often struggling on their own.

While business school was traumatic at first for almost all of the women, they did develop ways to survive, not only on their own but in networks and study groups. They learned much about how to get the best from the situation and were eager to pass that knowledge on. Some were stimulated and enjoyed school thoroughly, while others said that wild horses could not drag them back.

The Schools

There was little correspondence between women's opinions of the programs and the reputations of the schools involved. In this book, the top twenty or so schools are referred to as Goldmine, since they are marketed that way and represent riches to many people. That category covers everything from highly pressured and structured settings to much more informal schools. While I want to protect the anonymity of the women I interviewed, it is important to give the reader an indication of which women went to the most highly rated schools.

Distinctions could certainly also be made among the less prestigious institutions; the most obvious is between accredited and unaccredited programs. About half of the women I interviewed went to schools other than the top rated, but only a few graduated from institutions whose faculty and courses did not meet the accreditation standards of the American Assembly of Collegiate Schools of Business. By and large, the unaccredited programs are unlikely to grant degrees that will be helpful, except under very specialized circumstances (such as sponsorship by an employer with whom one plans a lifetime career).

Even among the accredited non-Goldmine schools, there is an enormous range from, for example, a public university well respected in its state's business community, to a private program that draws on a particular market, such as government employees, and is really useful only to them. What these schools have in common is primarily that they are neither Goldmine institutions nor the more obvious fast-buck operations. A number of the women I interviewed felt that one either went to a Goldmine school or somewhere else, and it did not much matter where, aside from the obvious extremes. Many observers feel that the gulf between Goldmine and all the others will only widen in the increasingly competitive market of the next decade. Therefore schools outside this category are referred to here as Generic, since, like generic drugs, they may be identical to brand name products, but are labeled and evaluated differently by MBAs (consumers) and employers (pharmaceutical houses) alike. (In the few cases in which a woman attended an unaccredited program, I have so indicated where it is relevant.)

Looking for Work

All the women I interviewed earned their degrees and most began looking for jobs. A few were in the enviable position of having recruiters come after them, but many had to mount an organized campaign, and they became expert job seekers. Even so, some were dismayed to find themselves back where they started, although they originally hoped the MBA would enable them to advance. Others found just what they wanted or took a job and discovered that it was right for them.

Although there was a time when MBAs automatically worked only for corporations and major financial institutions, the women who talked with me were employed in every sector and type of job. Some had the jobs I had always associated with MBAs; for example, a woman who was responsible for dissecting the tax problems of a huge conglomerate. But others were involved in commercial real estate, hospitals and rehabilitation clinics, universities, publishing, congressional and government offices, and nonprofit advocacy organizations. Some worked for themselves. When I asked them what should be included in this book, at least a dozen immediately asked, "What about a chapter on women starting their own businesses?" Most went on to say that they would love to go off on their own if only they had the money or the courage. Thanks to them, I interviewed some MBAs who had created their own establishments. The majority however, had to adapt to the established workplace rather than set up their own.

Coping with the Workplace

Once MBAs were actually employed, they learned a great deal about evaluating whether an employer offered women real career opportunities. They developed ways to cope with the situation as they found it, not as it was described in Pollyanna-ish magazine articles or self-help books. When one woman's project was about to be discarded because her boss did not have the courage to promote it, she learned to speak up rather than sit back and wait to be recognized. Others had taken it personally when they were excluded from men's lunches that appeared to be social, but were really meant for talking business; in women's networks, some found that they were not alone and that they could develop tactics together.

Evaluating the MBA for Women

Although the MBA did catapult many women into formerly male-dominated occupations, the outcomes were by no means uniform, especially for those who were older or who had to cope with prejudice based on race or physical disability. A number had suffered through periods of unemployment; several became so frustrated in their careers that they abandoned the business world altogether. A few did climb rapidly, but they were the exceptions rather than the rules. Recent graduates who were employed at the entry level were generally delighted to have access to the system, but those who had been in the workplace longer often found their careers stagnating. They were experiencing the same blockage and frustration as many women in more traditional jobs, but at a different level. As one woman put it, the MBA means that you reach a new plateau, but a plateau nevertheless.

Varied as they were, the women I interviewed both created and were caught up in major social trends. The most obvious of these was an enormous, and quite sudden, increase in the sheer numbers of women attending business schools. In 1973 about 1,500 women earned MBAs; a decade later, the annual number was over 15,000.[2] The change was the direct result of legal and political mandates resulting from the civil rights and women's movements. Previously, even the few business schools that were willing to admit women (such as Columbia in the early 1960s) found that they could not recruit them. Not until women could see real career opportunities before them—when discrimination became illegal, and both schools and employers had to allow them in new roles—did their numbers in MBA programs increase. Their absence as executives had often been attributed to barriers within the women themselves, such as fear of success, low desire to achieve, or lack of confidence. As soon as employers and schools began complying with equal opportunity laws, however, women could not fill in their business school applications fast enough.

They registered in such unprecedented numbers that their enrollment swelled by a factor of ten, or 1,000 percent, between 1973 and 1983; in contrast, the number of men increased by a mere 50 percent.[3] The net result is that, while the percentage of women differs greatly among schools, overall about one-third of MBAs graduating annually now are women.[4] Only a tiny fraction are women of color. For example, the Black MBA Association estimates that perhaps 2 percent of MBAs are black. Because of declining financial aid resources, the numbers of black MBAs overall have been falling recently. It is probably reasonable to speculate that less than half are women. Figures are not available for other groups.

The influx of women into MBA programs, accompanied by the smaller rise in numbers of male students, resulted in the creation of 200 new programs (now over 600 in all) in less than a decade.[5] The quality is variable;

only one-third of all programs are accredited as meeting certain minimum standards. Some observers (including some women MBAs I interviewed) say that the degree may not pay off for women who do not attend the most prestigious schools.* Some of the newer programs may go out of business as the baby boom supply of students runs out.

Meanwhile, back in the job market, what has changed? Employers have escalated the credentials required for many entry-level jobs. Positions that once went to bright high school graduates have long since been picked up by persons with bachelor's degrees, then by those with degrees from particular schools. Now certain entry-level jobs go mostly to MBAs, some only to those from prestigious programs. Distinctions have crept in. Once, the three letters alone were the Good Housekeeping Seal of Approval. But typical MBAs now come from another type of school. They are fundamentally different from the stellar Harvard MBAs produced in the 1950s; by 1979 only 15 percent came from the top twenty schools compared to 50 percent just nine years before.[6] There are more MBAs than ever, and no one could argue that the degree has not been diluted. It simply has not had the same punch for women as it had for men who held it ten years earlier.

Even so, the degree has given many women a crack at beginning jobs where females would have been almost unthinkable as recently as 1970. What it has not done is to provide them with opportunities equal to men's or access in any numbers to the upper reaches of management. The same wage gap that has been documented between female and male MBAs has been documented between female and male physicians, compositors & typesetters, bookkeepers, and virtually every other occupation the government counts. To say that women in the aggregate earn less than men in the aggregate does not signify that every man with an MBA automatically succeeds. Far from it.

Table 1.1. *Master's Degrees in Business and Management, by Sex*

	Men	Women	% Women
1959–60	4,645	169	3.5
1965–66	12,806	336	2.6
1969–70	25,506	1,038	3.9
1975–76	37,662	4,958	11.6
1981–82	44,359	17,069	27.8

Source: U.S. Department of Education, *Digest of Education Statistics.*

*See, for example, the discussions in John Byrne's "The High Price of America's MBA Mania: Some MBA Programs are More Equal than Others," in the April 1985 *Management Review* (26–29); or David Clark Scott's "What Is the Worth of an MBA?" in the September 4, 1984 *Christian Science Monitor* (25–26).

Men as well as women must contend with rising numbers of MBAs and, in many settings, decreasing numbers of appropriate positions at the middle and senior levels. Men must compete not only with each other, but with the influx of talented women who form an ever more significant percentage of job applicants. Nonetheless, the trends for women as opposed to those for men are clear. Men do make more money in virtually every field, functional area (such as planning or operations), and geographic locality.[7] A glance at the board of directors or senior management of almost any organization tells why: it is composed almost exclusively of white men, and there are few signs of change in that pattern.

Women MBAs may have made it to the ground floor, but the paucity of women in upper management is striking: there is still only one woman chief executive officer (CEO) in the Fortune 500 companies.[8] Even optimistic observers agree that there is only about one senior woman manager for every five large companies.[9] Income statistics show that women managers and administrators make only sixty-one percent of what men make. In fact, more than eight times as many men as women have more than $50,000 a year in total income, and that figure is distorted by the number of women who are independently wealthy.[10]

In addition to these harsh realities of the marketplace, other developments argue against the MBA for women: the ups and downs in demand resulting from an unstable economy, and increasingly vocal and pointed criticisms of the degree. Yet the women I interviewed had strong reasons for earning an MBA. Only a handful were initially interested in learning what business schools had to teach. What was almost universal was the desire for a credential that would admit them to the sphere of traditionally male jobs. Whether they wanted to go into health care or investment banking, women felt that they probably could not make it into management without the degree.

The MBA was billed as a foot in the door, a golden passport, a key to success. Most of the women were influenced by the same images that had affected me: in two years, a woman could be made over from another indistinguishable liberal arts graduate to a sparklingly employable future CEO, climbing the ladder as far as ability and hard work could take her. Every pressure is on women MBAs to believe that they have undergone just such alchemy. Even as their own experience contradicted the myths of Ms. MBA and the egalitarian workplace, many women continued to interpret their lives using those images. Earlier, they had often attributed career blockage to lack of qualifications rather than to the overt power structure or to the informal "old boys' system" that underlay it. But once they had the degree, that excuse was gone and they had only themselves to blame if something went wrong. Uncomfortable as that feeling was, it was preferable to the unappealing alternative of taking on the whole power structure, especially at a time when affirmative action was, at best, on the wane.

In addition, women MBAs have a strong stake in believing that the system is fair and will treat them well. They have, after all, invested several years of their lives, a lot of time and energy, and money (theirs and/or someone else's) in the expectation and belief that their credentials would help them advance. They are under enormous pressure to be successful in addition to fulfilling their traditional jobs as care givers not only to children but mates, relatives, friends, and even the community.

In the career realm, as in every other aspect of women's lives, there is a societal concept of what the ideal woman should be.[11] Stripped of her business suit and briefcase, Ms. MBA is wearing Mom's apron and a homey housedress or, if single, an alluring bit of casual silk—and beneath either is the sexiest underwear the market sells to respectable women. It is not enough for women today to raise children, bake cakes, and be playgirls on demand. The requirement of success has been superimposed on the traditional ones, and nothing has been subtracted, making the stresses on women greater than ever. In fact, the escalation of society's expectations of women has far exceeded the development of real opportunities for them to move up. Although they are told to expect equal treatment in the workplace, things often do not work out that way.

Many of my interviews began with women summarizing their careers and assuring me that everything was fine. One woman who talked with me by phone for an hour started off by a rapid-fire listing of her moves from one job to another, working gradually upward. "That's my story," she said. It seemed very straightforward. A few questions about why she had been stuck at her present level for several years revealed a different picture altogether. She had in fact hit a plateau despite good performance reviews, a mentor, visibility, and all the other factors that are supposed to work career magic for women. When I asked her what she thought would be necessary for her to move into the job above hers, she said, "A sex-change operation."

Plus Ça Change

By the time I had talked with fifty women about their careers and read almost everything published about MBAs in the United States between 1974 and 1984, my image of Ms. MBA had changed. Although they had sought to escape the dead ends of traditional female careers, in fact the patterns were all too familiar: access to entry, but little progress to the top, and a persistent wage gap between women and men with the same qualifications.

Historically, women's entry into other male-dominated occupations has tended to follow the same course. For example, nineteenth-century secretaries were originally young men in training for the boss's job. The position was a way station to prepare them to move up. It was seen as an ideal starting point, providing proximity to an experienced executive as well as an overview of the organization. As the occupation became more feminized, the status, pay, and career opportunities dropped. The entire structure of the occupation changed from the almost inevitable promotion of young men to the almost inevitable stagnation of women of all ages.

In the experience of my interviewees, the workplace is much less egalitarian than they were told it would be. They worked hard and well; sometimes they were rewarded, sometimes not. But whatever situations they found themselves in, these MBAs showed women's usual resourcefulness when confronted with unforeseen realities. Every step of the way, from making their decisions to starting their own businesses, they invented ingenious ways to cope. This book tells how they went about it.

Two

Making the Decision

The popular idea of a typical woman going after her MBA is a 27-year-old ash blond future executive. Perfectly coiffed and conservatively dressed, wearing just enough makeup to show that she uses it, she never loses a night's sleep over her decision to go to business school. Effortlessly, she tosses off the dozens of pages of essays that Goldmine Business School requires of its applicants. She takes the Graduate Management Admission Tests after a late night socializing in the finest clubs of New York. She is startled when someone suggests to her that she might not be accepted; it literally has never occurred to her. As it turns out, she is absolutely right: Goldmine welcomes her by return mail. If there is a minor setback in her ten-year career plan to become the CEO of a major corporation, it is the school's insistence that she work for a few years before she is admitted. Her father, a Goldmine graduate, introduces her to a friend of his in the field of her choice. He apologizes for offering her only $30,000 a year to accept a stimulating assignment that will do her credit.

Whatever their reasons for making the choice, most women who go to business school bear almost no resemblance to this mythical creature. They give this decision as much thought—and worry—as they do any other major step. The backgrounds of the women I interviewed were diverse: they were nurses, printmakers, bankers, secretaries, flight attendants, consultants, administrators, Ph.D.s in liberal arts, foreign language interpreters. Some had recently graduated from college with a business background, many had liberal arts degrees, still others had been out in the workforce for years.

For all their differences, business school was a major investment of time, personal resources, and money. Tuition at some Goldmine schools runs upwards of $20,000 or more a year. While other programs are cheaper or while employers may foot the bill, two straight years or an eternity of evenings (up to six years or even longer) are a real sacrifice. It requires that women really believe in what they are doing; for almost everyone, business school is a heavy commitment.

What finally pushed these women over the edge and motivated them to earn the MBA? They were stuck in their careers: a few at exciting jobs like foreign language interpretation in China, and many more at dead-end jobs in social work and other traditional women's fields. Even where they had enjoyed their work, most of the women felt that they would go nowhere in the long run. For all the variety in their backgrounds, they expressed similar reasons for going to business school: advancement, money, and credibility. What was different was the significance of their decisions: for some it was an almost automatic step, while for others it was a reach into a new world.

For most of the women, deciding to get their MBAs was a five-stage process: taking stock, getting advice, researching the degree, defining options, and weighing advantages and disadvantages. Most went through the process somewhat consciously, but many did not realize they were moving toward the MBA until the decision was nearly made. Some initiated a whole research plan, while others ended up in business school largely because a friend called at a critical moment and suggested it. A few cautious women did their homework thoroughly, but more were swept away on the rising tide of expectations for MBAs and their hopes to have an equal chance at powerful management jobs.

Only one of the women was clearly cut out from birth to get an MBA:

> My father is a Goldmine grad. He's class of '48, I'm class of '80. My mother was accepted at law school, and my grandfather wouldn't let her go.

This woman was taken to the Goldmine Club and pushed to excel from an early age.

The women who found the decision most troubling were usually constrained by family, class, or racial background, or by their sex. One revealed:

> I had no role model to work with, and that's probably why I wasn't interested in business until the eleventh hour. I had nothing to base it on. So this is completely new territory for me. . . . I have four sisters, and I'm the only one who got a college degree.

Another, a woman who had reached middle-level jobs in nonprofit organizations after ten years went through a torturous process in choosing the MBA. The whole concept of business was alien to her background:

> Nobody in my family was in business. . . . They just aren't business people: they're teachers, secretaries, a computer programmer. My mother was a secretary; my father was an engineer, but nobody really entrepreneurial. I was always fascinated by

business, though, partly because I never had any close exposure to it. At the same time I've been very intimidated, I did build up a mystique about it. . . . Though I found myself having entrepreneurial interests, I didn't know anybody very well who was actually engaged in profit-making business. That made the decision hard for me. The type of work I was doing had nothing to do with it either; I was in state government and nonprofits. Not being around business makes it all the more foreboding somehow.

Women who do not have a connection to the business world through their background do not have access to the information they need about career possibilities. They cannot call their Uncle Irv or his friend Ross to ask what investment bankers do every day and whether an MBA really makes a difference in that setting. Even the language is unfamiliar.

A number of women were "firsts" in their families, either the first to earn an MBA, or the first to have any graduate degree. For example, a telephone company employee who is a Goldmine graduate:

My father is a small-business man, but does not have even an undergraduate degree. I was really the first to get an MBA. I came from a Jewish family, and there are lots of doctors, lawyers, maybe even a smattering of accountants. Most of the women are nurses and teachers.

Being the first means more than simply lacking role models, contacts, and information. It can also mean taking a big leap in one's concept of what is possible. For women of every class who grew up in environments where women's aspirations were restricted, the MBA may signify an unfamiliar world. Almost no one was encouraged to go into business. An MBA working in a consulting firm told me about a colleague from an extremely wealthy family:

She is the daughter of the owner of a huge multinational company. She's married to a doctor, and they are very well to do. She has a brother who was educated and brought into the company. That was never a consideration for her. When she decided to go back to school for her MBA, her daughters were in grade school. Her father said, "What for?"

The restriction of women's aspirations is by no means confined to the upper middle class. A woman from an Eastern European working class family was also told that the MBA was out of the question for her.

Even when the family is intransigent, they can sometimes be brought around. A Chinese-American woman succeeded in securing her family's support despite the tradition of fostering their daughters' marriageability rather than their careers. Not everyone, however, was so fortunate; even on graduation day, one father was unbending:

> We go to the commencement and we go out to dinner afterwards. My father says, "My advice to you, now that you've graduated from business school, is to marry a rich doctor."

For some women, the "decision" to get an MBA was not really a decision at all; their employers offered them the opportunity to go part time at a nearby Generic institution, and they took it up. For almost all, though, the process of deciding to go to business school was a complex one that began with assessing themselves in several different ways.

First Step: Taking Stock

Some women consciously took steps toward a decision to go to business school. Initially, they often examined their lives to see where the MBA would take them. They had to look at their academic preparation and at their job experience as well as at career goals. Wherever they were in the labor market, they examined the long-term prospects for advancement as well as the more immediate issues of pay and promotion. Their assessments usually made them consciously decide to investigate the MBA as a possibility and pushed them on to the next steps.

Academic Preparation

About one-third of the women I interviewed had college degrees in business, economics, or related areas. Thus they often were blissfully free of the cares that obsessed those who were drastically changing careers. Some were able to skip a chunk of the MBA requirements and thus abbreviate their programs considerably. Because course requirements vary, many did research and chose programs because they could get more credit for prior academic work.

Women who came from the foreign lands of liberal arts were not as well prepared for business school. They had majored in just about anything you could name: international affairs, comparative literature, fine arts, various social and hard sciences, nursing, foreign languages, and so on. A number had not seen an algebra problem for several decades, much less a calculus book.

In taking stock of their academic preparation, these women often tried taking a course here or there to see how it sat or to fulfill prerequisites as advised by the schools. For example, a professional printmaker was told that she would have to toil in the vineyards of mathematics for years before she could approach the temple of the MBA. She did not accept the verdict, and found that she had more ability than she had expected:

> I started taking some courses at a school that was commuting distance from the farm where I lived. . . . Even though I had been in school a total of seven years, I hadn't taken any mathematics, any political science classes, any economics classes, marketing, management, no business classes whatsoever. It was really fine arts and liberal arts. There's very little use for that sort of stuff.
>
> [The business school I talked with] came up with a recommendation of six years of math before I could start. I took one year and skipped all the rest. I hadn't had any math since I was a sophomore in high school, but math was nothing more than a logical arrangement of numbers, so that was a piece of cake.

Not everyone had such a positive experience in evaluating her academic background and venturing into an unfamiliar field. One woman who, like the printmaker, earned a Generic degree ultimately, was traumatized by her first effort:

> I took a calculus course and went into a deep depression. I had a very stressful job at the time. I was taking time off from work, I was up nights, I was calling on all my friends for help. No matter what I did, I couldn't get [a grade] over a 50. So I just said, that's it, and I put it on the back burner for a few years.

Rather than allowing herself to be discouraged for good, she gave herself another chance when she discovered that not all schools require an extensive mathematical background. She set a much more realistic goal rather than doom herself to failure:

> I thought, let me take a course I know something about so I don't scare myself to death and never walk inside this place again. So I took a course in procurement and contracting, because I had dealt a lot with that. It turned out to be more like defense contracting, but a lot of the principles were the same. I didn't find the course too hard because it was something somewhat familiar.

Having evaluated her prior academic preparation, this woman was able to make up for the deficiencies by building on her workplace experience. Finally, she had a toehold on the full MBA program.

Workplace Preparation

Assessing where they were in the workplace played a large role in pushing women to decide to go to business school. Only a few made their decisions without any previous work experience. One woman who went straight to a Goldmine business school from the corresponding undergraduate program found out why the practice is usually discouraged:

> There are good reasons why they don't want you to do that. When they talk about things like inventory, everyone else understood, and I had no idea what it was. I didn't really know what I wanted to do with the MBA. I was just shocked that they let me in, so I went.

The lack of experience and the sense of direction it can provide hampered this woman and the few others who leaped straight from undergraduate to graduate school, although they had the advantage of knowing how to study, and simply continued the routine.

On the whole, the women I interviewed thought experience helped. One MBA program director counsels applicants to try business first, even if they have extensive backgrounds in other fields:

> You've never tested the waters. It may be that you get a job in business that you never want to do again. Why put that kind of money into the degree, plus all the study time and aggravation and so on, and then find that you don't like it?

When MBA candidates neglect to try the business world they often find they are ill prepared to adapt to its demands and change accordingly:

> They don't have a feeling for the work style expected, or what's expected in terms of time management. They don't have a feeling for the necessity of working as part of an organization, especially those people who come in from teaching. They really have been very independent professionally. They think they have had a lot of time constraints, but compared with the corporate environment, they haven't.

Women in Traditional Occupations

Most of the women I talked with came from occupations where women are in the majority: secretary, nurse, social worker, librarian, flight attendant, personnel, and so on. In other words, they were in jobs typical of the female workforce as a whole, and their jobs had certain elements in common—elements that often moved women to consider the MBA.

Traditional women's occupations are designed to be secondary in several ways: secondary to women's primary function as wife and mother, secondary in economic importance to husbands' incomes, and secondary to male authority figures in the workplace. By definition, these occupations were never considered to be "real jobs" in the sense of a male breadwinner's. Women were assumed to be working for pin money or luxuries, and were thought to lack ambition. They were perceived to be in the workforce only temporarily, and expected eventually to go back home where they belonged. Even before the huge influx of white women into the workforce in the last fifteen years, these assumptions did not reflect the reality of life for many women.

The assumption that women hold secondary jobs underlies the way that traditional female occupations are compensated, structured, and recognized. It is a commonplace that they pay badly, not only at the entry level, but over a lifetime. In fact, it is the huge number of women in traditional jobs that is usually considered the real basis of the wage gap between female and male workers (Figs. 2.1 and 2.2). Retirement benefits and other perks are generally rarer and poorer for female occupations: for example, compare the training opportunities available to many engineers to those available to secretaries.

The shape of opportunity in women's occupations is not the progressive pyramid in which some people are at the bottom level, slightly fewer at the next, and so on to the apex, which only a few reach. Instead, the great mass of women in traditional occupations is at the bottom or barely

Figure 2.1. *Median Weekly Earnings for Women and Men with Five or More Years of College (1982)*

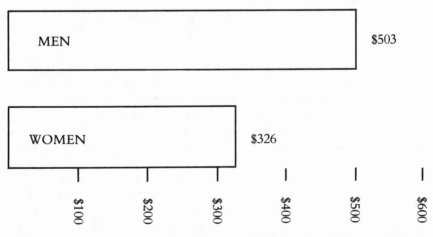

Source: Earl Mellon, "Investigating the Diferences in Weekly Earnings of Women and Men," *Monthly Labor Review*, June 1984, 18–.

Figure 2.2. *Average Weekly Earnings (1982)*

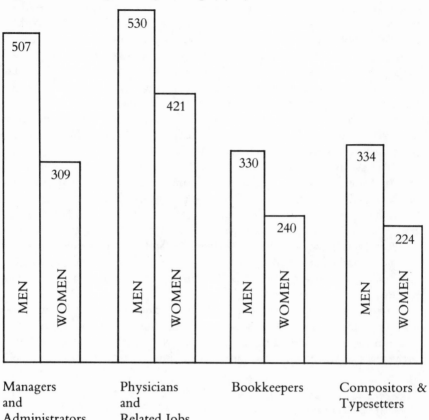

Managers	Physicians	Bookkeepers	Compositors &
and	and		Typesetters
Administrators	Related Jobs		

Source: Earl Mellon, "Investigating the Diferences in Weekly Earnings of Women and Men," *Monthly Labor Review*, June 1984, 18–.

above it—there is almost no apex to reach, and very few intermediate positions. These occupations are structured for stagnation, not opportunity. There is almost nowhere to go; where jobs are available at a substantially higher level, they tend to be filled by men. Teaching is a classic case: although four-fifths of elementary teachers are women, about the same proportion of principals are men. Much the same structure persists in other predominantly female fields.

Because women have so little opportunity to progress, their anticipated lifetime earnings in traditional occupations are much lower than those of their male counterparts. Although the content of their jobs is often very demanding, there are few material rewards for their labors. Some "women's work" is just plain dull, and women often react by expanding their jobs to include different functions or making simple tasks more elegant and complex. But no matter how well they perform or how much they expand their jobs, there are real limits to how far they are likely to go. Eventually, resentment often sets in, and some women turn off for good.

The women who decided to get MBAs often did so as a gesture of survival, rather than giving in to despair about their careers. One who was stuck as an administrative assistant—i.e., secretary—found that her growing responsibilities far exceeded her pay and title, a scenario most women will recognize. She could see that she was not going anywhere:

> I spent about three years working as an administrative assistant, which is usually a relatively low-paying job for the kind of responsibilities that were being doled out, plus low recognition and so on. At that time, I guess I started considering, "Well, you'd better start doing something, because you certainly aren't making much progress."

A woman who had gone straight from college into a defense agency as inventory manager moved into the classic field of personnel. At first she liked it, but once she mastered it, she felt smothered:

> I was working in personnel as a staff information specialist. It was very interesting, especially compared to my earlier job. It was fine coming out of college while I was learning it, but once I got the hang of it, it was really dull.

What she did was a typical response: she made the job more interesting by doing briefings and training, and looked for opportunities to move out of the office; fortunately, she was in a position to do so. She knew that there was no future for her there, though, and decided to try the MBA.

For her and many others, low pay and benefits and the limited opportunities to advance were only part of the problem. The other part was that they felt that people did not respect their work; and sometimes they themselves felt the same. A flight attendant reached a point of real crisis that had at least as much to do with her need to be recognized and to do valuable work as anything else:

> Although I liked the job itself, it didn't really satisfy me enough. I was moving toward my thirties and I felt like I hadn't accomplished anything. It was a real struggle with me because I really did like the lifestyle the job gave me.
>
> Also, I never felt that it commanded much respect from the public, and I had a hard time dealing with that. I was not married at the time, and I saw that I was just pissing my life away. So I thought, "I've got to start working toward something."

Women in traditional jobs had all of these valid reasons to move out. In addition, new developments made certain fields even less desirable than before: teachers went through major crises as public funding became tighter and as the social order that used to keep students under control broke down. Ironically, the feminist movement unwittingly exacerbated the denigration of women in traditional jobs by stressing the meaninglessness of the work rather than its value. Important as that observation was, it was incomplete. Some women moved out of their fields because of their own and others' low respect for their work. Combined with the more positive reasons to escape, it is easy to see how powerfully motivated women in traditional occupations were to consider anything that was billed as a golden passport.

Women in Traditional Sectors

Both government and the nonprofit sector have been major employers of women. Government was open to women, especially professionals, before many private businesses would hire them. In a period when women in management were scarce in industry, government was promoting them at least occasionally. While the same general patterns prevail there as elsewhere—women are concentrated at lower job levels—there has often been more opportunity for women inside than outside government. Women of color have found it a more receptive, although far from ideal, setting, and for disabled women in management it has been almost the only game in town.

Several of the women I interviewed had had jobs on Capitol Hill, and a number worked for executive agencies ranging from the Department of Labor to the Federal Reserve Board and the Environmental Protection Agency. One of them was in the strikingly atypical situation of having topped out in her late twenties in a job she loved:

> I had a tremendous amount of responsibility, working under a government contract. There was an agreement in principle to have cultural exchanges with China, and my job was to figure out what those should be and make them happen. I specifically worked on a series of study teams, going back and forth to China. I figured out what would be relevant, who the key players were, and either hired other people to travel with them or did it myself. . . . It was fun, but I was bored. I was fifteen years younger than anybody else with comparable responsibility in my office. There were two lawyers above me, and I wouldn't have been a candidate for either job.

While some other women also felt stuck, none of them had reached this woman's level of responsibility. Like her, however, they often enjoyed their work; they just felt that it was not leading anywhere. A young woman fresh out of an Ivy League school moved to Washington in hopes of using her Russian language skills and finally found an unrelated but interesting job with her senator. It was fine as far as it went, but at a certain point she knew she was immobilized:

> I was someone's assistant for about six months, then was made a legislative assistant, covering appropriations. The senator was on the Appropriations Committee. I prepared briefings, reviewed the budget when it came out in January, and wrote amendments to legislation. I was there four years. I reached the point where I wasn't getting any more responsibility. The way the office was structured, you could take on new issues, but the responsibilities didn't change.

Feeling stuck was only one of the factors that prompted women to consider business school. Some were fortunate enough to be exposed to issues and information that piqued their interest and made them want to learn more. A woman who worked on the Watergate case became intrigued with a number of possibilities that had not occurred to her before:

> I did everything from actually sitting through witness testimony to collecting the evidence to helping record data for computers. . . . I found that I had a real fascination with computer systems. I had a boss who was very tough; she recognized me and said, "Here, you can have the run of the place. Take what you want and do it. I need this kind of help. I'm not going to hold you back." She was very kind in doing so; she opened the doors to many different areas.

Women's experiences in the executive agencies were similar. An environmental protection specialist who had a varied background found that her horizons were limited. She could not find her way out of the government, and her specialty was only in moderate demand in a few agencies. Another woman in the Department of Labor used her economics degree to help businesses that were hurt by foreign trade: it opened new areas of expertise and interest for her and made her want to advance.

Women working in the nonprofit sector reached many of the same conclusions by a somewhat different route. Their careers were more plagued by financial uncertainty and organizational difficulties than by unsatisfying work or rigid hierarchical structures. Several of their jobs were fascinating and rewarding. A woman whose background was in social services succeeded in turning around a failing program to place people newly released from prison in jobs:

When I took over, there were supposed to have been maybe six-
teen people placed, and there had been one. . . . I have an overview kind of mind, and I had charts put up on the wall so I knew
where everyone was and where they should be. I knew how they
were doing at work and so on. I tracked them and color coded
them, so there would be little red flags when some problem was
coming up. . . . We exceeded our quotas dramatically.

On the whole, the women in nonprofit agencies also liked their work.
A project officer for a federal contract for a disability rights organization
relished both the human and numbers aspects of the job:

We put together a workshop that was a four day training session
to provide legal training and technical assistance to disabled people all over the country. We assembled a team of trainers and
technical people, personal care attendants, and sign language interpreters, and so forth. We all traveled as a team for about three
years.
    It was a wonderful job. I loved it. I was responsible for hiring
and supervising all the staff, monitoring the budget, and providing all the reports we had to send in. I got real interested in the
business aspects of the contract.

Her new interest stood her in good stead in business school. She reluctantly
decided that the organization was simply too small to provide other opportunities for her once the contract ran out, and like her colleagues elsewhere, she found that she could go no further.
    As much as the women in nonprofit organizations generally enjoyed
their jobs, there was another side to the story: not only the blockage that
is almost inevitable in small organizations, but the funding crises often
associated with the sector as a whole. One woman who later became a
CPA and MBA was at her wits' end trying to handle finances for a public-
interest group in constant upheaval:

I was doing all of this stuff I wasn't qualified to do—arranging
bridge loans to take care of cash flow problems. We would have
grants in September but we wouldn't be able to pay salaries after
April because we'd use up all the money right away, and so everybody would borrow from boyfriends, girlfriends, parents. I really
didn't know what I was doing at all, and it was like reinventing
the wheel. So I decided to go to business school. I thought I
would then go back to the organization and run it like an efficient
ship.

Even where a nonprofit was run as if by a tidy sea captain, familiar patterns could emerge. One woman who had moved around in the workplace frequently said:

> I didn't like where I was going or what I was doing, changed jobs again, and then suddenly realized when I became unhappy at that job that I wasn't moving anywhere except continually sideways, and in some cases even down.

Whatever their levels of job satisfaction in both government and nonprofit agencies, women often ended up feeling as though their lives would continue along the same flat plane, unless they took steps to make a drastic change.

Women in Traditional Industries

The women who had actually started their careers in the business world were all in fields where women are clustered at the lower levels: banking, insurance, publishing, and public relations. One did manage to work her way up through an insurance company, beginning at age seventeen:

> Right after high school I was tired of school, so I walked into town and saw a big sign over the insurance company: THE DOORWAY TO PROTECTION. I liked that, so I went in and got a job working in reinsurance. I became manager of that department and moved into accounting, working round the clock for six and a half years.

While a few others also considered that they had made some progress, most felt stymied. The major exception was a woman who had been admitted to a Goldmine school on the condition that she get some work experience. She took a special post-undergraduate program in publishing and was recruited right from the course. The variety and excitement made it a perfect introductory job:

> I worked in business offices, ad sales, circulation, market research. What I did was a lot of analysis along the lines of, "Are we offering the proper advertising editions [of the magazine]? What should we offer instead? Are we priced attractively? Are our discounts right? . . ." It was a varied sort of thing. I got to meet a lot of people. I really, really messed up a couple of times, learned my lessons, and thoroughly enjoyed it.

Although the traditional industries sometimes provided such positive experiences for women at the entry level, and although a few women did make their way up, on the whole those I talked with were not enthusiastic about their work. For example, a woman in her fifties who had made a career in public relations found that she just was not interested any more. Like the flight attendant, her work had lost its meaning and she was ready to do something else:

> It's not a very fulfilling job. . . . I wanted to do something that I felt would be humanitarian. I wanted to replace some of the things that I have gotten out of life: I owed something.

For her, it was time to move on. The few who were not employed in traditional jobs or industries reached this same conclusion.

Varied as they were in some ways, in the end all of these women were in more or less the same situation: on a boat to nowhere in their careers, circumnavigating the globe again and again at exactly the same latitude. Some were on a more southerly and comfortable course where the pay was better or the work more enjoyable or glamorous; others had a chillier sail. But in terms of getting from point A to point B, almost all were right where the currents of the labor market for women swept them: in traditional jobs, sectors, and industries, with limited prospects for promotion, pay, and recognition. It was enough to drive many to go to business school.

Second Step: Getting Advice from People You Know

At its best, advice from people the women already knew boosted their confidence, provided them with useful information and contacts, and helped them make decisions that took many aspects of themselves into account. Some advice, however, was based on false information and stereotypes about what the MBA could actually do for them. The women who did not weigh advice objectively against facts they gathered themselves often were in for some surprises when they went to business school. Others used advice as grist for the mill, checked it out through research, and made up their own minds. The few who let someone else convince them they should get the degree were disappointed at the end of the process.

The sources of advice were widely varied. For a few women, families were the most important. Several told me their husbands had pushed them to get the degree so that they would have "something to fall back on." One woman's family connections really helped her:

> When I began talking about MBA school the attitude was, "Oh, why don't we call Jane and have her give you a call [about her experience at Harvard]?" . . . It was really a simple thing to find

people to talk to, but it wasn't through the school. It was really family contacts as a result of everybody having graduate degrees, and all the women had worked [outside the home].

Here, the potential importance of class factors was apparent: because her family was well connected, she could get accurate information from someone who had actually gone through a top program. In contrast, a black woman who graduated from business school in 1974 told me that one of her most serious problems was that absolutely no one in her community could advise her about a career in business, much less the MBA itself.

Friends also helped women make up their minds about going to business school. They sometimes pushed women to learn about the option, even if they had not thought about it seriously before. A number described conversations in which they would rage about their careers being blocked and someone would say, in effect, "Why don't you stop complaining and get an MBA?" In one case, a liberal arts graduate who had pursued journalism was counseled about her lack of direction:

I hadn't really thought about business school and didn't know much about it. . . . A friend of mine called me up and said, "Why don't you go to business school? It's a credential, and you would get some quantitative skills. It doesn't commit you to anything, like the law or medicine."

While the notion of the MBA as the all-purpose degree for those who were vague about what they wanted is explored further below, it is clear that for this woman and others, the degree became an option simply because someone else mentioned it.

Bosses and co-workers sometimes initiated conversations about business school as the key to success, particularly if they had taken that route themselves. A Chinese-American woman found herself in a consulting firm that was failing, from which a group of fast-track MBAs wanted to set up a new business of their own. At first she resisted their suggestions:

They sat down and said, "Norma, what are you going to do? You need this credential. If we thought of a company, would you come in with us?" I started thinking about it, thinking that I was getting too old for this [late twenties]. I didn't want to go back to school.

Ultimately, it was her next boss who impelled her to decide:

I was working for a woman who was four months older than I, and she really pushed. She said, "You've got to change this. You're starting to limit yourself." I started looking at job opportunities and really got concerned. Things were looking hard.

While advice can be invaluable, women are most satisfied with decisions they make for themselves. According to a woman faculty member at one business school, some tend to pay too much attention to opinions of others rather than trusting their own instincts:

> I think too many women listen to other people, and what they think is best. . . . You cannot sit in an MBA class and give it your full attention, and work and be productive if that's not where you want to be to begin with.

Some ignored their own better judgment about whether the degree was right for them, especially when the person advising them was someone they depended on, such as a husband. For example:

> Even though I had a Ph.D. from Harvard, I was forced to go to MBA school by my husband, who said, "What would you do if something happened to me?"
> I just had a lot of people telling me that I should consider getting an MBA. My husband thought that I'd be good at it or it would be something that I should do. For practical purposes, I decided that I was going to toss aside the fact that I'd never wanted to do it prior to that point, and I really didn't know what I was going to do with it. . . . It was something to have another degree behind me and be able to get out of the rut. . . . My primary goal started out being a landscape architect but I decided my allergies were going to get the best of me. Now I wish I'd stayed with it, but that's beside the point.

Hearing advice from prospective employers tipped the balance for another woman, who had been unusually fortunate in gaining access to CEOs of major corporations: she was responsible for exchange programs with China in the early days:

> China was such a sexy topic then that you virtually had entree to everyone. I went and talked to these people because they were nice enough to share their time. They said, "We can hire you on. But in five years, you're going to be up against a Harvard or a Stanford MBA who will be chosen over you—probably not because of the quality of the work you do, but because that's just the way the system works."
> I said, "I'm not going to let some stupid degree get in the

way of my getting to where I want to be. I'm going to get this degree."

In this case, advice was a useful balance to media reports about the MBA; the woman learned first-hand what she would be up against. When a reporter for a popular magazine says that Harvard and Stanford MBAs get all the best jobs at the top corporations, that's one thing; hearing it from the horse's mouth is quite another.

Timing can be critical when women are trying to make decisions. A former teacher was at loose ends when she went back to her undergraduate college advisor. Like others, she posed the problem of feeling stuck in her career and, in this case, being out of a job:

> It was quite late in the year, probably a little late to find another teaching job, and I wasn't really happy teaching anyway. I called my old college advisor and said I needed something to do. I asked about law school, and she said, "Three years?" I asked, "What's business school?" She said it was two years. At that time [my undergraduate school] had an MBA program for management of public and nonprofit institutions, and I went down and had an interview. At the end, the Director of Admissions asked, "Would you like to start in October or June?" I said, "Don't I need to fill out an application?"

Both advice and chance played their part in her decision; if she had not called her advisor at the right moment in the business school cycle, she might have gone to law school instead or done something completely different.

Part of seeking advice is weighing the reactions of others, not only to the abstract idea of an MBA but to the combination of you as an individual in a real-life situation and that degree. Women looked to friends and partners who knew little about business as well as those who were more knowledgeable simply because they could offer a helpful perspective on their personalities and talents. At the same time, every woman had to make her own decision if she was to live through all the months and years, the boring courses as well as the interesting ones, and the long nights working on papers about how many tractors could be sold in New York City every decade.

Third Step: Researching the Degree

Except for a few women who had complete resources at their fingertips through people they already knew, most had to reach beyond their own small circle. A number of printed materials were widely used to provide basic information about the MBA and the various programs that were available (see the resources section). Even without seeking it, any woman who follows the business press or who reads magazines directed at career women is bombarded with speculation about the MBA. While there have been changes in the way it is inflated and reported, many women told me that they had read about the degree as a ticket to success. This conventional wisdom, while it has shifted at times, generally only encouraged women to believe that the MBA was an answer to all their career problems. Media reports often focused on the successes of white males from Harvard and other top business schools as if they were typical; when women or people of color were featured, they also were often from the top schools. Success stories abounded to show how much progress women had made into management, a tone that still dominates much popular literature. Borne on the tide of rising expectations in the 1970s, women believed it when they were told that they could do anything, that the doors were open if they would only walk in. They hoped that the MBA would perform the same alchemy for them as it had for the white men who poured out of business schools after World War II.

Because the law had begun to require equal opportunities and because a new market was opening up, business school advertising was targeted at women in particular, and it was highly effective. For example, a psychology major who was not sure just what to do with her undergraduate degree was easily snared:

> I was walking down the hall in the psych lab and saw a pink sign with black print, which I remember to this day, that said "Are you a psych major? You too can be an MBA." Up to that point I had never considered crossing that line. . . . From then on, that is what I thought I would do.

Crossing that line in this woman's case simply meant switching from one field to another. Business school marketing was calculated to escort women across many such lines: from women's to men's work, from traditional aspirations to more expansive possibilities. Women began to show up in catalogs in pictures of classes or among the featured students who explained why they went to that school. A look at the list of faculty at the back, however, or at the tiny number of women represented in the alumni magazine could give a different impression.

A few women checked on how employers responded to the MBA, how other people had used it, what kinds of jobs were open to MBAs, or which schools were most credible for different purposes. For example, a middle-level manager in the federal civil service did considerable research about the implications of her decision. The degree was to be the means to her switching into the private sector:

> I decided to get an MBA because I could see that all the jobs above mine in government were highly politicized, and I wanted to avoid that by switching to the private sector. I asked many people what I should do: friends who had made the switch, people in industry locally, teachers of business, and others. They told me that, with a Ph.D. in liberal arts and a limited number of years of experience, I could only get a staff job, probably in regulatory affairs. I didn't want that, so I decided to go.

By gathering information from a wide variety of perspectives, she was able to weigh others' advice and information based on her research. By asking people directly for their input, she coordinated a number of elements that would prove important later: academics, employers, and the persons who could identify directly with the change she was trying to make.

Considering the stakes involved, the women I interviewed did surprisingly little research that went beyond their own circle of friends and connections, and the obvious resource of business school marketing material. Few went on to do more than a handful of informational interviews. They seemed to think that media accounts and personal connections sufficed.

None of the women was familiar with the research already done about the outcomes of the MBA for women. Before going to business school, none had searched the literature to see what had actually happened to women who made the decision, as opposed to press reports of success stories and other anecdotal information that inevitably describes the sensational exception rather than the more mundane rule. It is an index of the power of the myth of Ms. MBA that women did not feel they needed to look at actual evidence about other women's careers. Considering how oriented MBAs are supposed to be to quantitative data, it was striking that they did not explore in advance to see what substantiation there might be for claims for the degree. Rather than checking it out, they went on to the next step.

Fourth Step: Defining Options

Once they had decided to consider business school seriously, women started defining their options. Most looked at the alternatives to business school and identified the constraints on their choices: finances, geography, and academic and experiential background. Only then did they examine the concrete possibilities, such as the program content and style they preferred, whether to go to a Goldmine or a Generic school, and whether to go full or part time.

Alternatives to Business School

For most of the women I interviewed, law school was the obvious alternative to business school. Although much has been made of their increased range of choices, the young women generally did not think beyond business or law. Those who did not have a strong preference between them chose business school because it does not take as long.

Others were scared off by the prospect of a glut of lawyers; one was told, "You're already an unemployed teacher; why become an unemployed lawyer?" Still, some women felt the appeal of a straightforward answer, "I'm a lawyer," to the constantly asked question, "What do you do?" and the social acceptance that goes along with it. One MBA still thinks wistfully of what it might have been like to be an attorney:

> Even now I always look back and say, "Now if you were a lawyer, people would respect that." If I tell my 86-year-old grandmother-in-law that I have a business degree, she thinks that I know shorthand. She doesn't think anything of it. Whereas a lot of people hate lawyers, but at least it's respectable.

The change in expectations for women in the business world is summarized neatly in the communications gap between the generations. Another woman's mother reacted in horror when she said she was going to business school: "After all that money we spent on college, you're going to become a secretary?"

In fact, the whole idea of business school was a new one to many of the women. Those who began their careers before the days of affirmative action were channeled into traditional occupations where most of them remained for some years. One woman's calculation of her chances was quite typical:

> I'm thirty-eight now. When I thought about what I might do with my life, it was in terms of teaching. Business school never even occurred to me. There didn't seem to be any point in going, since all the women were in low-level jobs anyway.

In considering what they could do with their lives, most of the women seemed to feel that business was the only possibility for advancement. Academia had dried up; funding for public programs was constricting; the public interest world was shrinking with the changing times. Sometimes their other options were not feasible, as for this woman:

> When I was in high school I decided that I would have to make my own living. I never planned on getting married. I looked at

my assets and figured that I would have to earn my living by going to work. So I thought about what I liked to do and what I was good at; it was accounting, art, or professional softball. I figured that being an artist is pretty chancy, softball didn't pay anything, so it was accounting.

Constraints on Women's Choices

Some women certainly had a much wider range of choices than others. For those who were employed and being sent to a particular program, the decisions were fairly obvious. But for most, the options were complex. Finding the right school is as exacting a matter of fit as choosing a garment, and there are no one-size-fits-all solutions. The range from which women can select is vast in theory, but in practice, many constraints operate in their individual lives. Finances are the most obvious; some women chose a particular program because they could afford it or decided against a Goldmine school because they did not want to go into debt for years.

Women's economic situation is the product of race, class, physical and marital status, as well as age, all of which limited their ability to choose the best program for them. Those aspects of their identity also reduced their choices in other ways; for example, one woman who uses a wheelchair was restricted by the failure of most cities and schools to provide fully accessible environments. She knew that business school was going to be challenging for her anyway, and she did not want to add to her problems by leaving the relatively manageable area where she lived.

Geography was another major restriction. Married women and mothers were by no means the only ones who could not go wherever they preferred. A single woman who went to a Goldmine school felt that she was jeopardizing a very important relationship with a man she later married. While she did not let it stop her, it certainly caused her some sleepless nights:

> I had been living with a man in New York whom I have since married. I'd been dating him for four years through college and then for two years in New York. . . . We were not engaged when I moved. I had quote-unquote faith that we would stay together, but I wasn't sure.

As it turned out, she commuted to New York on the weekends, like several other women who attended programs in distant cities and went home to their mates and children at regular intervals. Most women, however, chose to attend school where their personal attachments were closest, whatever those might be, rather than disrupt the lives of others.

Academic and experiential backgrounds also narrowed their options, both because these factors affected where they could be admitted to school and influenced their criteria for acceptability. For some women with a liberal arts background, a priority was finding a place where the dose of business would not taste too bitter, and where their earlier education would be valued. Some simply were not accepted by the schools they would have preferred, and had to settle for their second or third choice. Where a highly quantitative program was looking for students with extensive background in mathematics, the art historians generally could not compete and had to look elsewhere.

Concrete Choices: Program Content and Style

Because there are so many different types of MBA programs, women faced a confounding range of options. By shopping around, they could find programs that accommodated their backgrounds and preferences. Some simply wanted to add the three letters after their names as expeditiously as possible and looked for schools with minimal prerequisites; others were seeking a particular specialty, such as public accounting or arts management. Still others sought a credential to help them advance with their current employers rather than to look for a new job or field. One woman felt that she needed an "adequate" degree, but no more:

> Having a strong accounting undergraduate degree and knowing some of the people who had gone through the courses before, among the three schools I was considering the one I went to probably didn't have the best reputation, but it was acceptable.

In addition to examining program content, women preferred different styles of instruction. Some schools use the case method developed at Harvard, which presents students with actual circumstances that have arisen in a business context and requires them to analyze the problems and propose solutions. No specific teaching is offered in particular techniques except as related to the cases. Other schools offer more traditional instruction around a strictly prescribed program, and many combine the case and more conventional methods. The range of course content is immense; different schools have different specialties, and some have a much more quantitative bent than others. Women tested the fit between themselves and teaching methods on the basis of their past experience, reading texts, talking to current and former students, and sometimes by observing classes. Those who did not take the teaching methods into account were sometimes in for a rude shock, as the next chapter will show.

The overall style of an institution was a composite of more than the program and teaching methods. In addition to those relatively objective factors, one of the most important considerations in selecting a business school program was an intuitive sense of belonging, or fitting in, with the other students, the structure or lack of it, the prevailing values, and the social atmosphere. Many who did not take that factor into account felt very isolated as a result, particularly if they were mature students. A black woman could see the writing on the wall when she visited a Goldmine campus that felt unwelcoming to her. Instead, she chose a traditionally black university and had a positive experience there.

Concrete Choices: Generic vs Goldmine

For some women, Generic MBAs were the only option because they could not afford or get into the more expensive schools, or because only the Generic programs offered the logistical possibilities (part time or whatever) they required. Convenience was a big factor, especially for women with complex personal lives and/or demanding jobs. A number of the women who remained employed (and a few others) chose less prominent programs quite consciously. In addition to convenience factors, several mentioned their concern about overly theoretical Goldmine programs or curricula that would interfere with their leading their own lives.

> What was really on my mind was not having to go back to an ivory tower. I really felt that that was going to be a killer to my self-esteem. I knew in my heart of hearts that I just could not picture myself back on a campus, having a job there, and being thought of as a student with a part-time job.

Thus Generic programs are preferable for women in some situations, and it is not always better to go to a "better" school. Older women particularly valued the mixture of experience of their classmates, as Generic schools tend to attract more working adults than many Goldmine schools. A woman who went into debt and moved across the country to attend an accredited Generic program was apprehensive at first, but was pleased with the results:

> The admissions standards are very low . . . and I worried about that, but at the same time I got what I wanted. I got exposure to all the tools and techniques. You can learn those to whatever level you want. You miss the competition within the classes, but that was made up for by the work experience of the other students. I would rather be with someone with a 500 GMAT score who had

been in government or industry for five years than the 600-level person who is just out of undergraduate school and doesn't have any experience to talk about.

At the other end of the spectrum of options, a number of the women who were mobile and planned to go to school full time decided that they simply did not want to go unless they could attend a Goldmine school. They believed that anything else was not worth the effort. One art history major, now a banker with a Goldmine degree, says that her experience as an employer bears out her personal decision not to bother if she could not graduate from one of the top-rated schools in the country:

> When we have résumés, the MBA from Podunk really doesn't mean anything to us. It's important to go to a school with a very good reputation because there are so many MBA factories. So many poor people think the MBA is going to be the road to riches and stardom only to find out that nobody cares. They've paid thousands of dollars in tuition to support some small college that knows a business school will support it. A lot of programs are a real rip-off.
>
> It is unfortunate, because a lot of people look at the MBA almost like a dream to get them out of bondage. I don't think it's worth getting your MBA unless you go to a school that has a really good reputation.

Women who were particularly vulnerable in the workforce for any reason—age, disability, race, obvious lesbianism, class—often felt that they needed the most reputable degree they could get, since gender alone was not the only strike against them. Those who lacked a business background also believed that going to a top school was especially important in making them competitive:

> I knew that if I was going to go to business school, I'd better go to one of the top ten. Otherwise, it wouldn't do me that much good. I needed that, because I didn't have any business experience . . . to be at all competitive with anyone. So I only applied to good schools and would only consider a good school.

One woman felt so strongly about the differences among school rankings that she accepted a top private school over a top public one, despite the financial and personal sacrifice it entailed.

Yet some took a very jaundiced view of the mystique surrounding the top schools, including women who went there and discovered that they were not the shrines of all business wisdom as well as those who were outside looking in. A Generic graduate who was well trained in marketing felt that the Goldmine reputation was inflated:

> They have managed to put their name all over the place. If you gave a school half a million dollars and a creative PR person, they could probably do the same thing. Put a couple of ringers in there, graduate them, ship them off to other business schools, and get them to start writing. It's perceptions, not actuality.

A few who had the option of going to Goldmine schools rejected them, either because of personal constraints or because the additional costs (in every sense) were out of keeping with their career goals.

Concrete Choices: Full or Part Time

Just as there is no formula that says that every woman should go to the most reputable school where she can be admitted, there is no automatic answer to whether going full time or part time is better. While women's experiences with each are discussed fully in the next chapter, at the point of making a decision, most were channeled in one direction or another. Those whose employers were paying or who could not afford to attend full time usually ended up in part-time Generic programs.

Most made a clear choice between doing the program full or part time, although some switched in the end. One was in the very difficult position of having to choose between work she really wanted to do and a full-time program. She chose not to choose, and did both simultaneously. At the other extreme, a highly demanding job made one woman decide that part-time classes while working full time would be too much for her:

> I was thinking I should really go to business school, but I didn't think I had the energy to do it at night, particularly because in my job there was a lot of evening work. So it was a question of going full time, which was a huge economic commitment I am still paying for.

What finally convinced a busy professional woman to quit her job and go to school full time were the appeal of interaction with her classmates and the single-minded immersion in learning that only full-time study allows. Several women attempted to do the program part time and decided that it was simply too difficult to manage. Sometimes it was the combination of home, work, and school that added up to too much.

Although the option of full or part time has different implications for everyone, most women recommended full-time attendance for those who can afford it. The only ones who actually preferred part time were those whose personal lives were already complicated or whose identities were so firmly rooted in the working world that they would have been hard pressed to resume student life. By the time they had identified the range of options open to them, they were ready to begin weighing the advantages and disadvantages of making a final decision.

Fifth Step: Weighing Advantages and Disadvantages

For women considering the MBA, the business world suddenly seemed alive with possibilities. From a board game of concentric circles through which they could never advance, they felt they could escape to a game where the paths actually led somewhere. The MBA was the purchase price; the rewards were symbols of power and prestige: expensive suits, voluptuously furnished offices, specialized magazines devoted solely to business, and perks such as cars and even private jets. The chairman of the board never had to take the bus or make his own coffee, much less someone else's. The escape from a thousand small indignities was infinitely alluring.

Most exciting of all, women could see that the chairman was in the same system as they were. From the rigid compartments of women's work where one job is as tightly sealed from another as parts of a space capsule, the possibilities were suddenly open. Perhaps it would take a heroic effort to go from the entry-level management job to the top, but at least the two were on the same road. Unlike secretary and executive, flight attendant and pilot, or nurse and doctor, women and men did not generally appear to inhabit separate universes.

Women both rejected the female world of work and were attracted to the male world of business. They thought the MBA was all it would take to catapult them over the walls into the new territory. Above all, they wanted the money and prospects they thought the MBA could provide them. When asked what she and her classmates were after, one Goldmine MBA answered frankly:

> Mostly good jobs that paid well and lots of room for career expansion. I can't honestly say anybody was looking for a good education. You learn a lot, but it's more technical and mechanical things. It's not what I would call a mind-broadening experience. Most people viewed it as a ticket out to good jobs.

Sometimes the advantages of an MBA seemed immediately apparent. For some, it was a spoken or unspoken requirement to move up in their job. One commercial banker could see exactly how the lack of the MBA was holding her back:

There was a time when I was managing the corporate checks—
the checks they deposited, how much we charged them, and so
on. We were far more advanced in that subject than the international department. The same job came up on the international
side, and they were in fact trying to duplicate some of the computer systems which I had helped develop. . . . I interviewed for
the job and the head of the group said outright, "We only take
people with higher degrees." I said, "OK, it's time to go back to
school. If all I need to get into international banking is to go back
to school, I'll do it."

A woman in the health care field had much the same experience, although
the industry is structured very differently. She knew that she would never
make it into line management in her hospital without the MBA:

I'm a hospital risk manager, dealing primarily with insurance
claims, lawsuits, and a lot of off-the-wall issues that don't fall
into any category. I had eleven years of experience before I got
my MBA in human services management. The MBA was essential if I wanted to move into line management. I had a decision
to make when I was in medical records doing quality assurance.
I knew I wanted to run something. I decided, "If I'm going back,
I might as well go all the way."

Most women saw the MBA degree as a flexible credit that would help
them no matter where they were, particularly if they had a liberal arts
background. One who was making a big switch out of her government
job said:

My bachelor's degree is in psychology, so I'm basically liberal
arts. I felt at that point that if I wanted to get ahead, even within
the federal government, I needed some more business background. I didn't have anything. I had never even taken an elective
in business. So I really needed something along that line.

While some cherished dreams of reaching the top using the MBA as
their seven-league boots, others calculated the odds quite coldly:

I felt that at the time they were starting to differentiate in society
between those that had the MBA and those that didn't. They were
already differentiating between men. They were saying, "The guy
got a promotion. Well, he has an MBA." Now, if they are already
differentiating between men, what is my chance? I see what the
odds are just for men alone, so I'd better catch up.

Several did not want to give their employers any excuse not to take them seriously. According to one business school official, they are laying in an arsenal:

> We know that it's a male world and I'm competing. The young women in this program, I suspect, are on that track. "I'm going to get everything I can so they can't possibly say no."

The word "credibility" came up again and again when I asked women why they decided to get the degree. When they considered its advantages, they thought that they would suddenly attain a new status in the workforce. They would not be just one more woman who was out to earn pin money; they would be taken seriously as professionals. Because of women's status as newcomers in management in the business world, they hungered for credentials that would assure everyone—including themselves—that they really could perform in unfamiliar roles.

Because many who decided to get MBAs had previously tried to find jobs with real earning and promotion potential, they knew how hard it was, especially with liberal arts degrees. Some felt they needed the degree to legitimize their past experience or to give an employer a rationalization for hiring them. One woman saw the MBA as ammunition:

> I am never going up before a [interviewing] panel again with my English degree. I know what it cost me and I know what it took, but they are never going to recognize it. Next time I'm selected by men for a job, they're going to see MBA.

Adding the credibility they could get from the MBA seemed as though it could only help. A woman in her middle years, with extensive and varied experience, returned from some years overseas to look for a job, and began her search optimistically:

> I couldn't wait to get back to the States. I thought, "They will be so happy to see me." I'm in my middle forties, with sixteen years of fine work experience, and now I have middle-management experience with administration. I'm not getting pregnant; I'm just exactly what they are looking for.
>
> I walked the streets with my very nicely constructed résumé. I couldn't even get an interview. I sent my résumé out 120 times. For anything—anything.

Since the doors were closed, she decided to go to business school (and ended up in a job that did not require the MBA). For this woman and others, the idea of a degree that could spring them into a different job

market was irresistable. Even younger women, or others without characteristics that caused compound discrimination, sometimes found their way
blocked, even at the beginning of their careers. The MBA was a way out,
from the perspective of a woman who had specialized in a popular area:

> I got a master's in international relations specializing in Soviet
> studies and economics when detente was a big deal. It was also
> the beginning of the women's movement, so I thought I was
> really set with opportunities opening up for women and with my
> new degree. When I looked for a job, they usually handed me a
> secretarial application. Since I felt that if I could advise the pres-
> ident before he negotiated with the Russians he would do a better
> job, I didn't respond very well to that. I found that I was un-
> employable with a master's degree after one and a half years of
> looking. I said I would never let that happen to me again, so I
> got an MBA.

For women like these whose ideas of what they wanted from their
education were vague, the MBA sounded like a godsend. They thought it
would provide basic skills they could apply almost anywhere, without
committing themselves in a particular direction. A former foreign language
interpreter told me:

> Business school is so general. You come out with a business de-
> gree and what do you have? You're not necessarily a banker . . .
> You can do a lot of things.

She is now a banker herself.

Significantly, an actual desire to learn what is taught in business school
was one of the least frequent responses I heard from women who decided
to go. A few, however, felt they could pinpoint situations in which they
felt that they were using cumbersome, handhewn conceptual tools rather
than the state-of-the-art instruments available at business school. A woman
who had been administering a social services program felt that she was
stuck using ancient systems that could have been much more efficient:

> I was in charge of making sure the office ran well. I figured out
> my own inventory system. . . . It was all having to create things
> from scratch. I felt as though I was doing things much more
> slowly than I needed to. . . . I'd had all this on-the-job training,
> but I was counting on whatever leads people were giving me
> being accurate.

With the MBA, she hoped to be able to cut corners and become more effective in whatever sphere she chose, an advantage that a few other women also looked forward to.

In contemplating the difficulties they had or would have in entering the business world, a number of women mentioned not knowing the language of business. Like camouflage, it would help them be accepted as a real member of the team. One woman who went to Goldmine straight from undergraduate school felt that she would never at heart be a businesswoman. But she wanted to learn how to pass in that world:

> I wasn't very interested in business, I simply wanted to know the language and concepts, so I could talk with business people. I felt like I would never be one of them, but I would . . . not want to have them put me down as an academic or something. I figured that all the stuff you learned would be applicable to nonprofits and government work, and all these other things that I could see myself doing.

In the end, the biggest advantage women hoped to obtain was not so much the knowledge or skills or even the process of acquiring them and adapting to a different way of thinking. A woman who had given up her job and moved halfway across the country told me:

> The vast majority of the people I saw—at a second- , third-tier school—wanted the degree not for any great good of knowledge, but for three letters to tack on somewhere.

The Meaning of the Decision To Get an MBA

Women with experience in the workforce had every reason to decide to earn an MBA and to hope that it would mean fundamental change in their lives. The ceiling on their compensation and expectations was ground in daily by the way they were treated: often nicely, but rarely with the respect accorded an equal colleague with real career prospects and an important contribution to make. Even where women liked the work they were doing, the lack of room to grow concerned them. As one woman said of an earlier job:

> It was a wonderful experience, but it kept getting me away from any kind of goal. It was a happenstance kind of thing.

Many of the other women I interviewed also felt that they were "getting nowhere." The decision they finally made had very different meanings to them. For a few, it was a surrender to the inevitable or a logical step after college; for others, it was a carefully considered way station on a route they had plotted long ago. For some, however, it was an act of faith in themselves, an affirmation that they really could do something that was out of bounds. A woman who had been at home with her small children for some years when she went to business school said:

When I look back, I have to give myself more credit because I was afraid. When you're afraid, it takes a lot more courage to do what you are doing, and risk what you are in terms of personal relationships. But you have to grow.

For her and others the decision to earn an MBA was a critical turning point. It represented a deep reassessment of the direction their lives were taking and a repudiation of the employment society has traditionally offered women. One by one, they became discontented with a situation that seemed intensely personal but that is reflected in the broader statistics about women in the workforce. The decision to go to business school was an effort to take control, to provide themselves with the ticket they thought they needed to advance to a different destination. They were literally changing tracks: after simply being herded on the first train that came by and going wherever it went, they were leaping off and taking a chance on a different direction.

Whatever was to come when the women actually reached school and the jobs that did or did not lie beyond it, their hopes were high when they finally were accepted:

When I first came back to get my MBA, I basically thought that everybody I saw with an MBA degree at that time . . . was going gangbusters. I'd see these guys with MBAs, and they could do anything. Everybody paid attention to them and I sort of felt that was the answer to everything. Not that I didn't think you had to work and work hard, but it seemed to me that you had to be really good to get into school in the first place, and then having that credential, earning it, basically you had your life set.

The women whose lives you will be reading about came to the decision to go to business school from many different backgrounds and for many reasons; some proved to be well founded and some not. Unfortunately, their decisions were made with almost no information about what had happened to the majority of women who went before them. Those who researched the matter most thoroughly usually had an easier time living with the results; some of the more impulsive women did well, but the most disappointed had all rushed in and ignored their doubts.

Also, there was a wide spectrum of experience at business school. Some women spent the next several years absolutely delighted: one who had had a particularly boring job rushed off to school early in the morning and returned late at night, still beaming with energy and enthusiasm. For others it was a grueling time that tested their endurance almost unbearably. When I asked one woman if she could characterize her experience at business school in a few words, she said, "Um——brutal."

Three

Surviving
Business School

Ms. MBA swept into business school on a sunny September day, having installed herself a week previously in a fashionable apartment within easy walking distance of Goldmine. Her desk was placed to overlook a prime bit of riverside, and a tasteful but modest living space had been arranged to give the proper atmosphere either for study or for intimate dinners for two. (She was never more than a week behind in trying all the new recipes from the *New York Times Sunday Magazine*.)

With almost no forethought, Ms. MBA threw on a totally appropriate costume for registration: preppy enough to appeal to the more conventional among her classmates, but with a few little touches—handcrafted earrings purchased the previous winter in Switzerland—to reassure the others that she had taste. Registration was a breeze: no difficult decisions to make, since the courses were all predetermined anyway. Waiting in line, Ms. MBA made three lifelong friends with whom she immediately formed a study and support group—for their benefit, of course, not hers, since she was naturally brilliant and did not have to work that hard for top grades.

Her professors were not only stellar but personable, buoying her with constant affirmation as she aced course after course. Her two years of business school fairly melted in her mouth. In her speech as valedictorian, she wished all of her classmates the same success she had attained herself, a remark that went down especially well as she was by then married to the valedictorian of the class before her, had offers from several competing Fortune 500 companies, and was exactly eight months and twenty-nine days pregnant.

In contrast, Pat spent three years slogging her way from two small children and a demanding job to another city three hours away by train. She went to a Goldmine executive MBA program every other weekend, studying eleven nights of thirteen while her husband and kids learned to take better care of themselves. At the end, Pat decided that she did not like business after all and stuck with her old job, after three years of exhaustion and prodigious expense.

Jo-Ann went to a new but well-regarded program full time for two years. Although she had a boyfriend in another city, she had no family ties to keep her from throwing herself wholeheartedly into school after a series of jobs she had not enjoyed especially. When asked how she felt about business school, she said, "It was the most positive experience of my life."

For other women, business school meant everything from attending classes on weekends at an Air Force base to all the comforts of home at Goldmine. Some had fun and others were miserable. They studied hospitals, marketing, or arts management. They went to huge institutions with a cast of thousands pouring in and out every day or to intimate seminars. The schools were anonymous factories or close-knit communities, and everything in between. Women went after work or even during work, or consecrated themselves fully to graduate school for however long it took. At the end of these utterly different experiences, they all had an MBA.

The incredible variety and number of business school programs available now is the direct result of the upsurge in numbers of students. Since women's enrollment in the last decade rose 1,000 percent and men's 50 percent, much of the expansion and diversification are directly attributable to female students. Many other changes have taken place simultaneously over the last ten years in business education, some more directly related to women's entry than others.

Background about Business Schools

The first school to offer an MBA was Dartmouth's Amos Tuck, still one of the nation's top business schools. In 1900 the program began teaching the emerging science of management, a new field created by the rise of industrial capitalism, with its increasingly complex organizations. For about the first half of the century the number of business schools grew modestly.

The Harvard MBA, first offered in 1908, became the ultimate symbol of entry to the most powerful jobs in the country. Rather than the drudgery of studying accounting or management theory, Harvard students worked on the case method. They read and prepared comments on voluminous examples or cases drawn from real experiences, often of past graduates. In a classroom dominated by an illustrious professor, students vied for attention to push their theories about what so-and-so should have thought of or done. The avid competition, the absence of right answers, and the exclusiveness of the club were and are the keys to the Harvard system.

The first MBA programs all served by and large the same population: white men from upper- and middle-class backgrounds, with the occasional working-class striver who had done brilliantly as an undergraduate on scholarship. His presence only legitimized the system and showed that anyone could make it if he worked hard enough. Some state schools and less prestigious private universities began their own programs, which made the degree somewhat more accessible and expanded the total number of MBAs; however, there was no talk of "dilution" or "devaluation" of the degree as long as those receiving it were almost entirely white males.

The explosion in business education did not occur until the early 1970s. The student body changed immensely, largely because the push for affirmative action both in educational institutions and the workplace coincided with universities' need for cash and women's changing aspirations. The population of "business types" was diversified from the homogeneity of white males to include women, persons of color, working adults, and even parents and older people. A few students with disabilities and lesbians and gays also became visible in recent years. A large number of students, mostly women, came from traditional liberal arts backgrounds rather than undergraduate business programs or employment.

There are now about 600 MBA programs (although only 204 of them are currently accredited) compared to a total of under 400 in 1974.[1] While there are many reasons for the sudden popularity, including and especially women's new opportunities, the money crunch in all institutions of higher learning was a vital factor in producing the present crop of graduate business programs. Unsavory as the expression "cash cow" may be, it perfectly describes the way some universities have milked the surge of interest in business courses to preserve their more esoteric pursuits from destruction.

Not only are more programs available than ever before, they are incredibly varied in both content and format. Harvard still uses its case method and virtually locks students up in the same seat in the same classroom week after week, with professors rotating in and out. The part-time adult students in newer schools would probably be incredulous at the idea of spending days on end in the same institutional green room, rather than dashing in and out of a downtown office building with classrooms on one floor and businesses on the others. Adelphi University even offers an MBA on the commuter train to Long Island. The only type of program I did not run across is one that plays cassettes to you in your sleep and tests you in the privacy of your automobile by car phone.

The content of business school programs has been expanded far beyond the world of business itself over the last twenty years. Many respectable programs focus on the arts, hospitals, nonprofits, government, and a host of other subject areas. For example, the Public and Nonprofit Management Curriculum at Columbia was initiated in 1977–1978 not only in response to the tightening of funding for those programs, but to promote an interdisciplinary approach appropriate outside the profit-making sector.

Other schools changed their content to focus on the needs of specific industries. For example, high-tech degrees are offered by the Polytechnic Institute of New York, Stanford, Purdue, MIT, and others; NYU has devised a program for the financial services industry that provides one full week of classes in each term and classes one day a week on alternate Saturdays and Fridays.

While the Goldmine schools clearly aim at the national market for CEOs and other top managers, some Generic schools cater specifically to local markets, such as an industry that wants to provide some professional training for employees or a government agency with a major installation where training funds are available. For all the diversity, the lack of programs to accommodate women specifically is striking. Only one business school, the Simmons Graduate School of Management, devotes itself exclusively to women. Statistics are not available about the numbers of schools that still offer courses focusing on organizational issues for women and men or on women in management. But most observers agreed that they were scarce, and I met no one who had taken one in the last several years. Although business schools have accommodated the needs of women somewhat to ensure that they would enter, the content has hardly altered despite this totally new population.

Overall, changes in format have been more significant. Even Goldmine schools have also shown great flexibility. The University of Chicago, for example, introduced an alternating work/study option aimed at the star employees in local firms who would normally give up their jobs to study full time for two years. (The option offers the possibility of alternating between periods of full-time study and of evening courses.) Others have added part-time and executive programs.

Generic business schools are the real innovators in offering what students need. Because they were often founded to train working-class women and men, they are well accustomed to providing what the market wants. At Pace University, "volume merchandizing"[2] is the key to success, where location, schedule, attractive prices, and the opportunity to waive up to one-third of the required credits combine to make it as convenient as possible to earn an MBA. Pace even provides "late start" courses for those consumers who postpone enrollment until after the registration deadline.

Golden Gate University in San Francisco also thrives on recognizing and meeting the needs of a growing market. Now installed in a handsome, open, modern building in what will soon be the center of the financial area, Golden Gate has the air of an adolescent who has already spurted to twice the height you would have thought possible and is now gathering herself for still larger bra and shoe sizes. It caters to working adults, accommodating them by planning class times to fit schedules as nearly as possible to the working day and offering courses in outlying suburbs so that people can go directly from class to home.

Although they are criticized as crass and unscrupulous, riding the wave of enthusiasm for the MBA while it lasts, and paying little attention to the disappointment of human aspiration they may create in the process, Generic

business schools have made the MBA degree more accessible and less eli-
tist. In a system that rewards competitiveness and entrepreneurship, they
have made it possible for many persons, especially women, to get a degree
that seemed completely beyond their reach just a few years ago. A recent
issue of the Golden Gate alumni magazine pictures three beaming women
on the occasion of their graduation with MBAs. Could these three sisters,
whose father owns a credit finance company and car dealership in Malaysia,
have earned the degree even ten years ago?[3]

Whether the increased access to the MBA degree provided by the
Generics will ultimately prove to be a valuable service or merely one more
broken promise to the disenfranchised remains to be seen. As these young
women and thousands of others have poured out of business school in ever
greater numbers, the education they receive has come under mounting
attack. As early as 1959 both the Carnegie and Ford Foundations published
reports bemoaning the quality of instruction and the lack of academic expertise of both students and faculty. By 1981 criticisms had reached such
a pitch that the *Business and Society Review* printed an article with the blunt
title, "Do Business Schools Teach Absolute Rot?"[4]

While many arrows were shot at MBAs and their training over the
years, three seemed to hit home more than others: overemphasis on theory
rather than the real world, lack of training in communications and other
people-oriented skills, and insufficient attention to ethical, social, and political consequences of organizational actions. Even with the case method
now incorporated into most school programs in some way so that actual
situations are discussed, many still feel that business school is too theoretical.

The lack of training in communications and related skills goes hand
in hand with the stereotype of the MBA as an automaton obsessed with
the bottom line and short-term results at the expense of any other values.
MBAs have been accused of causing the recession and bringing corporate
America to a crisis through their shortsightedness. They are sometimes
seen as insensitive to the wider context of their actions. Several of the
women I interviewed brought up these issues quite spontaneously; one
even decided against going into business because she was so unnerved by
her classmates' unscrupulousness. Another recalled a case involving a European mining company devastating the ceremonial burial grounds of In-
dians in New Guinea; she reacted strongly against it and was put down by
both the professor and students.

As numbers of students and programs in the late 1970s escalated, the
voices of critics grew louder, the demand for MBAs began to fluctuate and
gloomy statistics about a glut appeared. Companies that were delightedly
clamoring for all the MBAs they could get one year changed their tune the
next. While many organizations continued to recruit only at Goldmine
schools for some or all of their positions, others quietly began looking to
the Generics. Some hired undergraduates and others simply looked for the

cheaper price tag and adequate preparation that Generic MBAs could offer. Depending on the organizational culture, some felt it was more important to have a trainable hard worker—the image of a Generic graduate—than a highly ambitious Goldmine MBA who thought of himself as a future CEO and acted accordingly.

These trends to more students and programs, criticism, and erratic demand meant that the women I interviewed were coping with a shifting scene at business school. Ironically, the elite quality of the degree that attracted many of them in the first place lost its shine a little more with each additional thousand new graduates.

Women's Starting Points

Women make up the great bulk of the new population that has swelled business schools in the last ten years, and they are expected to account for any increase in demand that survives the spurt of the 1970s and 1980s. One would therefore expect the avid market researchers at business schools to have compiled a wealth of statistical and qualitative data about their women students: work experience prior to business school, undergraduate institutions they attended, attitudes about the MBA, why and how they chose it, and so on. In other words, no more and no less than any competent advertising executive would find out about her customers.

As I began asking business school officials for information about female students' backgrounds, especially as contrasted to men's, it was evident that they did not have such data. Almost everyone told me that there were few if any differences between male and female students, but when I pressed on specific points, like whether there might be more men than women with technical backgrounds, they allowed as how that might be the case. This experience did reinforce how invisible gender differences are at business schools, even though women will probably continue to be an increasingly important percentage of students. While the invisibility could be interpreted as lack of bias, in the context of the workplace and given the large male majority at many schools, it shows an obliviousness that will not stand women MBA candidates in good stead when they enter the real world. The schools I talked with had not educated themselves about the specific characteristics and needs of women. Instead, they expected women to conform to the norms established by and for the male population.

Although broad quantitative data by gender were not available, the informal observations of the persons I interviewed confirmed what I was learning directly from women MBAs: because of their backgrounds, women entered business school with some disadvantages as well as some powerful assets. Their starting points were usually different from men's, whatever their backgrounds. Some, especially the younger ones, started business school with academic and experiential qualifications virtually identical to men's.

Coming in with the same backgrounds by no means guaranteed women the same experience at school, however. Whether they were aware of it or not, a learning environment almost devoid of role models in the faculty, administration, cases, and textbooks could not help but affect them differently than the men for whom the system was designed. Men could identify with the faculty and vice versa, and could effortlessly envision themselves as chief executive officers with a large body of popular and scholarly literature to uphold them. Women still had to scramble for role models at top levels, and, as will be discussed, even today they will not find many in business school. For all those reasons, even women with backgrounds apparently identical to men's entered school at a disadvantage.

Most of the women I interviewed had different backgrounds from their male counterparts. They were often older and came from more diverse academic and work histories, some of which served them better than others. Their previous employers included the public and nonprofit sectors as well as the business world, and covered a wide range of occupations. Where they had been in management at all, the women were generally at or just above the entry level, except, of course, for the few in executive programs. Those who had followed the most traditional female paths occupationally and personally had the most strikes against them from the start. According to Dr. Joanna Mulholland, a faculty member at the Philadelphia College of Textiles and author of a major study of women and men MBAs,[5] women often enter MBA programs substantially less prepared than men; the differences start with choices against math courses early in life and continue all the way to business school. Often, the language and basic concepts of business are more familiar to men than women. While there are traditional MBA candidates and career changers of both sexes, most of the former were men and most of the latter were women. For example, an investment banker in her early thirties told me:

> The women's backgrounds were much more interesting. Of course there were a lot of interesting men, but most of them had done it the way you're supposed to do it . . . so they knew the language. We showed up, and we didn't know what a debit was and a credit was except in our check books. That was the difference in experience. So they had a real advantage, at least in the short run.

Because their opportunities were more limited, even women who had had business experience often did not have the same qualifications as men.

While these disadvantages are apparent, less has been said about the particular contributions many women could make in business schools. First, because they are far less than half of all MBA candidates and are a minority at most schools, there is still a "creaming" effect. The average female MBA is likely to be more motivated than her male counterpart, just through the law of averages. Similarly, a woman with one of the already mentioned extra strikes against her usually has had to overcome even more barriers and is therefore even more likely to be exceptional. For all of them, to earn the degree is a conscious choice that is still against the grain of many traditional expectations of women, however much those may be changing. Men, on the other hand, may drift into business school in much the same reflexive way women fall into marriage.

Thus many women MBA candidates had the advantage of strong motivation. Although some lacked quantitative skills or higher level business experience, many brought valuable perspectives and qualities from their previous experiences, not to mention the communications skills MBAs have been criticized for lacking. Time and again women told me that their ability to listen closely and respond to needs of others had served them well. Even in unfamiliar business subjects, their writing skills gave them an edge. For example, one banker felt that she and her support group of women were able to pick up the vocabulary of business and use it because of the abilities they cultivated in more traditional jobs.

While women considering business school should recognize that most enter it with some hindrances, the qualities and skills they have already developed can more than outweigh the lack of business background. A woman with a strong sense of herself and what she has to contribute is much more likely to overcome barriers than one who is determined to conform to whatever is expected of her and feels that she has nothing to offer.

Making the Transition to Business School

Except for a few women (such as undergraduate business majors), the transition to business school was demanding. Whatever their circumstances, almost everyone had to contend with fears about not being able to do the work, about classmates, or about the school itself. There were major changes in lifestyle, both for part-timers adding study to their already complex lives and those who were switching from employment to school full time.

When I asked women what their first few days or weeks at business school were like, they admitted to moments of real terror. They were prey to doubts about their ability to perform, particularly if they did not have a strong quantitative or business background or were in competition with the crème de la crème. To some extent their fears were well founded. Some schools, both Goldmine and Generic, pride themselves on giving students a hard time. Many women were put on the spot and made to look foolish. For example, a woman in her mid-thirties who had been out of school for years felt like an ancient matron on her first day at Goldmine. A young male professor really terrified her:

> He was droning on and on about something, and all of a sudden he said, "Isn't that right, Mrs. Roslyn?" There must been over a hundred people in the class. I thought, surely my name can't be the first one on the list, and I hadn't even heard the question. I came home that night and told my husband, "I can't deal with this."

Ultimately, though, she changed her mind:

> It was very intimidating, but I decided that all of these people who had just come out of undergrad school were no smarter than I was. I worked very hard and it paid off. I found out that people around me just talked a good game. I went to school at the right time in my life and I loved it.

In fact, many women discovered later that the persons, especially men, whom they had viewed as having everything so well under control were in fact just as scared as they were. In one case, the stereotypical young male executive confided to a female classmate that nothing he had known earlier had helped him a bit.

As they coped with their fears, most women were also contending with basic adjustments in their daily lives. Part-timers suddenly found that any free moments they had had were eaten up, either by going to class or studying; all the extra time they counted on for refreshment and recreation suddenly evaporated. Often there were major changes in personal lives and routines, particularly for those who had others depending on them.

For full-time students, the adjustments were often even more extreme. Some moved over long distances and had to find lodging, with little institutional support and few if any friends in a new setting. One who had had a demanding job traveling around the country to train people about disability rights found it taxing to go to school full time:

> It was a big adjustment. The first thing I noticed that I didn't like were the constraints on my time. . . . While I was working, I felt that I had a significant amount of control over my time. But my class schedule was dictated to me for the first quarter—really for the first year—because we didn't even choose the classes.

Despite the fears and adjustments the transition inevitably entailed, everyone did also comment on positive aspects of her experience. At its best, business school was an exciting time to absorb new information and ideas. Many women enjoyed the challenge, especially if they had been doing repetitive work for which they were overqualified. A former flight attendant told me that there was no time in her life that she enjoyed more:

> It was marvellous. I was like a sponge: "Tell me more, tell me more"—an information junkie.

Another who had worked at a boring administrative job before going to school full time was so high that she was never even tired:

> I would start out my days—especially when I took computer courses, where you have to spend hours and hours on the computer—at 8:30 or 9:00 and not come home till 10:00 at night. I was never tired. I could just go and go and go, whereas when I was working I would come home at 5:00 and say, "Oh, God." It was just incredible. It was very invigorating.

On the whole, women discovered that they could handle business subjects better than they feared, and some found they could excel. When I asked a former schoolteacher about her most satisfying moment at business school, she told me about her classmates' amazement when she, from a totally nonbusiness background, received one of the five As in a course taught by a distinguished former dean of her Goldmine school.

In making the entry into business school less traumatic, women should anticipate some of the changes that are inevitable in their daily lives and discuss them with the important persons around them, whether they are family or friends. Talking with an MBA who has already been through the process can help in thinking through what the change could mean in practical terms. When it is possible to visit a campus in advance and meet even a few potential classmates, the setting seems less hostile and unfamiliar. Just knowing that it is normal to be afraid and uncomfortable at the beginning can be reassuring, rather than feeling that doubts and fears are indicative that business school is just too much. Forming friendships as early as possible can take the edge off the difficult first few weeks, especially if you form groups, as discussed later.

Differences between Generic and Goldmine Schools

Contrary to the conventional wisdom, I found that Goldmine schools were not uniformly praised, nor were Generics routinely put down. Women had both positive and negative experiences no matter where they went. While the most satisfied women went to both types of schools, the least satisfied nearly always had attended Generic institutions. Just visiting the schools is telling. The Goldmine schools I saw were all real campuses, complete with lawns, campus bookstores, majestic trees, and the amenities of a middle-class environment. Women as well as men were affected by the setting and services that were designed to make graduates feel special. The alumni and placement offices were often wonderfully efficient, keeping close tabs on virtually every graduate. Because they generally depend on their alumni for financial support, the Goldmine schools have a strong reason to look on their students as potential friends for the long haul.

In contrast, the Generic schools seemed utilitarian. The ones I visited were all in downtown areas of cities and were often concentrated in a few buildings on roaring urban streets. They had a practical, down-to-earth tone about them. Anyone could walk in or out, and the most obvious feature of the offices was the profusion of marketing literature. With one notable exception, the placement and alumni offices were a far cry from Goldmine's. Being a student at many of these schools would feel more like a continuation of high school in terms of its overall institutional tone, complete with inadequate cafeteria. While not all Generic schools even approximate this descripton, many do.

The faculty was a very important determinant of a woman's business school experience, no matter where she went. Although the Goldmine professors are often better known, many women told me that that was no guarantee at all that they could teach. Sometimes the elitism gave faculty permission to treat students unkindly or unfairly, as one very dissatisfied woman in her twenties told me:

> There was respect for people as they are, but [there were] put-downs of you as the student. Not because you're Marian, but because you're the student and I'm the teacher, and that's the fun factor. Sometimes sadistic, sometimes really sadistic. And I think these guys say, "Well, this is Goldmine Business School. I can do this; I can be really tough on these guys if they are supposed to be the best."

On the other hand, some women were stimulated by the excitement of learning from persons who were in the forefront of their field and who were developing the theories and ideas that would be put into practice.

At Generic schools, the quality of instruction also varied, from capable state-of-the-art management skills to incompetence. Sometimes, because of the shortage of faculty, people were selected to teach subjects about which they knew little. One woman was totally exasperated by an instructor who had no apparent qualifications other than having made a million dollars by buying cheap and selling high. At their worst, some Generic programs virtually marched MBA candidates through in lockstep, having them stand at attention in the appropriate classrooms for the precise amount of time required. Most Generic MBA programs are not accredited because they do not meet the minimum standards set by the American Assembly of Collegiate Schools of Business for quality of faculty, students, and other criteria.

The positive side of instruction in the Generic schools, when it was good, is that it was firmly rooted in what was happening in the workplace then. The faculty may have been practitioners who taught on the side rather than the reverse, so they had a wide store of examples and cases based on real experiences. Because students often came from a variety of employers, they brought many perspectives, and were valuable sources of information about alternative careers or workplaces.

Differences between Part-Time and Full-Time Courses

The decision of whether to go part- or full-time was highly individual. For many, the choice was dictated by finances: they did not want to go into debt any more than necessary and could have some level of support from their employers. For those who had to do it on their own, part-time courses were often the first choice. Some women did risk a great deal to quit their jobs completely and use a combination of their own savings and large loans to go full time. Others spread the expense out over a period of years. The most privileged women were those who were supported by others while they pursued the degree.

Some who went full time suggested that other women not consider any other option. They found it invaluable to be able to concentrate undividedly on their studies. Contact with other students outside the classroom was as valuable a part of their education as formal classes, and there was a cohesiveness among those in full-time programs that was very rare for part-timers:

> Part of it is lunch. You can sit at lunch talking to people in a different class than yours, being surrounded with the people you are partying and playing with. You are all going through the same program. . . . People make jokes where the punchline is a technical business term. . . . You don't even realize what happened from the day you walked in to the day you walked out, because you have been surrounded by it.

Making the opposite case, however, a few women felt equally strongly that part-time programs helped them keep their perspective, and maintain balance in their lives between school and other activities. Yet the process at times seemed endless. Two critical variables in making a part-time experience as positive as possible for women were the support they had from their employers and the attitude of their schools.

A few had almost ideal employers: one paid nearly all the costs and provided flexibility in work schedules to allow for classes at odd hours. Some women succeeded in integrating their work and study lives so that each built on the other; they enjoyed the opportunity to put their learning to work immediately and often were able to use material from their jobs in their papers. Many, however, did not receive that level of support from their employers. A woman who graduated in the mid-1970s approached her company before it was commonplace for them to send women to business school and was summarily refused. More recently, a woman in her fifties was told that an MBA was a requirement for her to do the job for which she had been hired as a trainee. Yet she did not receive any support at all, and ultimately was laid off right before she graduated from the program she had pursued at her own expense.

Just as some employers were much more helpful than others, schools varied greatly in accommodating the other demands in part-time students' lives. When they had to travel on business or miss classes for other good reasons, faculty and students could be understanding and helpful—or the reverse. Often, part-time students felt satisfied with some aspects of their program, but not others:

> The school tried to be very sensitive to our needs in tutoring and class schedules. I will say that they bent over backwards to accommodate evening students and not treat us like some kind of appendage. . . . But placement was an area where they fell down, and I was very frustrated with the career services there.

Some found the pressures of an eternity of evenings too much and shopped around for alternative schedules. One MBA who is now a government training officer earned her degree at a special weekend program. Instructors were actually flown out from an accredited Midwestern program for weekend blitz courses. Three weeks before they started, each student received the text and assignments; on the weekend itself, classes ran from approximately 6 P.M. Friday to 5 P.M. Sunday, when the midterm was administered. (Each course occupied two weekends.) The woman I interviewed simply rented a motel room nearby and collapsed at the end of each day, but still found it less exhausting than going to school four nights a week on top of her job. In the end, her MBA had nothing to do with the work she found after a long job hunt.

Others for whom the pressures of part-time study became over-whelming chose a different way out: they switched to full time, borrowing money or relying on someone else. I did not talk with a single woman who regretted making the change. One who had done the first phase over several years part time and then took the course full time told me:

> You forget a lot and it doesn't connect as well. . . . When I went
> that full year, I got so much more out of it.

All things considered, the choice between full and part time depends not only on an individual's finances and preferences, but on support from employers and schools. Some women were satisfied with both types of experiences, but the most dissatisfied were those in part-time programs, and most felt that full time was preferable when it was possible.

The Context of Women's Business Education

Women's attitudes toward their business schools varied greatly, but they all agreed that men are the vast majority of the administration, faculty, and often student body; men have written the great bulk of the texts and cases about a world in which women are relative newcomers in management.

Women sit next to men in classes, but they have arrived at business school by different routes; their context is different. While both have some of the same reasons for being there—career prospects and money—credibility is a far more important motivator for women. They know they need the degree more than men do. Men might be stymied in a particular job or industry because of a recession or because there were cutbacks in that field, but not because the job was capped off by gender discrimination, as it is for librarians, teachers, social workers, nurses, and secretaries.

Even if women and men arrive at business school with identical work histories, their prospects once they leave are statistically quite different. Individuals vary, but the overall pattern of lower earnings and attainment for women is as true of MBAs as of females in any other field. While many industries have become more accessible to women, there are still areas, such as heavy manufacturing, where women managers are all but unknown. Some women go through business schools believing that those patterns will not affect them, but their lower aspirations[6] show that they internalize the realities of the labor market. Most female MBA candidates have already assumed the caretaking identity society has groomed them for. Now that they are also expected to have careers, and successful ones at that, another burden has been placed on their shoulders, with no release from their traditional responsibilities. They are caught in a welter of conflicting messages about being "real women" in the old sense and being "successful" in the new one.

The content of business school courses is enormously varied across different programs, but very little of what is taught reflects these and other specifically female perspectives and concerns. The subjects that MBAs study are not neutral, scientific topics that need only be presented accurately; much of the criticism of the education centers on the point that it is approached too much in that spirit, with little social, political, or ethical content.

When I interviewed the first female faculty member at one of the most highly regarded schools in the country, she could not recall a single time when there was any discussion of how the curriculum content should change because of the influx of women: never at a faculty meeting, department meeting, or even in private conversation. It simply never came up; the school assumed that women would be fed the same diet as the men.

While some schools do offer career-development courses, most use men's lives as models for goal setting and planning. In the long run, women MBAs may well prove to follow career patterns more like those of other women workers, particularly professionals. Dr. Betsy Jaffe's study[7] of management women in transition compares women's career patterns to men's, finding that many of the adult and career development models that categorize people by age and stage do not fit women. Even looking only at the immediate future for the women MBAs I interviewed, they unquestionably faced different pressures and prospects than their male colleagues; yet none of them mentioned that these had ever been discussed in their formal coursework. Considering the shock that some expressed later when they found obstacles to their progress, it was clear that few had been prepared for the workplace as it is. A faculty member confirmed that observation:

> [The women] don't know how tough it's going to be out there. They really don't. . . . Unless somebody actually asks me or comes to me for career counseling, I don't make a point of mentioning it in class, because I have male and female students and would therefore not want to turn them off.

Thus to her the gender aspects of the workplace are defined only as woman's concerns, not features that any manager has to understand. They cannot be discussed publicly for fear of alienating the men. What is omitted is at least as significant as what is included.

The cases or examples discussed in class are very rarely geared to the particular situations women are likely to encounter in the workforce. Many women MBAs who become managers will have to contend at some point with a male subordinate who has difficulty taking orders from a woman.

How should she handle him? More important, in terms of her career development, a woman needs to study cases in which a hopeful new MBA like herself is gently, noiselessly passed over for promotion again and again—and what she can do about it.

Women MBAs usually lack preparation for organizational game playing based on sexist assumptions, and for counteracting it assertively and effectively. A seemingly neutral classroom case can and should be treated very differently depending on whether the manager is female or male. For example, employees might be confronting a manager for being indecisive and taking insufficient initiative to protect their welfare during a cutback. Because of the way women are stereotyped, employees could perceive the manager's behavior as waffling when in fact she was being clear, but not being heard. She would use different strategies to counteract the situation than a man; if he spoke overemphatically, it would probably put the point across, while the same behavior on her part might earn her the label of "tough broad" or even "hysteric".

Business school prepares women to play the game as men have always played it, armed with the same weapons, rather than developing the specific skills they need to survive as women. Aside from obvious differences such as the need to handle sexual harassment, women must be alert to a different set of organizational signals; if a woman is excluded from a business lunch or denied permission to attend a professional association meeting, it may have an entirely different meaning than it would for a man in the same position. By not recognizing differences between female and male experiences in the workforce, business schools do not prepare women for the realities they will face.

The message that women did not belong at business school was sometimes overt. The use of masculine pronouns in reference to anyone who is not a secretary, for example, reflects historic patterns of employment that have changed somewhat and, in the hopes of women MBAs, will only change further. Sex-biased language is still the norm in many written materials and in classroom instruction. Often faculty members are completely oblivious to the fact that they speak only of men in professional or leadership roles, and of the significance it holds. Here is what happened when one woman asked a professor to include her half of the human race:

> There was one finance professor who would constantly use examples of stockbrokers who were always "he." Finally one woman wrote him a note and asked if he had noticed that half the class are female, asking if he could just switch. He was a good-humored person, so he came in the next day and took a vote. He said, "This has been suggested to me, and frankly I never even noticed that I did this, and I don't want to slight the women in the class. *It's just normal for me* (italics mine). As some of you may know, it is proper grammar to use the masculine form."

One woman attributed some faculty attitudes in her 1984 Goldmine classroom to nostalgia for a bygone era:

> A lot of these older professors are used to having primarily men in their class. There are some that aren't used to women students. I had one who would tell very off-color jokes. I'm a big girl; I'm not offended, but it's just not appropriate for a class. I had one gentleman who was very open about the fact that he didn't think women belonged in business.

Lack of Women Faculty

Most of the women I interviewed found it utterly normal to have all male or almost all male faculty; similarly, most adults do not question the appropriateness of a picture in which a man is a doctor and a woman a nurse, although they may well query the reverse. Most women had not given it a second thought until I raised the question. They began to count the women in authority roles in their business school experience, usually on one hand. Statistically, their data seem to be quite accurate. What difference does it make? One woman said:

> I had one woman in both my undergraduate and graduate programs. I had one woman during the entire time. You don't have anybody to look up to.

Looking at it from the other side, a female faculty member was genuinely startled at how important it was to her students that she was a woman and willing to talk with them about issues related to gender. As a black woman in a white institution, she was somewhat taken aback at how hungry students were for her insights:

> The role model is still so important. I was surprised, because we are talking about upper middle-class, affluent, white young women, and they were so receptive to me. . . . I've had female students come to me in a way that I don't believe they would have come to a man. Sometimes they have even said so (directly). When I first got to campus, sororities would invite me over. They were so glad to have a female professor.

Other women faculty may not be so willing to raise issues of interest to women; indeed, they may be the last to do so for fear of being labeled. Even so, at least their presence establishes role models for women in authority, which are essential to students of both sexes.

At times, simply having another woman to talk with can help immeasurably. A woman who was beginning business school in her forties was wringing her hands in the school bookstore; she could not see how she would ever survive microeconomics:

> The man in the bookstore said, "Wait a minute. I'll call this woman professor for you and you can talk." She said, "Don't clutch up. Here's the book you should buy." I took her course second semester, highly recommended by everybody, and she was excellent.

When business school offers as few models as the workplace, women do not have the opportunity for the rich relationships between student and teacher who can identify with each other. The most striking example of business school attitudes was observed in a Goldmine women's room:

> They don't really accept women as being part of the MBA program. . . . You know the classroom building there? There were urinals in the women's bathroom. Every women's bathroom has urinals in it. The very simple reason is that the school was not coed until the late '60s or early '70s. They converted a couple of bathrooms to women's bathrooms. They've got four urinals and two stalls. They've never seen a reason to change it.
>
> I've told a couple of guys in my class who have called me up to give money to the school: "Tell me if they've taken the urinals out of the classroom building, and then I'll tell you if I am going to give money. I refuse to until then." They've got enough money so they could take those things out if they wanted to. There's no way in hell they are ever going to need them again—hopefully.

By leaving the urinals in, this well-endowed school reminds women that they may be a temporary aberration.

This signal, like many others, is perceived only by those who are really attuned to sensing women's opportunities and the limitations on them. Some observed the dynamics in their classrooms closely—who was called on, when, and how—and of study groups. One observer who has watched the scene change over the last decade feels that many issues are more difficult to detect:

> So many of the issues are so subtle, about being handled differently in class or a male model being put out as the one to have. If you deviate from that, it's wrong; you can't look at many different styles of management.

To some women it was obvious that business school was a fundamentally masculine environment. Several had been to undergraduate schools that were in the process of admitting men, so that men were in the minority and had to adjust to a female norm. One woman said:

> At college they had to learn how to deal with women as equals,
> and as friends. . . . At business school they certainly didn't need
> to learn that. They absolutely didn't. So if they weren't predis-
> posed to doing it at the beginning, they sure as hell didn't end up
> doing it at the end.

The issues women raised when I interviewed them were by no means confined only to the mid-1970s, to less reputable schools, or to geographically isolated programs. For example, Berkeley, hardly a laggard in business education or a cultural desert, was taken to task for sexist and racist practices by the MBA Association co-vice president in 1984, and others echoed her concerns.[8] Within the last two years, a woman I interviewed was sexually harassed by the dean of a Goldmine school who told her that he could make things easier for her. No doubt he could have, but she did not give him a chance.

How Women Responded

For some women, being in an environment so little shaped to their needs added to the stress of going to business school. It could be a real endurance test intellectually, emotionally, and physically. For others, it was as easy as breathing. There was absolutely no correlation between how trying the women found the experience and the quality of the school as conventionally defined. For example, one of the few women who went straight from undergraduate school to one of the very top business schools found that she hardly had to work at all:

> Most people will have told you that they worked really hard. I
> don't know why it is, but I was able to get through. I never
> prepared a case. There was very little work besides preparing
> cases, and I just didn't do it. I'd sort of read over the first
> page. . . . I didn't cover myself with glory, but I made it.

At the other extreme, some women pushed themselves through "easy" Generic programs by sheer force of will, having decided that they would somehow make it despite lack of academic preparation and experience. Most women eventually made their peace with business school, wherever they went, but they often had significant adjustments to make in all three spheres of their lives: academic, personal, and social.

The Academic Sphere

What was business school like academically for women as diverse as those I interviewed? The sheer volume of work was a shock to most of them. Many vividly remembered looking at the size of their first assignments in horror. One woman was so piled up with cases on her first day that she could hardly carry them all. A woman with very strong mathematical skills who was going to a Generic program found that she was just this side of coping.

While some were enthralled by their course work, a number told me that they found it unbearably dull. The problems simply did not interest them, or they found the level of instruction so low that they could not rouse themselves to care very much. It was the boredom, not the difficulty, that upset someone like a philosophy major who had always enjoyed the intellectual excitement of exploring complex issues. Yet a few women had just the opposite experience, discovering that business was more interesting than they had expected.

Whether they found the work easy or difficult, boring or interesting, everyone was affected by the level of competition at their schools. There was a broad spectrum, from the very high-powered Goldmine schools with their long lists of grade point averages worked out to the fourth decimal place, to others where cooperation is the norm and students are urged to work together as much as possible. Some women had thought carefully in advance about where they wanted to place themselves on that spectrum and were comfortable with their choices.

At the top schools, women were in classrooms filled with valedictorians from all over the world. The pressure was sometimes intense:

> Everyone who is in that program is used to being at the top. When you get thrown into that kind of situation, somebody is going to be in the middle and somebody is going to be on the bottom. For those of us who weren't at the top, we were continually worried that we were going to flunk out. But we didn't, and you make it.

At other schools, with either a different philosophy or a less selective student body, grades were still often a worry to women who were accustomed to "doing well." Some had to struggle to pass. One who had a graduate liberal arts degree from a top school prepared carefully for an accounting exam. She received an F for the first time in her life. First she went into a panic, but then she coped:

> I thought, this is really it. This is where you separate the people who can do it from the people who can't. . . . Now I'm with

the real competition and I can't do it. This is horrible. Then I asked myself why I made an F.

Rather than flagellating and blaming herself as she might have done when she was younger, she began to analyze the test and concluded that it was a very poor one. She went to see the professor and insisted that the test be revised. From that day on, the tests improved, and she never got anything but an A (except once!) for the rest of her business school career.

For most women who made lower grades for the first time, the problem was not so readily resolved. It was usually a matter of time until the vocabulary and context of business sank in, although in the meantime the blows to the ego could be hard to take. One reentry woman was moaning about getting a C when her eleven-year-old son consoled her: "C's not so bad, Mom. B is good and A is better, but C's not so bad. It's average."

Even the passage of time and newly acquired skills did not always help. One woman put off the course she dreaded most until the very last minute. She ultimately passed, but she had her doubts:

> Right before graduation I sat down with the dean to check the requirements. He said, "You haven't taken statistical analysis?" "Well, no, I haven't." "Why are you waiting until the end?" I said, "In case I die first." When I got into it, I thought I may not even pass this course after spending three years in business school.

The academic sphere was infinitely easier for women who had an undergraduate degree in the business area or experience in the profit-making world, or both. The career changers simply did not have the same orientation. A woman with ten years' experience as an administrator in nonprofits found that she lacked something even more basic than she had expected:

> Some of it is a mentality that's very hard to grasp. I was at a very big disadvantage because I had never worked in a for-profit institution. A lot of what other students took for granted was not obvious to me.

One of the few generalizations that can be made is that women's academic experiences at business school became easier over time. One faculty member told me that the first semester was 50 percent of the battle, the second was 25 percent, and the whole second year was only a quarter. By then, the necessary adjustments had been made to the routine, women knew how the system worked, and they had made a start on the basic skills they needed.

The Personal Sphere

Substantial commitments outside business school, whatever they were, took more than time and energy away from women's studies. They also divided their attention among conflicting priorities and curbed the social life that would often have contributed to their education. Both single and married women, mothers and nonparents, had responsibilities to others, and the level of support they received varied tremendously.

   Only one woman told me that she was totally free to pursue her studies. After a year as a practicing artist and administrator, she cut loose completely from her old life and moved across the country to live in a city she had always wanted to explore. She registered in an accredited Generic program and immersed herself for two years:

> I had no responsibilities or attachments per se, so that made it very easy. I had attachments, but I didn't have a husband, I didn't have a kid, I didn't have a house, I didn't have a dog or any debts. I was pretty much a free spirit. . . . Any decision I made was not based on someone else.

Other single women did have commitments that influenced or even dictated the quality of their experience. A young black woman who was working full time cared for her grandmother while she was also taking a heavy course load, until other family members insisted on taking over. Although single women were less likely to bring up the importance of the personal sphere, they often had numerous responsibilities that affected their academic and social lives. A lesbian woman found it difficult to maintain her intimate relationship through the years that she was going to school at night and working full time at a demanding job, just as some other women reported strains in their relationships with men.

   Some women had excellent support from their male partners. A few even said they could not have completed the program without it or that they would not have entered business school if they had not known they would have enough support, financial and emotional. They also made trade-offs; one woman in her forties struck a deal with her husband that she would iron his shirts if he would type her papers. On the other hand, she was also typical in trying to discharge her home responsibilities just as she had done before going to school, rather than securing support and dividing the duties differently. She went to extraordinary lengths, as others did, to adjust herself rather than asking anyone else to adapt to her new schedule:

> I used to get up at 5 in the morning because I didn't want to disrupt our life. . . . I didn't change our social pattern. We still had people over for dinner; we still went out and on trips. I just

dragged books wherever we went; I didn't cut anything out of our lives. My husband didn't like it, because he didn't like to hear the alarm go off. I thought, "You don't like to hear it, but I've got to get up!" That went on for four years, which seemed endless.

Other women also attempted to do most of the adjusting themselves rather than put demands on male partners who might respond unfavorably. For example, while she and her husband were both working and studying, one woman continued to take charge of their food:

I just switched to frozen foods. I didn't worry so much about nutrition. . . . I just made things convenient and I used to do a lot of juggling.

Often, the sacrifices involved in earning the MBA were made by taking away from the small amount of time that women spent on themselves.

Women with children had particular burdens. Although it was very demanding, some actually chose business school as a convenient time to have a baby. If they went full time and had a partner supporting them, it worked out quite well; they could be home some of the time and still keep up with their studies. Some went back to school immediately; others timed children between the first and second years, took a year off, and returned. It sounds smooth relative to the lives of those who leapt straight from childbed to lecture hall, but there were still complications in arranging care, especially when children were sick. In the great majority of cases, it was mothers rather than fathers who discharged those responsibilities.

Sometimes the women who were mothers, students, and often workers as well felt like multiple personalities. The only housewife in the taxation program at her Generic school felt that she changed identities every time she drove from her sweltering suburban home into chilly San Francisco:

I had a baby at home and I was commuting from a suburb where it was very hot. I'd drive into the city and everyone was wearing wool suits. It was a cultural shock on almost a daily basis, switching from one mode to another. Plus being in a situation where you were competing with attorneys and CPAs who were dealing with the subject matter daily as part of their job, and I wasn't dealing with it at all.

The contrasts were even more extreme for a mother who left her family behind during the week so she could attend a Goldmine school full time, then commute home several hours on the train for weekend visits. She even had to write a paper during a family vacation visiting relatives and Disney World. Yet several women felt in the end that their children benefited from having their mothers pursue their own goals:

> I think it has a real impact on my children's lives. They know now that moms can do other things. They know moms go to school.

Close relationships were often stressed. Even without children and the unique problems of single parenthood, juggling personal lives, school, and work can be very demanding for women with partners and friends who are important to them. Choices and trade-offs must be made daily if not hourly, and they can be difficult to explain. One woman who had been the life of the party in her day found that some people just did not understand her new situation:

> It was hard for me to explain to my friends that it wasn't that I was being unfriendly, I just don't have time for you or my husband or anybody. I can't even talk to the cat.

Some women found strong support from both their friends and their families. A black single mother sent her child off to her mother, a history professor, when she needed a few weeks of straight studying; others were soothed through the terrible nights before exams by friends who reassured them that they really would survive. One woman's husband, although he was threatened by her new-found independence, helped her with her homework night after night.

Generally, though, women managed to get through business school with much less support than they might have had from employers, friends, family, and others. Many tried to handle their personal situations on their own, making ever more exorbitant demands of themselves rather than seeking assistance from others. It was partly that pattern that dictated their lives in the social sphere of business school, especially for those who were working part time and trying to keep their personal lives more or less the same as they had been.

The Social Sphere

Social life at business school was an important part of many women's learning experience. Not only did they study with others, but they had an opportunity to help each other through the occasional crises in confidence that plagued almost everyone. Only a few found friends immediately. A woman who had left her boyfriend behind in New York was feeling very lonely as she walked across campus a few days before school opened. It was Sunday, so she bought the *Times* and soon found a few similarly exiled women reading their papers on the lawn. The friendships that formed that day persist. Not everyone was so lucky, however.

There were all kinds of reasons why women felt set apart from their classmates, particularly at a time when many were fearful of what the program was going to be like. Since the percentage of persons of color in business school is low and has always been, any woman who was not white could feel quite out of place. It was not until a black woman made her way to school that she realized the full extent of the economic disenfranchisement of her community and how it would affect her education:

> I knew that I didn't know how little I knew, because those things had been so closed off from certain segments of society.

Although she ultimately succeeded, it took extraordinary time and patience to overcome the barriers.

A disabled woman told me much the same story. She found herself isolated initially by the fearful reactions of many of her classmates. Some shunned her during the early adjustment period, when everyone admitted that support was important. Eventually, however, most of them accepted her:

> Once my classmates got to know me, they pretty much treated me like everyone else. But for the first few months, people didn't tend to talk to me a lot, and those who did were generally people who had some experience with disability. This happens in life in general. They're people who have had a disabled family member or had a disabled roommate in college. . . . But people who have not are very afraid at first. They tended not to talk to me until they saw me over and over again, doing the same things they do, like participate in class. That's when I really began to break down barriers, by continual exposure.

Age difference can make a woman feel alone, whether she is older or younger than her peers. Some of the women who returned to school after raising families or starting their careers in another field told me that they felt ancient beside their classmates. A nurse with several small children used to seek out another older student in each of her classes, sit with her, and team up on homework assignments. Although they sometimes knew little about the technical subjects being discussed, often they could offer insights on the broader issues. Younger women sometimes felt inferior and dumb because they had little experience in the business world and had the additional disadvantage of having less authority outside the classroom.

In programs where people were expected to contribute their points of

view, a woman without prior business experience could feel particularly
exposed and inadequate. Other differences also made women feel as though
they did not belong. A Jewish woman with a strong Democratic background was jarred by her classmates' reactions to her husband's job as a
legal aid lawyer. A lesbian found no one who openly shared her experience.

Any of these factors could make a woman wonder whether she had
really made a terrible mistake in coming to business school. An art history
major who became an accountant felt disoriented when she started at Goldmine. It was like being in a foreign country:

> Absolutely the first day I knew I was in a different culture. That
> day all they do is go through the hype of going through a job
> interview and getting a job, negotiating salary—that shocked me.
> Here I had come from the Seven Sisters where you study for
> study's sake, to learn how to think in the liberal tradition, and
> God forbid you tell an admissions officer that you want to get a
> job after you graduate.

Whether women were able to overcome these barriers and others to
make friends, colleagues, and sometimes lovers depended heavily on
whether they were going full or part time, as well as on the atmosphere
of the school. Many part-timers had their social lives already established,
and between job and other responsibilities the last thing they needed was
another crop of friends. They approached business school, in general, as
consumers, coming to class and then leaving. When they did connect with
other students, it was usually over a specific assignment rather than a social
friendship. People often simply did not see each other again after a brief
encounter in one course or another.

Although many women found friends and even boyfriends among
their male peers, both MBAs themselves and business school observers
reported a distinction between women as colleagues and women as women
with social and sexual identities. Single men preferred to consort with
undergraduates rather than with their peers in some schools:

> The guys went to the local undergraduate girls' schools. They
> made expeditions. They'd come back, and you'd hear the funny
> story about how the car broke down, they left a buddy at the
> dorm, and God knows what happened to him.

According to an alumni office staffer, women's expectations about what
their relationships with male classmates will be like are somewhat naive:

> Many of them are not aware of how tough it is. . . . Women
> who are going through programs like this are still greeted with a

certain amount of skepticism from the male population. The MBA men are often not looking for women in terms of long-term relationships who are similarly educated. That is obviously a real generalization, but I think to a certain degree that this is true. . . . The men here have an enormous amount of respect for the women intellectually, but that is a very different thing from saying, "I want to spend a lifetime with one of them."

Most women felt that the men included them socially to some degree, but they differed about exactly where the cutoff was. Some said that it was in casual group situations where men preferred each other's company; others noted a classic division between female classmates and girls to have fun with. (Contrary to the stereotype of greater enlightenment at Goldmine schools, there seemed to be a stronger male culture at the more established institutions.) Because women's situation was so ambiguous, they adopted different tactics to cope with it. One even took on the safe camouflage of marriage to keep herself from being classified as intellectually threatening and sexually available:

I pretended I was married. I say that now and my friends think I'm crazy, but I thought I'd be less of a threat to the men in my classes if they thought I was married. . . . I don't even know what made me do it. The first couple of weeks I was there I just did it. I guess I just didn't want any trouble. I just wanted to go to class, and I didn't want to have any problems of any kind.

On a personal level, women sometimes felt out of place, even when they belonged to a generation that is supposed to be more aware. According to an alumni office staffer:

They are at a point where they are feeling significantly confident about themselves and they also didn't grow up at a time when there was an enormous amount of discrimination. It's still there, of course, but not blatant. I think they are often surprised at the kinds of subtle forms that discrimination can take, because I don't think they expect it, in personal sorts of ways.

Just one example: a group of women were sitting on the lawn one September evening, and one of them was feeling very hurt because the men she worked with on a project had excluded her socially:

I started to question myself: am I a nice person, was I really awful? how come they don't like me? All kinds of taking it down to a personal level. . . . I looked around the group, all attractive women with nothing apparently awful about any of us, and we began to notice a trend. As long as we were working with the men we were equals, but when it came to social life, they wanted nothing to do with us. They didn't want us around when they were hustling.

Only one woman I interviewed identified herself as a lesbian. She was open about this to her classmates and found them accepting, if not enthusiastic, about her identity and lifestyle; she did not look for or expect to find intimate relationships among her peers, although she did form a number of strong friendships with both women and men. On the other hand, several other women said their lesbian friends at business school were very careful of what they revealed to peers (their future business associates) and faculty; while I heard of a few who formed relationships there, they seemed to be the exceptions rather than the rules.

The social side of business school was a more important part of business education than many women realized at the outset. Although most went through some lonely times at the beginning, they generally made at least some connections, a process that was understandably much easier for full- than for part-time students.

Changes in Business Schools

Business schools still vary enormously in their level of acceptance of women students as serious career persons. Overall, some real changes have taken place in many schools in the last ten years; the most obvious is the increased number and percentage of women students, which in itself has no doubt created a more comfortable environment for them. Dr. Betsy Jaffe, who received her MBA from the University of Connecticut in the early 1960s as the first and lone woman, has a class picture showing her demurely seated among her male classmates; she looks unbelievably out of place unless she is misconstrued to be the token woman. (In reality, she was number one academically in her class.) Most programs now have enough women so that anyone can be sure of finding an appropriate toilet. A woman is not an isolated anomaly whose every action seems to accentuate how different she is, nor is she painfully conspicuous simply because she is female. One hopes that the more open-minded professors who had preconceptions about women students have now taught a sufficient number of them to overcome some of their prejudices.

One effect of women's increased presence is that the language of some cases has changed. A recent Generic MBA who also holds an undergraduate business degree feels very encouraged that the cases are no longer always about men, at least at her school:

When I went to undergraduate school, all the cases were Mr. Jones and Mr. Smith. There were no women in them. Now they've changed them to "Miss" here and there. You think it's really stupid, it's silly, and just women complaining, but it makes a big difference. . . . You know when you're reading cases, it's a subtle thing, but you are always reading about men being in charge. Men are the ones who are the supervisors: Mr. So-and-so is in charge of personnel, and Mr. So-and-so is in charge of accounting. They're changing it now and maybe they think it's silly, but it really does make a difference.

Only a few of the women could cite examples of business schools responding positively to the new population of women. For example, Howard University was given credit for raising both gender and race issues and how they would affect MBAs' careers. In some other schools, women's organizations were able to change both student and faculty awareness of some of the barriers women faced. But special programs to address women's particular situation at business school are generally a thing of the past. In the 1970s the American Assembly of Collegiate Schools of Business used to offer a $10,000 award (funded by the Sears Foundation and the Business and Professional Women's Foundation, then Sears and the American Association of University Women's Foundation) to increase women's enrollment. It has now disbanded the one committee devoted to women's concerns. Only Simmons was founded to serve women exclusively and still does.

Pronouns may have been altered in some cases, and the percentage of women students may be creeping up toward just half of what would be their fair share as 51 percent of the total population. What is most striking, however, is how little the drastic change in the student body of business schools has affected the substance of what is taught, how it is taught, and by whom. Most adjustments have been geared simply to drawing women in. Schedules have been made more flexible, and marketing literature now often depicts female as well as male students. Otherwise, many barriers are still firmly, if sometimes subtly, in place.

If business schools had been fully committed to being part of widespread change in women's opportunities, what would they be like now? Students today would be reaping the benefits of a long-standing affirmative action program to cultivate and promote women faculty. Course content would include a realistic view of the power dynamics between the sexes in the workplace, and cases would represent the experiences of female as well as male managers, including situations that are particular to women, such as most types of sexual harassment. Courses in organizational behavior would cover patterns of workforce distribution by gender and race and how those affect everyday life in organizations. Schools would be working closely with recruiters not only to clean up their act in interviews (as many have) but to publicize their practices on child care, family leave, and other issues of special concern to women, and their statistics about management positions by gender and race.

By now, the knowledgeable reader is laughing. While each of these items has probably been addressed somewhere at least theoretically, business schools as a body have not even approached this level of commitment to equal opportunity for women. Instead, they have complied with the legal requirement that they admit women on the same basis as men. Most have stopped right there. Because informal barriers remain in place and because the content of what is taught has changed so little, women have had to develop strategies to make their business school experiences more successful, not only on an individual level but as a group.

Strategies To Cope with Business School

Those who tried to go it alone in business school were almost invariably sorry that they had. Whatever their circumstances, most women were wrestling with what to do next in their careers, which implicitly involved the many ways that being female would affect them. All kinds of support systems were critical to their pulling through an experience that was often challenging and could even be downright painful. Connections made all the difference: study groups, informal networks, outside organizations and support systems, and networks women created specifically for themselves. Using those strategies, many found that maintaining a confident, assertive posture was the most effective way to contend with business school.

Speaking Up

As individuals, women developed some specific techniques they wanted to pass on to others. One of the most important was speaking up, whether in class, in the study group, or wherever. A woman in a Generic program went so far as to make an appointment to see every professor on the first day of class, to explain what she was looking for and to ask their advice about the program. Instead of sitting in the back row, as she felt tempted to do as an older woman, she made her way to the front time after time. Some women also coped by letting others know when they felt left out or offended. A stellar student confronted a "sweet old guy" on the faculty when he made up an example of a man's company going under because he had no sons to take over, only daughters. As the daughter of a small-business man, she told him how his lecture affected her:

When you say something like that, it makes me feel like I don't belong here, that maybe there is something wrong with me for being here. But I know I work just as hard [as the men].

Speaking up in all of these situations and others was considered essential by many women. By doing so, several women from Asian backgrounds felt that they were frowned upon even more than their WASP counterparts, because they were not expected to stand up for themselves. Being assertive and persistent depended largely on women's maintaining their self-esteem, which could be difficult in circumstances in which they felt inept or uncomfortable. Some who really became stuck found that the help they obtained from other students simply was not enough, and they hired tutors or bought elementary textbooks to help them.

Working Together

While these techniques worked well for individuals, almost every woman found that she could benefit both personally and academically from participation in groups. Schools vary tremendously in the degree of emphasis they place on group projects and participation in class. In some it is an established and rigorous part of the curriculum, while in others it is left more to chance. Again, there was a big contrast between part- and full-time students. Most part-timers wanted to get on and off the campus as quickly as possible; the logistics of coordinating a study group were often too difficult to overcome, although some managed. Most MBAs who participated in groups found them valuable. A telephone company employee who went to a Goldmine school that stressed cooperation felt that it really helped her on the job:

You need to depend on the support and expertise of your fellow students to get through. That's good, because it's exactly what it takes when you get out and get into a job. You can't go by yourself in a corner; you have to work with other people. Fostering that attitude while you are in school is probably one of the best things they could do. The people who shared common interests naturally gravitated toward each other. We found ourselves studying together more, and being a support group for each other.

Working together was an opportunity for women and men to know each other in settings in which they had a common professional purpose, rather than competing in the classroom. At their best, these groups transcended the issues that sometimes prevented colleagueship, as they did for this MBA:

We did so many projects together that nobody could afford to start thinking in terms of male and female. . . . If there weren't so many group efforts, I think it would have been a different situation . . . the guys would not have had to face the fact that you were wearing a skirt. They were more interested in what's going on in your head. Under those circumstances, they had to be.

For women with liberal arts backgrounds where the premium is often placed on individual accomplishment, it could be difficult to adjust to the idea that students should help each other. It was not until her second year at a Generic school that a woman who had previously been employed in the nonprofit sector finally began to work with others. She even overcame the scheduling problems of working adults by talking with people by phone and meeting for coffee for twenty minutes before class. Although she first feared that she would have nothing to contribute because she had no business background, others valued the insights she had gathered from her sociology training.

Similarly, informal groups were essential to success at a prominent executive MBA program. I was told about one woman who was isolated from the male group:

All the guys were housed with four or five in a dorm around a central lavatory, so they all lived together. Every day, they would come to class prepared. She wouldn't be, even though she had spent half the night and really worked hard. All these guys would be ready.

One day she was ready to quit. . . . She was going across the campus and one of the guys said, "Why don't you join us for breakfast?" She went, and what she found out was that each of the men—one in finance, one in marketing, whatever—had read the case studies and the information in their field. Then they got together every morning and told each other what they needed to know for the day's class. From that day on, they found out that she was an economist, and they were all vying to have her at the breakfast because she had very valuable information to give.

This woman might have given up on the program without ever learning that the game was being played at breakfast, not in the classroom. She was so left out that she did not even realize that she was left out.

Finding Support

In part because the barriers were often invisible, some women found support groups specifically for themselves especially important. A future investment banker told me that she picked out some of her allies just by looking through the book of photographs and biographies of other students. She started a group right away:

> [Most of us] were concerned about our ability to do heavy-duty quantitative stuff. In classes like accounting and math, we would study together and . . . we were meeting all these men who had been commercial and investment bankers. I had never even heard of all this stuff. It was very intimidating. . . . We felt comfortable with each other, and we managed to do fine. Perhaps not the best, but we didn't have to rely on the men to carry it through.

Sometimes participation in a group that had nothing to do with business courses helped women cope, especially when they felt on shaky ground academically. For example, soccer saved one woman's sense of self. When I asked her how she had contended with business school, she said she did not totally succeed. At a time when her confidence had been knocked out of her by exorbitant academic demands, it was comforting for her to do something she was good at again.

For others, simply maintaining their working and social lives while attending a program part time provided them with the necessary sense of balance. Some general student groups, such as MBA clubs or associations, were also a valuable resource for women, especially in putting them in touch with alumni. (Most of these, however, were a great deal more accessible to full-time than to part-time students.)

Forming Networks

When women first entered business schools in any numbers, they began to organize associations and networks of their own, most of which are active today to varying degrees. Some simply allow women to meet each other and discuss common concerns; others also act as pressure groups to make people in business schools more aware of how their practices and policies affect women particularly. Whether they are set up as alternatives to the old boys' network, as social groups or as support systems, women's associations and networks are often the only groups on campus that pay specific attention to their needs.

The five organizations I learned about recognized the need both for formal programs to raise awareness and for informal opportunities to exchange ideas and offer support. The formal programs often included speakers and seminars on a whole range of issues, such as the classic dilemmas of work and home life and panels on career strategies or which employers were promoting women most fairly. Some groups also met socially; for example, at one school the second-year women invited the incoming students for a potluck dinner where the newcomers could ask questions about which courses to take, what workload to expect, and how to make it through the first shock of the program. Whatever their format, women's group meetings gave participants a chance to talk about their career plans, to air out issues that were arising in class, or to strategize about how to handle themselves in interviews.

Affecting the School Community

At some schools, women's organizations reached beyond their own immediate concerns to affect the entire school community. In a relatively new program where women were 50 percent of the class, it was the older students who kept raising issues about integrating women's experience and perspectives into the curriculum. Those with less experience first questioned the approach, but in time came to understand their careers from a different perspective. Male students and faculty also benefited from discussion of issues, such as balancing personal and professional lives, and helped make other campus groups more responsive.

At another Goldmine school, only about one-fourth of the students were women, but they recognized some patterns of behavior they wanted to change:

> If you sat in a classroom and observed what was going on, you would hear a woman say something and it would be ignored. A few minutes later a man would say the same thing and the comment would be attributed to him. Even in the small study groups, there was a lot of that. . . . At first, it was really hard. There were a few of us who really stuck our necks out.

The few who spoke up took the next step and organized a planning committee of students, faculty, and administrators; they were helped by the dean of students, who must have been aware of the university's legal obligations. An open meeting drew a large crowd to discuss not only issues in placement, but also the language and structure of cases, and the questions recruiters ask women. After the meeting and follow-up activities, everyone gained from the awareness of issues that are too easily brushed aside as being only of concern to women:

> Married men in the class began to have an appreciation of what their wives were going through. A lot of the women who had experienced discrimination . . . were really delighted that there was a formal mechanism in business school to recognize it as an issue when corporations dismissed it.

Reaching Out to Alumnae

Even beyond the function of women's organizations within and during business school, they can form the foundation of a network that reaches beyond it. Connections between alumnae and students are fostered yearly at another Goldmine school, where the women's association gives a large cocktail party. One of the organizers told me that women in particular need such opportunities to meet on an informal but work-related basis:

> You're used to having girlfriends since you were a kid, but professional friends are something else. . . . At alumnae night, you can just come and talk to them, not to grease their palm and say, "I want to get a job from you," but, "What's it like to be a real estate person or an investment banker?"

Looking beyond school years, women cannot start too soon to connect with those who are already involved in networks in the business community. One woman from a nonprofit background wished that she had begun her outreach much earlier, since she simply was not connected to people who could help her. In retrospect, she would have liked to link up with some businesswomen's organizations in the area where she wanted work, to begin to know local people who shared her interests and had similar careers.

Why Women's Groups?

Those who question the continued value of women's groups in business schools argue that they are no longer needed, and that women are better off putting their energy into student government and other mixed groups. Unquestionably, women now have some different priorities than those who organized such groups did in the mid-1970s. For the most part, they do not have to cling to one another like the only two women in a pioneer community. Because the needs are less apparent, many groups are still defining their roles and tactics.

Administratively, the groups are hard to sustain. Women are, after all, going through one of the most pressured periods of their lives. Two years is barely long enough to make a commitment and pass leadership into new hands. While women who are employed, studying, and handling their personal lives are around for longer, they are unlikely to participate. It is no accident that all the groups I talked with were at better-known schools that have a higher proportion of full-time students.

For all the difficulties and potential criticisms, the women I spoke with said their organizations were necessary. They felt a strong need to keep their ties both with women's and with mixed organizations. Although the percentages of women in business schools have increased substantially, they have only reached parity in scattered institutions. On the whole, women are still very much in the minority. It is quite possible for a woman to be one of two or three in a class or major. She needs a support group for the same reasons as the pioneers of ten years ago: to be reassured that she is not alone and that she is normal, and to share tactics for dealing with a male-dominated environment. She might be motivated by the same concerns that caused this woman to become active:

> Just because they were men and went to games and spoke the same language, they had the sense of belonging and automatically supporting each other. We women have been taught that we were each other's rivals. . . . From that point of view I felt it was very important to create a sense of belonging and . . . a system of information and support.

Although I interviewed some at schools where women were well represented, they still felt that they needed to discuss issues that are not on the regular business school agenda. The obvious ones were child care and traditional female identity in the home, but there were many others: corporate games as they affect women, the structure of career opportunities, early detection of blockage, and so on. Of course these issues should be an integral part of what is taught and talked about, inside and outside the classroom. Everyone is affected. For now, however, such questions are discussed only sporadically and in a few schools, and if women's groups do not raise them they will probably be ignored.

Why did women commit themselves so heavily to these organizations? One of the prime movers behind one group put it this way:

> My concern was that I was going to have to work with these people for the rest of my life. If they don't respect me, and if we can't gain that mutual respect now, in fifteen years we'll be sitting across the table from each other and negotiating. They won't understand then either. So we'd better start today. It was always to lay a base for the future.

Women with the same strong motivation from all over the country have gathered annually since the 1970s as the National Network of Graduate Business School Women. Organizations from a wide variety of schools send representatives to address career-development issues particularly affecting women MBAs. A report of the Network's 1979 meeting gives a flavor of what was most important to women at that point, when they were asked how they would use the knowledge they had gained at the conference:

> Women indicated that given their greater awareness, their interviewing and employment choices would be more selective. They would carefully screen the companies' performance as to the number of women in management positons, the upward-mobility patterns for women, the general visibility of women, and the job climate.

In the last few years, the Network seems to have stressed individual development, according to Beth Pinlin, organizer of the 1984 conference. The need for a broad focus is greater than ever.

The Results

Business school built confidence for most women. They found that they could handle the math that they often had not taken at earlier levels of school. Whatever they might have been told about their ability to perform in a highly competitive business environment, many learned that they could stand the various tests that business school represented for them. Whatever rough periods women jostled their way through, particularly when they felt lonely and left out, completing business school was, in the end, a success for most who finished their degrees. Attaining the MBA broke new ground for many of them. Almost everyone did gain skills, learned the language of business, and was exposed to a broad range of careers.

Except for those with strong undergraduate business credentials, the MBA was a real accomplishment, the more so when women were conscious that they had a shot at a degree that would have been virtually off limits to them a decade or so earlier. Those who had to sacrifice to make it could not help but respect themselves more when they had attained their goal.

What they did not get is a golden passport or any of the equivalent notions, and the sooner they learned that the less likely they were to be disillusioned later. As one Goldmine placement office director said, "My role is to watch the students take the yellow brick road to the diploma mill, and it's my job to tell them what Kansas is really like." "Kansas" was experienced differently by different groups. Business school almost totally neglected major areas of work experience that vitally affect women's later careers, such as traditional patterns of female employment in business, organizational dynamics, and the implications of gender.

Even where women students were a substantial fraction of the class, women faculty were a rare, if not an unknown, species. What does the failure of business schools to hire more women faculty mean for students? First, it indicates that they have not made room for women in powerful roles, although they allow them to come and go as students. Schools have needed more faculty than ever to meet the demand created by women students, and female MBAs are more numerous than ever. Many schools have resorted to hiring people with lesser qualifications; in the early 1980s, national surveys showed that an average of 20 percent of faculty seats were empty. Both supply and demand thus argue for hiring women faculty; if business schools are not doing so, the only apparent explanation is that they place a low priority on the particular contributions women could make.

No one familiar with recent history could argue that the mere inclusion of women faculty would transform business schools and remove the barriers to female students' career development and male students' treating them as equal colleagues. Nevertheless, business schools are missing an opportunity to hire some of the most qualified persons in the marketplace and to reflect and facilitate changes in broader career patterns. The failure to cultivate women as doctoral candidates and then to recruit and promote them can only support the view that most business schools intend to remain predominantly male institutions.

While the numbers of women MBAs have unarguably grown, the question is how much influence they have had on the curriculum. Where there were strong women's organizations, there has been some impact. Left to their own devices, however, business schools have done precious little to adapt their approach to the new population of women, aside from redesigning their marketing materials and erecting new classroom buildings.

Some women were employed throughout business school, but many began looking for work just after the beginning of their second year. They began testing the receptivity of employers to their new qualifications. Some pounded the pavement, while others attended the modern equivalent of royal audiences as recruiters visited business schools to inspect the new group of courtiers. No matter what their circumstances were, looking for work was a real challenge—sometimes an overwhelming one.

Four

Looking for
Work

Ms. MBA just couldn't understand what other people meant when they said they dreaded interviews. To her, fifteen minutes in the recruiter's booth was more than enough time to explain her goals, and demonstrate how perfectly they fit that particular organization. Since she wore only the most businesslike clothes daily, it was no problem to add her pearl earrings and freshen up briefly before each interview. Because she was completely clear about her goals and had been since birth, she knew that she would accept the perfect job the instant it was offered—and she did, at an astronomical salary with outstanding promotion potential. As her classmates struggled from airport to airport, Ms. MBA quietly aced all of her exams and turned her attention to the dashing, totally supportive husband she had acquired over the summer. The week before she got her job offer, Ms. MBA discovered that she was pregnant. She had plenty of time to hire a full-time nanny, thus avoiding any unseemly disruptions in her career.

No one could blame a woman MBA who simply sat back and waited for the world to kneel at her feet, proffering up a series of devastatingly lucrative job offers. Since the degree had been sold as the key to success, those who have it may assume that they need only wait for Prince Charming, in the form of a major organization, to sweep them off their feet. For most, nothing could be farther from the truth; looking for work was at least unpleasant and often gruelling. Some of the women I interviewed stuck with jobs they had while studying for the degree part time, but most did look for work, both after business school and later in their careers.

After they decided what kind of work to look for, sometimes through making a deliberate decision, but often taking the obvious or expedient route, women began their job searches. Some went through school placement services, but a number initiated their own process. By whichever route, they ended up in interviews where they had to evaluate employers and search for both positive and warning signs about possible careers. Several strong influences shaped women's varied experiences at each of these junctures: the structure of the labor market (for MBAs generally and for

women in particular), the school they attended, their backgrounds, and
their social roles and identity, including traditional expectations of women
as care givers.

First Influence: Structure of the Labor Market

In addition to trends applying specifically to women, the overall job market
affected all MBAs. As it became tighter or looser in a particular field,
women would shift ground or take a detour toward the job they ultimately
wanted. After an extensive series of informational interviews, one woman
concluded that she was not going to be offered a job in either of her two
real passions: international trade and environmental issues. She had called
alumni from her formerly male Ivy League undergraduate school, as well
as friends of friends. Since she had no experience directly related to either
of her main interests, on the basis of their advice she concluded that a job
might not be forthcoming for some time, especially since both fields are
popular. Instead, she decided to construct an intermediate step for herself
in a government agency that had been courting her. She took an apparently
unrelated position because she could see how it would be useful to her in
the long run:

> I saw this job giving me a chance to use a lot of the skills I learned
> in school and getting some generic experience. . . . I realize that
> I may not move into that area; it may just be an interest that I
> have. But I think things will come together at some point. You
> never know. This sort of experience would be really good in a
> nonprofit setting, on the financial side.

In addition to the general picture of which jobs are available to MBAs,
some labor market trends are predictable influences on women's careers;
some individuals escape them and some do not. More than one-third of
women MBAs are hired into just three industries: commercial banking,
electrical/electronics and accounting. Following the three industries at some
distance are energy companies, food and beverages, consulting, and government and nonprofits. All the others fall below 4 percent.[1]

The Association of MBA Executives conducted a career and salary
survey[2] concerning 1979 and 1980 graduates, collecting data from both
schools and companies. While the results are necessarily incomplete, since
reporting was partial and definitions of which industry is which are slip-
pery, the survey does give an overall picture of where women MBAs work
and for how much. Aside from the question of their remaining confined
to lower-level positions in most organizations, many women MBAs are

also generally concentrated in a few segments of the labor market and in certain functions, the lower-paid areas in both cases, generally speaking. It is not surprising that they earn less than their male counterparts across the board, with much greater differences in some geographic areas and occupations than others.

According to the data schools submitted on 1980 graduates, more than half of the 36 hiring industries took only a handful of women MBAs, 2 percent or less.[3] Thus in many industries they still are rare. My own interviews confirmed that, while the numbers of women are increasing at the entry level, there are still pockets where they are virtually absent.

Many women said that they were the first females to do their jobs or that only a few others were working at their level. While these percentages give some indication of where women MBAs are concentrated, they also no doubt reflect the economic fluctuations of 1980 and give an only approximate, although useful, idea.

In line with other evidence that women MBAs are paid less than men, the survey found an overall salary gap at entry of $1,555.[4] That figure is less than half the differences between female and male MBAs in the Southwest ($4,182).[5] Women were concentrated in metropolitan areas, and were notably absent in the Central/South region, where 80 percent of the 1980 hires were men.

Looking closely at the differences between female and male MBAs' salaries by industry in 1980, one sees that the bottom for women was lower than the bottom for men and the top for men was higher than the top for women.[6] The least lucrative fields for men included two of the most female-dominated industries, commercial banking and accounting. The functional breakdown showed that women earned less than men in all but two categories: lending and personnel. Where the rewards were high, in consulting and general management, there was also the greatest gap between women and men.[7]

In attempting to explain the wage gap, the survey said, "Different 1980 functional, industry, and regional patterns of 1980 female hires explain some of the salary differences between female and male MBAs."[8] The survey did not address the issue of how much those patterns reflect discrimination rather than choice; why, for example a woman in Boston should be worth $3,409 less than her male counterpart at entry. If women are excluded from certain functions, industries and regions, of course that explains part of the difference in their salaries. A degree from a top school, a conventional business background, or an undemanding personal life can mitigate the effects of discriminatory trends somewhat, but these elements do affect everyone. For all the variety, patterns still emerged, particularly in the levels where women work and their small numbers in the most highly paid industries and functions.

Second Influence: School Attended

The differences in job search outcome between Goldmine and Generic graduates are not nearly as clear cut as they are made out to be. The Generic programs include some good regional schools that serve a particular geographic area or market very successfully, so that their graduates are well linked to the local business community or to a particular sector. For example, persons attending the military procurement MBA program at Golden Gate University end up with a degree that is prerequisite to moving up in their specialty. The public accounting program at Rutgers serves a very specialized business community and finds jobs for its graduates in a variety of firms. Although neither is a Goldmine program they both do place people successfully. Among employers more generally, there are periodic reports of a reaction against the inflation of salaries and expectations of Goldmine MBAs, so that some who recruit at the national level actively seek persons from less exalted circumstances. Some Generic schools cultivate their list of recruiters assiduously and work closely with employers to make their graduates as marketable as possible.

Others simply do not care. Many of their students are in jobs already, and putting out any additional effort to improve their career prospects does not directly bring cash into the school's coffers. Whether an MBA degree will actually result in a career leap for someone who is already on a particular track is at best open to question; it depends largely on the employer's attitude toward the MBA rather than the quality of services from the schools. Nevertheless, the question is more pressing for Generic school MBAs because they are more likely to be employed than students at Goldmine schools.

Many students in the Generic programs did not look for a new job soon after they graduated. According to one woman:

> Most of the people who were in there were staying in their jobs. They got the MBA in order to move maybe later on, but they weren't looking for a job right after graduation. That was true for both men and women. The one and only woman besides me who actually quit work to do an MBA went into banking. . . . Everybody else had jobs.

Some of the most satisfied women I interviewed had gone through Generic programs. For many, getting an MBA was a leap farther than they had ever expected to go, and they savored the accomplishment of finding a well-paid, if not ideal, job. On the other hand, virtually all of the most dissatisfied women came from Generic programs, that is, those who were particularly underemployed or who went through long periods of unemployment.

Yet a Goldmine degree was not foolproof. It did provide access to certain types of employers who hire no one else: one well-connected woman from a top school leapt straight into the hierarchy of one of the most prestigious firms in her field, and a few others had similar stories. When I asked her about the importance of her education in making the outcome so successful, she said, "----the coursework. It's the contacts that count." While there are certainly some differences in curriculum between Goldmine and other schools, they are probably not as significant as the feeling of being treated as an elite and of being prepared for the top jobs in the country. Certainly, some Generic MBAs also make contacts through their programs, but on the whole they operate in a different sphere.

Contacts came through for a Goldmine MBA who found that business interviewers did not take her seriously because her background was in teaching, a traditional female occupation which they did not view as a "real job." When she was despairing, she appealed to one of her professors.

> I said, "Help me. I'm having trouble; I can't find a job." The next week, he ran into a buddy of his at a cocktail party, who had just taken over as head of finance. He said he was looking for half a dozen MBA types for a troubleshooter project team.

The Goldmine degree did not assure women of the job of their dreams; while it made them more credible in general than Generic school graduates, there were some purposes (such as entering management in a locally based concern) for which the MBA may not have been so important. Many of the Goldmine graduates were positive about where they were, but some felt stuck and disappointed, particularly those who had been out in the workforce longer and experienced more barriers.

Third Influence: Background

Women with a business background—academic, experience, or both—had an easier time in almost every way than the career changers. They knew the language of business already, had contacts, had tested the waters, and often had a sense of direction. Some simply stayed in the jobs they were doing before and hoped for advancement. Anyone with a technical undergraduate degree was at a particular advantage, even if she had no experience. Those who had been in the workforce for a number of years often had a realistic idea of what they were up against as women in a relatively new field. Many had developed strategies, including networks, that were immensely useful to them as they looked for work or promotion.

The outcomes of the MBA were much more uncertain for career changers or for women with no experience. A few succeeded admirably in making major switches. A Goldmine graduate who was trying to escape social services told me wistfully about a classmate who had made an even greater leap, from midwifery to investment banking.

The lack of a business background was often more readily outweighed by a Goldmine than by a Generic degree. Even so, it did not always work. A woman who was trying to switch from prison programs to banking could not make the transition:

> I don't think I really had a shot at very much. I really knew that I had to start my own job search. . . . They are looking for someone who has a clear understanding of banking. . . . I had an odd background, as much as I tried to neutralize it. Most people were able to pick up that it wasn't quite what they were expecting, and because there were a lot of people who did have banking experience, I would really have had to be somebody who jumped out at them.

If having the wrong experience was a problem, lacking it altogether was equally hard to overcome. Women who had gone directly to business school from undergraduate work felt caught in the classic bind: no one would hire them without experience, and they could not get it unless someone hired them. When I asked a woman in that situation what held her back, she said she felt that lack of experience was harder for women to overcome than for men.

On the whole, career changers and women with no experience had to work harder to get good results from their MBAs. Only occasionally were they able to incorporate skills from their past lives directly into their work, such as a nurse who keeps track of developments related to hospitals for a law firm. But many women who had had traditional jobs were told that their past work had no value or applicability to the business world. A former teacher was outraged by the reactions she had in some interviews:

> I believe that no matter where a person works, there's a big difference between someone who is fresh out of college and someone who has worked, even as a teacher. I say *even* as a teacher because when I went for interviews for jobs after business school people would say, "Oh, I see you've never worked." "I was a teacher for twelve years." "No, no, *worked,* at a real job." But teaching was a real job and, to the extent that it made me appreciate what was going on in the classroom, it helped.

Some women who were trying to make changes from their earlier backgrounds could not go directly from one point to another. One woman's goal was working in university foundation relations. After spending some years at home taking care of her children, she could not overcome potential employers' attitudes. She had to take a very circuitous route that she felt would not have been required of a man:

> I found a lot of male chauvinism in the university world. They kept asking, "What could you possibly contribute?" when I applied for jobs in foundation relations. . . . The MBA didn't make me an automatic shoo-in to a lot of glamorous jobs. I had to detour to health care and advertising to get back into the non-profit sector.

Ironically, just as too little experience could be a problem, so could too much. Women who went to business school after only a year or two in the labor force were in a very different position with respect to changing careers from those who had moved beyond the entry level. A woman with a Generic MBA who was trying to switch from the nonprofit to the profit sector had about ten years of solid experience. She ended up in a job she could have obtained without the degree, as administrator in an advocacy group:

> I'm very discouraged about getting my foot in the door when people are looking for MBAs, because I just get this sense that they take one look at my résumé and say who are you kidding? Here's somebody with ten years' experience in the nonprofit sector. They can hire somebody with no experience who is probably less threatening to them; it's not the money, but more a psychological thing of having someone with a lot of experience come in. You can't really treat the person as a trainee.

Summer and other temporary jobs sometimes gave women a chance to try out different possibilities, to see what working in the business world really felt like, and to show what they could do at work in which the risks were relatively low. The experience could offer skills, contacts, or even a job. For example, the woman who could not get away from her social services background found a job in the publishing company where she had had a summer job between her first and second years.

No matter what school the career changers and women with less experience went to, the transition was rough, but the outcomes were more likely to be positive for those who went to the more prominent schools. It is no surprise that going there is closely tied to class and social background, which had an enormous effect on the outcomes of the MBA for women. Not only did women with higher social status have more contacts and often more models for business careers, but their aspirations were in keeping with their class. They were at ease with the middle- and upper-class white males at the higher end of organizational pyramids and, perhaps more important, they were the types whom men in management were accustomed to dealing with. Their manners, dress, leisure activities, and other cues all bespoke a common culture.

Fourth Influence: Social Identity and Roles

The outcomes of looking for work also depended heavily on women's social identity and roles. Although the concept of roles is often used to describe women's moving from the personal to the professional world, the reality for the women I interviewed was more complex. At work, they were often treated in accordance with traditional functions, and they inevitably took some of their working life home with them. Women cannot simply step in and out of roles; they are taught to fulfill them from a very early age, which forms their very identities. Like an actress who is typecast, neither they nor the persons around them can distinguish where the woman ends and the role begins, and vice versa. Everything women do, including searching for jobs, is affected by their gender identity, which in turn affects the outcomes. A woman has a compounding disadvantage to overcome if she is a woman of color, is older or much younger, is disabled, or fits stereotypes of working-class women or lesbians. Those who surmount these barriers must be exceptional indeed.

Among the women I interviewed, mothers of young children predictably felt the most constrained by their social roles and identity in looking for suitable employment. Most were, in effect if not in fact, single mothers; if there were adjustments to be made, women were expected to make them. Their experiences documented the extreme difficulty of finding child care arrangements compatible with a demanding career. Even with their considerable financial and other resources, child care was a major obstacle. At one extreme, a few women dropped out of the business world altogether. One decided that she could handle a single child, but not two:

> I started looking for jobs, but I decided it was too much to have a toddler and a job and be pregnant again. I would be too worn out. Contrary to what a lot of people think, I did it for me, not my kids.

Another woman seemed to have an ideal but most unusual child care set-up. She was working part-time as a management consultant in a woman-owned business. She had been looking for a job and considering becoming pregnant at the same time, and knew that if she made a decision or had a breakthrough in one area the other would probably come through at the same time. After nine months of unemployment she finally found her current employer:

> When I interviewed with her, I was pregnant with Paul, but I didn't realize it at the time. It worked out perfectly. I worked there through my pregnancy, so I wasn't bored. He was early, so I worked up to the last minute. I was on the phone with her one afternoon, and we were talking about what I was going to do when I came in the next day. I hung up, went over to the sink, and my water broke.
>
> I called the doctor, who told me to come to the hospital, and I called my boss back. I said, "Rubye, my water just broke." She said, "Does that mean you're not coming in tomorrow?"

Although the child was eventually placed in day care when he was older, initially he went to the office with his mother, where his presence was welcomed.

Even though many other women have small children whom they prefer not to leave in someone else's full-time care, there are surprisingly few arrangements as constructive as this one. Because the workplace is so dominated by the model of the full-time professional with no life outside the office walls, women simply do not expect the possibility to exist:

> I would never have thought to look for this kind of thing. You would never think to set your goal as "I want to find a professional job part time." I would never have thought that the possibility existed.

As a measure of how desperate women can be for part-time work, one Generic school graduate accepted a student internship after she had her degree simply because it was part time. By then, she had spent months of futile searching:

> I did all the hunting of what firms around here I might be interested in and tried to get names, and sent out résumés. I had zero response, unbelievably bad response. I had better response when I had no MBA and I was looking helter-skelter.

Ultimately, she found her job through someone she met at a cocktail party. For a student salary, the corporation hired an already trained, fully qualified MBA with the advantage of prior experience in other fields. When I met her, she had left the job because she could see that it was leading nowhere, but had not been able to find another part-time situation.

While mothers were the most obviously affected by expectations of women outside the workplace, others had thought about the price of a life devoted solely to a career. One of the most reflective women I talked with expressed her desire for autonomy and challenge by working in the telecommunications industry, where she felt that the newness of the field would stimulate her with flexibility and constant changes. At the same time, she felt that the strong ambition that drove her career before her MBA was not enough:

> When I went to business school, I thought [U.S.] Secretary of State sounds nice. I felt the way to get there was by establishing myself in the private sector. That was my focus in terms of where senior management would lead. In the process of business school . . . I realized that I might never reach that end, so it's important for me to be happy with the means. I think that's what takes me off the track of working twenty-four hours a day, seven days a week.

A number of women made deliberate decisions about their careers on the basis of traditional expectations, sometimes sacrificing income and advancement potential. For example, a researcher in a publishing firm evaluated her employer in terms of her desire to have a baby:

> I have been thinking about the issue of where I would want to be if I were to have a child. This would probably be a good place to be. There's a certain amount of flexibility about working at home.

Because she already had a family of stepchildren and many other outside interests, she chose publishing rather than a more lucrative but more taxing career in investment banking:

> I'm making half of what investment bankers made in their first year. They can probably triple their salary in the second year, and I'm going to get about a 10 percent increase over inflation, which is pretty good, but clearly not what I could get. At the same time, I've left at five o'clock 90 percent of the time since I started working, and I usually get a full hour for lunch; I can leave a little early on long weekends. . . . I can basically count on doing what I have to do when I want to.

Similarly, one woman is putting off moving into the field she really loves because she now has a very responsible part-time job and cannot find anything comparable. While her two children are small, she feels that the flexibility she has now is more important to her, although she sometimes questions whether they are the reason or just an excuse:

I'm the director of a department at the rehabilitation center, and I work about thirty hours a week. It's not where I want to be long term because I'm not managing clinical areas, and that's what I want to do. But it gives me the flexibility that I need right now.

The results of many such decisions were described to me by a black graduate from the mid-1970s who told me about a number of the women in her class. Each chose to put her family first, such as one who moved to accommodate her husband's career every few years, or another who stayed in a less challenging job. In contrast, the woman I interviewed had made her way up through a bank on the West Coast, where she was hoping to move into senior management. She had succeeded in maintaining a long-distance relationship with her fiance back East, and eventually he moved to be closer to her.

Women's decisions were most clearly influenced by their social roles in terms of geography. Some single as well as married women confined their job searches to the cities where their boyfriends or husbands lived. Although I only heard about a few men who followed women to a new location, many women had done the reverse. Young women fell into the same pattern as older ones.

For some, the decision to go wherever the man in their life was living was reasonably easy and did not exact too high a price. When the location was favorable for the kind of job they were interested in, the conflict was not acute; however, for some it was both apparent and painful. After much agonizing, one MBA in her mid-thirties with an excellent business background turned down the job she really wanted so she could live with her boyfriend in another city. Although she was working in his family business, a high-tech start-up, she did intend to find a job of her own. When I talked with her several months later, she was not sure of her direction:

> I'm still not 100 percent certain what I am going to end up doing. . . . I had done a substantial amount of job searching elsewhere and had an offer that I was very excited about, working in the treasury in a large corporation. It has a woman at the top level, has a very strong commitment to women. I came here and put myself in a situation where I didn't have . . . I hadn't looked [for a job] here, and I haven't started. It was a very painful decision.

For her, there was a very direct trade-off, particularly as the city where her boyfriend lived was not a base for the kind of large corporations for which she preferred to work.

Even when both members of a couple are MBAs, the woman was often expected to make way for the man's career. A woman who graduated from Goldmine in the same year as her husband deferred getting a job until he knew where he was going, by which time everyone else had a job already and opportunities were shrinking. On the other hand, choices can be mutual rather than conflicting. One woman decided, together with her husband, that they did not want the high-powered New York lifestyle, although it was the leading city in the country for her as a finance MBA and for him as a specialized attorney.

Whether or not they had children, the results of women MBAs' job searches were strongly influenced by their social roles and identity, in addition to the other factors discussed here—the structure of the labor market, the school attended, and background. All affected how employers reacted to the candidates, creating or diminishing their career possibilities, and shaped both stages of women's looking for work: decision making about what to seek and the job search itself.

Stage 1: Decision Making about What Kind of Work To Seek

Some women were well launched in their careers before they got an MBA and simply continued along the same trajectory as before. They hoped that they would go farther or faster because of the degree, but their career patterns had already been established. All the others were faced with decisions about what kind of work they wanted and in what setting; some resolved the issue by making expedient choices based on panic or by taking advantage of luck and accident. Other decisions were textbook examples of careful self-assessment leading to deliberate career moves.

Obvious Decisions

Women who already had business backgrounds were at an enormous advantage in avoiding the agonies of narrowing their goals. Some were already lodged in reasonably comfortable situations at the entry level, and the weight of their experience had inclined their careers in a certain direction. While they had expectations of the MBA, they did not see it as a reason to make major switches in direction.

The director of compensation in a consumer products manufacturing company, for example, had no intention of changing jobs after she graduated from a Generic program. She had been with the same company for six years and wanted to stay there. Because of their strong affirmative action program and years of rapid growth, she had progressed dramatically since she was hired. For her, it was the skills she could gain from the MBA that were critical, rather than the credibility offered by the degree. Despite a change in the economic climate that had affected the company drastically, she still felt there were good opportunities for her.

Yet an obvious decision like hers may also be an untested one. Few women had chosen a conscious career direction previously. Many simply were following along a path that was laid out in the fields and industries that were open to women. Others were also strongly influenced by feeling that they had to accommodate traditional female responsibilities and therefore sought part-time work. Decisions that appeared to be choices may really have been the only options offered in the labor market, particularly for women who were employed for some time.

Expedient Decisions

A few women simply fell into their jobs. One interviewed with a company she would never have otherwise considered only because she had a hole in her schedule and felt that she could use the practice. As it turned out, she was glad that she had, because it was the only job offer she received, despite being a Goldmine graduate in the early days of affirmative action. While her accidental decision might have produced good results just through the perversity of fate, in fact it turned out disastrously. She was miserable and isolated.

When women made expedient decisions more consciously, they were usually based on sheer panic. After the sacrifices of time, energy, and money that the MBA entailed, many felt that they had to find a good job fast. Some had debts, all had hopes. Women from Goldmine schools sometimes panicked because the highest expectations were heaped on them. Those women who were first in their families to do anything like earn the degree also felt the pressure keenly no matter where they went to school. A black 1974 graduate took the first decent offer she got:

> I was the oldest of five children, raised by my mother and her family. I was the first to finish college and at that time the first to come through graduate school. It was important to me to come out with a job, and a good job. Maybe I should have waited, but my family's situation had changed and they needed financial help.

Although she later recuperated from her mistake, one woman made an expedient choice because she did not believe that she could get a "real job." While she had a strong field of specialty to combine with her MBA, she graduated in a year of low demand for that combination. She knew immediately that the job she was offered was not right for her: she could foresee conflicts with her supervisor, and her summer job had taught her that the field did not excite her at all. Yet her fears took over:

> I was so nervous. I kept thinking I wasn't going to get a job, so I should take the first thing that came along. . . . I didn't have

enough confidence that I could really get a normal job. Of course that's horseshit, but it's my feeling that I'm really no good, or that I'm not going to be as good as the others. . . . I should have taken a much more general, nuts-and-bolts business job.

The MBA was not a magic formula for self-assurance. Although some women gained confidence because they attained a goal originally beyond their grasp, many still sometimes felt unequal to the task of establishing their careers as MBAs.

While everyone is prey to making hasty decisions, low confidence combined with legitimate apprehensions about the job market for MBAs can push women in directions they regret later. Both of these women ended up in destructive jobs: the first stayed almost seven years, until she was laid off, both to her horror and relief; the second left as soon as she could, making the leap to investment banking successfully. Expedient decisions are not necessarily the end of the world, but they can certainly cause a detour from a woman's goals.

Deliberate Decisions

Women who made their decisions more consciously began with self-assessment. In the final throes of preparing for the job hunt, a number did some real soul searching. They had to assess their own values and where they wanted to put their work effort. They had to be realistic about their personalities: were they fighters who could make it in a scrappy corporate setting or did they want a more supportive working environment? Did they see bureaucracy as an intriguing game to be played or as a multidimensional web that enmeshed anyone who tried to move within it? Was three a crowd or was anything less than a skyscraper full of people a two-bit operation? Was it stability that they sought or the turmoil of being on the shifting forefront all the time?

Women asked themselves all these questions and more. Those with more experience in the workplace, especially in business, had a better basis for knowing what they were looking for. Often they began by eliminating what they disliked, as in, "I'll never work again for a director who doesn't have prior management experience," or, "I never want to be the only woman at my level in a big company." Establishing those outer limits helped women narrow down what they were seeking. Some found it difficult to establish criteria, either because they were inexperienced or because they had no backgrounds in business. One young woman felt that she was at a real disadvantage compared to others who were more focused:

I knew that I was basically a finance type, but I didn't know specifically what I wanted to do, and that's the lack of experience. . . . That made it difficult finding a job, to tailor your interview to suit the company you were talking to. I wasn't like some people who say, "The minute I was born I knew I wanted to be an investment banker and I've been eating, sleeping and breathing investment banking since then." I'm sure you could tell the difference between me and people like that.

By evaluating the gaps in their experience, some women found a sense of direction. They figured out where their weaknesses lay and understood that certain settings could be congenial to them. For example, a woman in her mid-thirties with an erratic employment history decided that she needed an employer with a good training program in a company where older women were accepted at upper management levels.

Once they had made their decisions about what kind of work to look for—whether they did the obvious, fell into it accidentally, took the expedient route, or thought it through deliberately—a long process was still ahead of them. Much depended on whether they were at schools where they could simply appear at the recruiters' booths or whether they had to initiate the job search themselves. At that stage, their decisions were tested and sometimes changed.

Stage 2: The Job Search Process

The job search process was difficult for almost everyone. Women who went to Goldmine schools, and some Generic graduates, had the advantage of recruiters coming to them and even courting them. Goldmine MBAs had a relatively wide range of choice among different employers, compared to the much smaller band of recruiters at most Generic schools. Some of the Goldmine women also found that they could not get the kind of job they wanted without initiating their own search, as many of the Generic graduates had to do. No matter how they went about looking for jobs, everyone faced interviews, whether in the recruiter's booth for fifteen minutes, or in a marathon all-day tour in a distant city.

School Placement Services

The conventional way for many MBAs to find work, especially those from Goldmine schools, is to run from one recruiter cubicle to another in a sorting area like a stockyard. Prearranged appointments for fifteen minutes to half an hour provide just enough time for the interviewer to get an idea of the candidate and decide whether or not she is asked to play the next round of the game. By the end of such a day, interviewers can understandably be jaded by any but the most vivid candidates. Since business school only lasts two years and interviews begin in the fall of the second year, a woman without a business background may be just beginning to understand what she wants; suddenly, she has to dazzle recruiters. The competition can be fierce, depending on the school, and peer pressure can make questions about who has been offered what almost unbearable.

The initial cuts are especially cruel, made as they are on the basis of snap judgments. Since there is so little time, much depends on the appearance and image of the candidates compared to the ideal or the norm that is expected by a particular employer. The first step in the process is necessarily quick and dirty because of the sheer numbers of candidates. If there is a next step, it often involves visiting the organization and meeting many more persons, and undergoing a much more thorough examination.

On the whole, business schools did little to help the women I spoke with prepare for interviews, although a few did offer an opportunity to practice or, in one case, a career counseling course. Placement services at Goldmine schools were predictably superior, partly because many are private institutions that depend on alumni for their funding, directly and indirectly. For some women, placement offices were invaluable, because they enabled them to skip the step of seeking out potential employers and to get a lot of practice at interviews. Those with relatively conventional goals, especially in the corporate world, often benefited. At their best, placement services provided counseling and a broad range of written information, such as corporate annual reports and materials on how to interview or do research about prospective employers. Feedback about résumés was also helpful to some women. Graduates who were looking for jobs outside the usual formulas of the corporation were often disappointed in the help they received from placement services, no matter where they went to school.

With exceptions, the placement services at Generic schools were given bad reviews. The worst marks went to schools at which MBAs were handled by the same placement office as all the other graduate and undergraduate students. Companies are often reluctant to put the money into hiring an MBA rather than a BBA. Another problem for Generic graduates was that some major employers look only for certain majors or types of people. One woman who had put her heart as well as her budget into grinding through an MBA program for years while employed full time was sorely disappointed. By the time she had eliminated the recruiters who wanted entry-level persons or those with bachelor's degrees, technical backgrounds, or MBA specialties she did not have, the results were nil:

> Although at first I thought it would be a great thing, I never did end up with any interviews with recruiters because for various reasons there was nobody for me to talk to.

Much the same thing happened to another with a Generic MBA who even worked in the placement office. Both of these women, as well as a number of Goldmine graduates, had to launch their own job searches to have a real chance of finding what they were looking for.

Looking on Your Own

Women start their own job searches for many reasons. Some are looking in an unusual area, like international trade with a particularly obscure country, or simply a field in which their school does not specialize. Those who are searching for their fourth job rather than their first may no longer have placement services available or may not want what they can offer. Women who least fit the standard mold of the hard-driving young male executive were often the ones who had to look beyond the recruiters' booths. The three key ingredients to a successful self-initiated job search were self-assessment, research, and networks.

Self-assessment
Knowing what they themselves wanted was critical to convincing employers that they should be hired, despite whatever strikes were against them. A Goldmine MBA with prior experience in the public sector wanted to switch into the corporate world and decided that government relations would be the right choice for her. While she did not immediately end up with exactly what she wanted, she was able to convince the telephone company that she could do a related job in state pricing, which could lead to her goal. Before she reached the point of negotiating with them, however, she had investigated the possibilities in her own area thoroughly.

Research
Solid research included not only finding out as much as possible about an employer before interviewing, but discovering whom to approach in the first place. The woman who ended up at the telephone company knew that she wanted to stay in the area where she lived and had gone to school, both because it was a supportive environment for her as a woman who uses a wheelchair and because her friends were there. She tracked down all of the relatively few local corporations with government relations departments and pursued them one by one until she got results. Systematic research based on self-assessment paid off.

Networks
Many attested to the worth of networks as a source of both information and contacts. One woman even said she felt that her contacts were more valuable than her degree:

> Frankly, if I didn't have a job, I wouldn't get a degree. . . . I'd join every club I could find, and every organization, and meet people. That's the only way you're going to get a job.

Career changers may have to start their networks early, since they are at a disadvantage:

> I look at my friends, and I see they're not working in business either, so they can't give me the contacts or explain to me how what I do could be used somewhere else.

For many, getting in touch with people who could help them and persisting in their job searches over time finally yielded results. The woman with a Generic MBA who went through a dismal nine months of unemployment after graduation really thought that she had tried everything. It was extending her network that ultimately found her a job. She began by talking with a few people she and her friends already knew, and rapidly found herself busy with informational interviews. She found many people who were willing to help, including those at higher levels:

> Once I started this network, I was so amazed at how well it worked. The people I talked with who were the middle level of management, the people who have all the work piled onto them, would spend fifteen minutes with me. . . . But I talked with vice presidents of banks who got me coffee and talked with me for an hour about what I wanted to do. They'd ask for copies of my résumé, saying, "I'm going to lunch with some other guys [sic] today. I'll pass it around and see what I can do."

In addition, women in many situations were receptive, and it was through one of them that she found her present job as a management consultant, working part time in a small woman–owned firm.

Networks from past jobs and social life can also help women who are looking on their own. A summer job was key for a career changer who had been rejected by Goldmine recruiters because of her unconventional social work background. When she contacted the company she had worked for, her former boss responded well, although he thought she was overqualified:

> He was able to say to me, "Yes, I'd like to have you back, and in fact you deserve better. You should be going to an investment bank. But if you want to take this job—." So I ended up there.

Friendship networks paved the way out of difficult situations for several women, who quietly let their friends know they were ready to move before they announced it to the world. Others used the professional network of headhunters and several felt they had good results, although at least as many were disappointed.

The same techniques were used by women who were trying to escape extremely demanding jobs, in situations where it would seem that they literally did not have time to look. One who was on the road most of the time hired a secretary who typed and mailed application letters in her absence, and an answering service with whom she checked daily. Another simply badgered the bank she wanted to work for over a period of months, calling at least weekly.

While these approaches seem to be necessary to good outcomes for most women, they are not sufficient. Too many uncontrollable factors intervene for any woman to believe that she can ensure success, and the first hurdle is the interview.

Interviews

Whether women look for work through their schools or on their own, they all go through interviews—at uncomfortable lunches as they try to chew and talk at the same time, or in booths with only a room divider between them and the next anxious MBA. No matter where they were, most of the women who spoke with me disliked interviews. The stress came partly from knowing that the employer makes the final decision, often based on an ideal image of the men who traditionally have held management jobs. (For specific information on self-presentation at interviews, see the bibliography.)

A few women were very obviously ruled out of a certain job because their gender was incongruous with that image, such as one who was repeatedly told that she would have to deal with blue-collar men who would be alienated by her background. It was clear that gender, not background, was the issue, since she came from a working class family. The more unlike the ideal a woman is, the more effort it takes to counterbalance whatever other strikes are against her. Even so, she may not be able to overcome a potential employer's attitudes in spite of excellent self-presentation and interview techniques. For all that the interviewees put into making themselves as acceptable as possible, the employer ultimately decides.

Women found that it was not enough simply to respond articulately to the questions that were asked. A career changer in her mid-thirties had always considered herself a good interviewee, but learned that the techniques that had served her well in nonprofit settings did not work as effectively in the business world. She had to prepare much more actively and decide what points she wanted to emphasize, identifying possible weaknesses in her background and deciding how to deal with them. Rather than waiting to be asked, she would raise areas that could be of concern. Searching for a point of common interest, however bizarre it may seem, also paid off. One woman included on her résumé a summer stint playing blackjack in Las Vegas. When she was offered a job in consulting, the second in command told her that they had talked with her only because his boss loved to gamble.

Contrary to the advice that tells women to conform to whatever expectations the interviewer has, one MBA took the opposite tack and told them what she was looking for:

> My approach to the interview process was, for example, "I understand that you are starting an international group, and I'm interested in that." I would tell them what I wanted, which was a different approach than many people took. I wasn't interested just in a job. I wanted one that fit my list of criteria, and I had enough confidence to do it.

While not everyone could use the same technique effectively, most felt that practice, good advance preparation, and strong goals were important ingredients in successful interviews.

For all that, the quick once-over is especially deadly for a woman who is at all out of the ordinary, since her unconventionality may well be the most obvious thing about her. Women of color had to make special efforts to prove that they were credible professionals. At a time when affirmative action was stronger, a black woman with top marks from one of the best public business schools learned about both the informal and formal sides of interviewing:

> By that time I had established my grade point, and it was one that let me have entrée to all the corporations. . . . In one interview, when I started talking I mentioned that my brother was a scholarship student in one of the prep schools down in Ohio. The atmosphere just changed in the interview. I became somebody he could relate to.

A disabled woman was also treated with suspicion, despite her 1984 Goldmine degree and a polished, confident approach that showed her years of experience in conducting and then directing a major national training program:

> You could tell that in the back of their minds they were having all these questions about, "I just don't think she can do the job." If they are going to be closed or afraid, there was really nothing that I could say in that short period of time—half an hour, fifteen minutes—to change anybody's mind. If they had fears, I'm not going to break them down in half an hour.

Similarly, a reentry woman with years behind her as the power behind the throne in her husband's political career was viewed with suspicion by younger managers. She had difficulty making it past the initial interview. These three women could identify the source of their problem: interviewers' reactions to their race, disability, and age. When gender alone is the issue, women are often less astute about catching on.

Whether they knew it or not, many women were affected by the interviewers' traditional views of women as wives and mothers. The signs can be as subtle as body language that anyone could overlook. This management consultant, a young woman married to an attorney, tried a friend's suggestion:

> One of my friends told me I should take off my wedding ring before I went into interviews. I tried it a couple of times, just to see what would happen. I realized that the very first thing they do—the very first thing—is look at your left hand.

Most people know that it is illegal to question a woman about her marital status or plans to have children, or the place those factors have in her working life. A number of women, however, found that interviewers have ways of getting the information. A young married woman told me:

> If I were going to an interview, the first thing I would think about is what my answer is going to be to the questions they're not supposed to ask. I've been in situations before where they don't specifically ask you, but they can find out on the way to the elevator or at lunch. . . . I think you need to decide ahead of time. If you get all huffy, you're not going to get the job. The question is, do you want to work for somebody to whom that is important?

She recommended telling interviewers that career is the top priority for the next five or whatever years; others simply said that they had always integrated the various parts of their lives successfully and that they intended to continue to do so.

Some business school officials told me that illegal questions are almost never asked any more; one could not even recall the last complaint, it had been at least several years ago. Another was less sanguine about the way women are evaluated in interviews, whether or not the obvious illegalities are as prevalent as they once were:

> I'm not sure this [evaluation] is something the women are prepared for. I think they come in feeling they have a right to this [MBA] as a person. It's a time of great opportunity and I'm going

to grab it. I think they don't realize that they are still going to run into that very subtle examination, but they still do.

Dean Maryann Billington of Northeastern University, one of the six women business school deans in the country, agrees that there are still discriminatory practices at interviews, obvious and otherwise. Because women have an interest in the outcome, she feels that they often do not complain when it would be appropriate.

Because everything is supposed to have changed, women who do suffer illegal questions or harassment may have trouble believing the evidence of their own senses. One woman was incredulous at the way an interviewer treated her. She tried to explain his behavior by speculating that he was sick or drunk:

> I had a terrible interview at [one of the Big Eight accounting firms]. . . . As a matter of fact, I ended up complaining to the dean, as did a number of other women who had similar questions asked of them. For example, he asked me and another person, "It looks like you're wearing very expensive clothes. How can you afford that and the fancy tuition?" Then he asked me what I would do if my big brute of a date was waiting for me and I had to tell him I had to work on Saturday night and cancel a date. It went on and on and on.
>
> He evidently is not that type of person. . . . The dean, who knew him, was shocked. I would have thought I was hallucinating if it weren't for the fact that other women complained about him too, that same day. Evidently, supposedly, he's a star interviewer everyone likes.

As in so many other situations that come up both at business school and the workplace, the support and perceptions of other women were critical. Since the dean knew and respected the man in question, would he have believed just one woman's isolated account, or would he, like her, have tried to excuse the behavior?

Advice to Women MBAs about Looking for Work

At the end of the interview process, negotiating for title and salary is a sticking point for many women. Often, they simply accept what they are offered. In some fields, such as public accounting, the salaries are fixed, but in most there is some flexibility for those who ask for it. Dr. Richard Thain, who is at the University of Chicago Graduate School of Business and author of numerous books (including *Think Twice Before You Accept That Job*) and articles on management subjects, advises MBAs to negotiate for what they want:

> Where in doubt, and where it seems promising, don't hesitate to ask for more money. It's usually a weakness if you take the first offer. Don't shoot out the hand and shake, and be all flattered that they at last have recognized your genius. If you think the salary's too low, tell them you like the company and you like the job, but there's one little thing that seems dissonant. Can that figure be reexamined? Most of the time it can.

Titles can and should be negotiated as well as money:

> If they want to call you an analyst and you've had some experience and want to be called a something else, tell them. That's the time to tell them. Get it right there or forever hold your peace. Once you start working for them, it's going to be hard.

Because future pay and advancement, at least in that setting, depend on where a woman starts, it is especially important to get off on the right foot. She must ask herself whether the employer has made a reasonable offer that reflects the market and the general picture for what others from her school are earning. Are they matching responsibilities and outward labeling by a title, or is the job too loaded for the authority it carries? If they respond well to assertive negotiation on pay and promotion issues it is a good sign that they expect and want her to be as strong in promoting her career as anyone else. She may also want to ask some "what if" questions, such as how certain ideas would be implemented if she tried a new program, to gain a feeling for their responses when she begins to take charge of the job rather than simply function in it.

To achieve the best outcome from looking for work despite all the uncontrollable factors, every woman must evaluate whether there is a good fit between her and a particular employer. She can only make a sound judgment if she has set realistic goals based on knowing herself. To learn as much as she can about employers, she must do preliminary research and look for both positive and warning signs during the interview and in other contacts.

Some of the women who had bad working experiences or who felt they had made mistakes probably did take some of the steps that are recommended here, and some who love their jobs may have relied more on luck than on self-assessment and research. Nothing can guarantee that a woman will find the job of her dreams, not even a Goldmine MBA. She may follow all the suggestions that emerged from the histories of the women

I interviewed and still not come upon the right job for her. She will, however, increase her chances of finding what she is looking for considerably if she pays attention to the women who have gone before her. What follows is advice that is drawn from their experience.

Unless a woman has thoroughly explored her own strengths and skills, foibles, appetites, and eccentricities, she will be leaving her career to chance. The first job after earning the MBA must be chosen with as much self-knowledge as a mate or a house in which one plans to live for years. Unless the match is intricate and accurate, it will chafe and constrain rather than provide growth and success.

In setting career goals and looking for work that will make them possible, women must examine the whole constellation of circumstances that can affect them, beginning inside and moving outward. Just as essential as knowing themselves is understanding the system they are entering: what it will demand of them, where it is likely to place them, and whether it will advance or obstruct them.

Evaluate the Employer

Over and over women stressed the importance of research before entering an interview. Even when time is short, it is too important to neglect. A banker working in Washington hopped on a plane to San Francisco for an interview on a day's notice, but she was ready:

> The first thing I did was research on the bank itself. I started with all the statistics, financial statements from way back, biographies of the top managers, and management style. . . . I compared the bank with the large New York banks, and my experience [in auditing banks] came in handy because I could actually see how well or how badly the bank was doing.

No matter how well prepared a woman thinks she is, there is always more to learn. It seems obvious to know the background of the interviewers, but many women have been surprised. One Goldmine graduate who had been pestering an investment bank weekly for months to give her an interview found that she was not nearly as prepared as she had hoped when the time came. The interview was far longer than she had expected and had an unforeseen purpose: she was being examined as to her potential as a banker, while she expected specialists to be evaluating her in her own field.

Dr. Betsy Jaffe, formerly at Catalyst (a women's career-development organization) and now a private career counselor, suggests that women do a thorough preliminary evaluation of an employer, including both organizational and personal factors:

It is essential for women to understand the concepts of line versus staff, and bottom line responsibility, and who is really making a difference in this company. It will vary company by company: whatever makes that company run, who are the movers and shakers. First of all, do your homework. Know about the industry, and read articles about the specific company and what their plans are, what decisions seem to be emerging. You might be able to pick that up from looking at the sources of company profits. Look at it by division and by product. Talk to people who work there, perhaps go to some meetings of professional organizations for that industry. Do your homework before you get there, so you can ask about growth areas and what they are really doing in long-range plans. . . . The economy, the company, even the division may be expanding or contracting.

Once women actually make their way in the door and have an opportunity to check the employer out, some positive indications can help establish that the organization would be suitable for women MBAs in general—as can some warning signs. Only the individual knows whether a place feels right in terms of her own values, but the signals discussed here should help in terms of the larger context.

Positive Signals
Some women will decide to be the pioneers in working environments that have been predominantly male at all levels; they expect and hope to break the patterns that have prevailed thus far. For most, however, assessing whether there is real evidence of progress for women in management is an important step in evaluating their long-term career prospects. It is not enough to receive verbal assurances. A career changer who had worked earlier in a very male-dominated industry went over prospective employers with a fine-tooth comb; she felt that she had already done her time in places where she was not welcome. She ended up in a very supportive firm, working in product management:

> I looked for a corporate environment that was very pro-woman, where they could show me tangible results of that attitude. You have to find your fit. . . . I found tangible examples of women moving up in the corporation who were very highly respected, and who in many cases were moving up faster than the male counterparts they came in with. Looking at that, you feel very positive. Plus they have plans for the future, like the child-care center.

Seeing whether or not women are literally in the picture can be an indication of whether they are present at any level above the ground floor. Jaffe suggests:

> Look at the annual report. How many women are there on the board? How many are pictured there? As you go through the company, where are the women sitting? Are they part of the group you are going into? How many women are above that for the next couple of levels? What would your initial assignment be? What is the possibility of advancement and what kind of visibility would you have? Is this boss someone who seems to promote people? . . . Ask where other people have gone from this position.

If the last person to hold the job moved up, particularly if that person was female, it shows that the job is a possible launching pad. Several really serious job problems could have been prevented if women had asked more closely about the fates of their predecessors. In one case, the situation was so difficult that four different employees had come and gone in a few years' time.

Watch to see if the people who are hiring you really know what they want and have the authority to make their decision stick organizationally. Again, women who ran into barriers felt that they should have cross-examined their interviewers more closely about the lines of authority. If employers are absolutely clear about what the job entails, its purpose, and boundaries, you have a much better chance of turning in a stellar performance—or at least a capable one—than if they are unsure of specifics but know generally that they want a miracle worker. Because of the propaganda about MBAs, expectations can sometimes be very unrealistic.

Seeing how the prospective employer responds can also be telling, particularly when it comes to negotiating over salary and title. One useful test of an organization's values is the salary they offer initially, and how they respond when women press for more pay. While women can expect some resistance, they should feel that they are being treated as respected equals. Negotiating for salary is a critical skill for women to develop, not only because their work is generally undervalued, but because they can only begin to challenge assumptions by demanding to be paid what they are worth. Starting off on the right foot is indispensable, and much easier than hopping around once on the job.

Warning Signals
Without cultivating an overly suspicious attitude, women should maintain a healthy skepticism as they evaluate employers. The following are some of the questions the women I interviewed wished they had asked more often.

Am I being taken seriously at the interview? Even with years of business experience, women still are not taken seriously in some interviews. One of the most qualified women who talked with me, who has both law and business degrees from a Generic school, had a rude shock when she was interviewed by the vice president of one of the leading banks in a major city:

> I didn't realize then that this firm was one of the strongholds of the old-boy situation. After my first interview I came back for a second. He told me that they were not interested in me for commercial real estate. I asked why. He said, "We don't feel that you have a business background." I said, "You don't consider an MBA and a law degree and four years of practicing tax law, hiring and firing secretaries, setting up and liquidating corporations and partnerships, doing syndications, and advising people on estate planning—you don't consider that a business background?"
>
> He just looked at me and sort of shrugged. It was then that it hit me: My God, it must be because I'm a woman.

Are women channeled in a certain direction? Will this happen to me? A woman with a Generic school MBA had applied to be a consultant with a consulting firm:

> I had three interviews, and at the third one with the vice president he said, "What we really want is for you to work in our research area." This is after I have already had these other two interviews under the impression that I was being considered for consulting.
>
> It's fairly common to start in research, but not for long. [I asked for what period of time], and he said, "Five years." That's absurd; the maximum would be eight months. I just noticed that all the women MBAs they had were in research. . . . It was apparent to me that the men were steered into consulting and the women into research.

An MBA-program director who had been interviewed at a number of business schools learned that things are not always what they seem when she began asking questions. Her own degree was from Goldmine, and she was being considered by a Generic school. She asked:

> "What do you have in the way of women around here?" [They had just made a major appointment of a woman] so they told me that, very proudly. . . . I said, "Is this a problem? I want to know this. If you're going to bring me out here for a top administrative job and you've got a team here that's all men smoking

big cigars—" "Oh, hell no," he said, "when I showed them your
résumé, at first they said, 'You're just bringing a woman out and
all that stuff,' but I said, 'No, just look at this résumé.' "

Tokenism, in other words, should be a warning sign, and employers who
consider themselves enlightened should be looked at as closely as any others.

**Is the employer aware of where the women in the organization
are?**   There is a big difference between real awareness of the issue of equal
opportunity in the workplace and outward compliance with the law, as
one CPA/MBA discovered:

> When I was interviewing at another accounting firm I asked them
> what percentage of the partners in the New York office were
> women. The man said to me, "Oh, I don't know, we have women
> partners—let's see, we have about a hundred partners, and there's
> one woman." Here's this accountant who can't calculate 1 percent.

Where are the women at the top?   Another telltale point is the positions
top women hold. Are they where you would expect to find them, or have
they moved into unconventional areas? The MBA-program director quoted
above warns:

> When they tell you, "Oh, yes, our affirmative action officer is a
> woman, or our director of personnel is a woman," find the door.
> I suppose everybody knows this, although maybe they don't know
> right away when they get out of school. . . . If that's their idea
> of a good place for a woman, you're in alot of trouble.

Sometimes, of course, there are almost no women at all outside of clerical
positions; if an MBA decides to work in such an environment, she should
be prepared to make her way against powerful structural obstacles, and
should examine the reasons given for women's not being recruited or promoted before. If the real issue is lack of supply in a specialty, that is a very
different matter from being told that women cannot handle the demands
of a technical job.

Will my background be valued?   Some interviewers react negatively to
a background outside the business world. It may indicate that the employer
will not appreciate the contributions that someone with a different history
can make to the organization. An accountant whose experience was in the
nonprofit sector found that most of the people who interviewed her felt
that she would have nothing to offer from her earlier experience:

The firm I decided to work for was the only one that asked me about, and seemed interested in, my background. Everybody else was skeptical about it and thought it was not even worth discussing. They thought, "Oh, you couldn't make a living in non-profits so you're going to business school."

Can the employer handle assertive women? Some interviewers also showed negative attitudes when women asked hard questions researching the organization's employment policies and practices, or negotiating salary and title. In one case, a woman who is now an investment banker ignored clear signals that her future boss could not handle a strong subordinate and was sorry she had:

She immediately criticized how I was at the interview. She said, "You're very good, but you didn't do this and you didn't do that." That's really not what you do at an interview. She said she was giving me feedback, but it's not the appropriate time to give feedback. It was immediately establishing her telling me how I should be. I knew that I had an immediately negative feeling about her.

Because the MBA was outstandingly qualified through her past experience in a highly specialized field, she was hired. Unfortunately, she accepted the job despite strong misgivings—because she did not have the confidence that she could get a more suitable job if she kept looking. She leaped for the first offer that seemed at all acceptable rather than holding out for what she wanted. Soon, she found that her boss, like many others, wanted both a yes-person and someone who thought independently, and every sign of assertiveness on her part was met with resistance.

Do I feel comfortable? Feeling uncomfortable is probably the most serious warning signal and one that women tend to ignore. Too often, they dismiss the irritation when something just does not seem quite right, whether or not they can put their fingers on it precisely. What is mildly uncomfortable at the interview stage may be a real source of anguish later on. To dismiss intuitions about persons and organizations is often a mistake.

Even making a move from a summer or temporary business school student job to another within the same organization requires an assessment of whether the personalities and values of organizational culture are comfortable. For example, a banker told me:

When I was on my temporary job, where I was with more upper-level people, the climate was much more relaxed than it is here. They are new, pushy MBAs and they all want to prove themselves. So even within the same culture, within the same structure, you go through various personalities. Sometimes you just have to stick it out and say, "OK, I'll get through it, and then I'll look at which area I like, where I like the environment." So I think it's a combination of asking how much I am willing to go through for what I want to get. And how much am I willing to give; am I willing to compromise myself and how much do I stand to my own values?

Another woman, a Generic school graduate, had a shattering experience with an arts organization that ended in her being fired. While many levels of organizational politics were involved, she had stumbled into a snakepit of old relationships and loyalties. She would probably not have been able to find out exactly what was going on in advance, but she did sense some strange factors at work from the very beginning:

> When you get into an institution where people have been for thirty or thirty-five years, they control with an iron fist—the old thing of who is sleeping with whom. The sooner they teach that at business school, the better off it's going to be. That's what makes things run in old-line institutions. It was a major disaster. They interviewed and hired me as a marketing person, and they brought me in to make sure the windows were clean.

Where does the prospective employer fit into the power structure? In this case and others, the informal structure and formal power structures were at odds. Sensing where someone who is offering you a job fits into both is indispensable to assessing her or him as a possible employer. A woman from a good state program discovered that it was not enough to have a clear agreement about what a job would consist of if the person in question did not really have the authority:

> My first job was very disappointing. At first I thought, "This is really great." I thought I had a chance to update the system for handling the sales force. But it turned out that they really wanted someone to maintain the system. Anyone out of high school could have done what I did. I learned that the lines of authority don't always go with the organizational chart. The people who hired me had the titular but not the real authority.

From the outside, it can be almost impossible to evaluate who really holds the reins in an organization. Even so, this woman felt that with more experience and sensitivity she could have been more perceptive in her interviews.

A 1976 Goldmine graduate pushed herself ahead despite her misgivings, with disastrous results. She had assessed herself and set her goals very thoroughly, and decided that she wanted to enter consulting by way of marketing; because she had lived on the East Coast all her life, she wanted to prepare herself for national marketing projects. It all sounded very sensible, but the reality of working for an auto company in the Midwest was something else again. Most of what finally undid her career there (although she left honorably) would have been predictable: she was the only single woman in the entire installation where she worked, and her travel schedule was killing. Even hard work and determination could not make up for the deep alienation she felt while she was there. She was both socially and professionally excluded; neither fish nor fowl, she did not belong either at the boys' drinking bouts or at the secretaries' lunches. Like anyone who is isolated, she became plagued by self-doubts and lost confidence in herself. Only with a supreme effort did she manage to move on to a better job. If she had paid more attention to the social fit between herself and her employer, she might have been spared several very rough years.

Every woman has to decide for herself which personal preferences and values she wants to put first. On that basis, she can define her own positive and warning signals, in addition to these general points. For example, someone with a shy personality would watch for a job in which she would be gobbled up by much more aggressive people as opposed to a cooperative atmosphere. A woman whose top priority was career progress might choose a company where there were few MBAs who had positioned themselves successfully, so that her talents would be more sought after. Another might consider criteria for the size of organization, the physical environment, working style (participatory or hierarchical), and the degree of social contact with colleagues. Such choices depend largely on the individual, and should be made on that basis rather than in keeping with the conventional wisdom. A larger, more complex or prestigious organization is not the best choice for everyone. Whatever direction a woman takes, it will be tested in the reality of her workplace.

Five

Confronting the Realities of the Workplace

After securing her job in entry level line management with a Fortune 500 company, Ms. MBA took two weeks off to have her baby. Delivered into the hands of an English nanny, little Dorigen promptly became a child prodigy, thanks to quality time with her mother. Meanwhile, back at the office, Ms. MBA was making strides. Her boss could not have been happier with her: weekly they sat down to discuss her accomplishments and possible future directions.

In board meetings Ms. MBA always got credit where it was due. Sought after by all departments in her company, she advanced rapidly, but not so much so that others resented her. To a man, her colleagues supported and applauded her, for she had reached the level where she had almost no female peers. A network of professional women in her city nevertheless kept her well informed and provided companionship. By the time she was appointed the first female senior vice president who was neither somebody's daughter nor in personnel or human resources, Ms. MBA could honestly say that she had had nothing but support all the way. Certainly she had never been discriminated against.

A surprising number of women expected that their careers would be as untroubled, if not as stellar, as Ms. MBA's. Many believed that hard work would be the key to their success and that they would have as good a chance as anyone to advance. They thought that the world had really changed for women.

They would probably have approached their careers quite differently if they had entered the workplace with their eyes open to what had actually changed and for which women. In retrospect, they often thought that they could have avoided mistakes and heartaches. Like inexperienced sailors who don't know where the lighthouses are, they often missed the warning signals that would have told them to take another course. Once they stopped allowing themselves to be buffeted about by the tides and began actually to steer, women discovered all kinds of strategies that would have helped them even more earlier.

Some of women's collective wisdom is reflected in this chapter. They were eager to pass on what they had learned to others, both to help them avoid problems and to create as positive a route to their goals as possible. This chapter examines how women MBAs have coped with the workplace as they have found it, not as it is depicted in positive-thinking literature or as it was experienced by bright, young, white male MBAs in the 1950s. For women, the workplace differed from their expectations. Although the atmosphere is now supposed to be favorable to them, they shared many of the same issues as other women workers; discrimination still existed, both overtly and subtly. The workplace was affected by the traditional value that women belong in the home, an expectation reinforced by the lack of a coherent child-care policy and the small scale of efforts to provide child care outside the family.

Taking both the workplace and their personal identities into account, women learned a great deal about what to watch out for. Primarily, there are two underlying warning signals: the lack of positive, active support and encouragement (including constructive criticism), and the lack of adequate resources to do the job. Like everyone else, women MBAs have had to develop strategies both to counteract problems and to keep to their career paths. Against a background that is supposed to provide equal opportunity for everybody, they must watch for ever subtler signs of career blockage and create increasingly sophisticated tactics to deal with them. Some women tried to cope with everything on their own, but most found both friendship and professional networks indispensable, not only within their workplaces, but locally and nationally.

Expectations of the Workplace

Many women started their careers as MBAs with high expectations. At first, they chugged away at daily tasks, showing what productive employees they were. Many enjoyed their work; they liked being out of school and in a different setting. Unlike many of their female predecessors in business, few were totally isolated, although the earlier graduates reported that they were often the first women in their jobs. All things considered, most were satisfied at the entry level.

Many extrapolated that the rest of their careers would go smoothly because they had not encountered significant obstacles in their first few years. They expected the system to recognize and support them, with advancement inevitably following. They thought they could make it on their merits, assuming that people who treated them fairly at the entry level would do so again when they competed directly with them for higher jobs. To these women, the concept of discrimination was a thing of the past.

Although presently satisfied with entry-level jobs, others did recognize that they were not yet far enough along to hit the barriers that could halt their careers. A woman who worked for one of the most active corporate affirmative action programs after earning her MBA felt that the obstacles did not really arise until later:

> My guess is that the resistance is not at the bottom. It's not in entry-level jobs. It's not in those first few weeks, it is as the pyramid narrows, when you are really talking about putting women in decision-making roles or where the real power in an organization lies, that you begin to get resistance. I find that many organizations are very successful in promoting women in management jobs and certainly in technical and professional roles. The wall really is when you talk about women in top management.

The women I interviewed at middle level were usually well aware that they and their friends were hitting the brick ceiling and making lateral moves. After years of feeling that they were exceptions who were not going to be held back, they suddenly found themselves at a barrier, like this woman who learned that the often-repeated maxim that a woman has to be twice as good as a man applied in her company:

> In spite of all the changes going on and everything you read and hear, there's still a lot of discrimination against women. It's easy to get your foot in the door, but it's not so easy to get a real position of power in an organization. You just have to have a realistic understanding of that.

A faculty member put it another way, that there is a change of veneer, but the same men are still in power as were there fifteen and twenty years ago.

The notion that women need only wait for advancement, since they have not been in the pipeline long enough to expect to come out the other end, is popular among optimists. They contend that the top ranks of corporate management and boards will be desegregated by sex as soon as enough women are sufficiently senior to attain those positions. Certainly that argument has some merit, especially in the case of technical business specialties that have genuinely lacked supply in the past.

There is no reason, however, to assume that the passage of time alone will overcome all obstacles. To continue the pipeline analogy, any good plumber knows that when water does not come out the far end, you assume there is a blockage along the way and look for it, rather than rushing back to see if the reservoir has run dry. The experience of secretaries and teachers in entering these formerly male-dominated fields decades ago does not support the concept that women MBAs will automatically move up in course of time.

Barriers at the Top

According to Dr. Myra Strober, author of the first study of women MBAs and an expert who has interviewed many women in management, it is well-placed women who perceive the invisible barriers most clearly:

> The women I see who are most likely to understand this are women very close to the top. The women who are "the top woman in their company" realize all too well what the difficulties would be to try to move any further. They will tell you, "Yes, I'm very successful. Sure, on any criterion of success I'm successful. But I can't get any further. I'm blocked."

Similarly, women in one of the Goldmine alumnae networks told me that the major concern of those who were at least five years out of business school was that they had not advanced beyond middle management and felt stuck.

A few were fortunate enough to be in settings that approached an egalitarian workplace. They felt valued for their current contributions and were treated like strong candidates for advancement. They saw more than token numbers of women moving ahead. They felt that they had a fair chance, and a glance at the top managers bore out that feeling. For example, after several miserable jobs, one accountant expressed her satisfaction with her current employer:

> For me and the women I know who work there, it is very close to an ideal place to work, with a reputation for being very fair and reasonable to women. There are women in very important positions.

While most women did not have such a supportive working atmosphere, they did not routinely suffer from the blatant harassment frequently reported by the earlier graduates.

MBAs Not Immune

Although the women I interviewed often hoped that their degrees would immunize them against the usual fate of women in the workplace, they faced many of the same issues. They were generally paid less than their male counterparts (as the studies discussed in the final chapter show). Like women dockyard workers, librarians, engineers, and others, they were underrepresented at the top. They experienced subtle as well as overt discrimination. And, like all women, their careers were strongly influenced by men's perceptions of them in traditional roles and their own efforts to integrate the personal and professional spheres of their lives.

While women continue to experience overt discrimination that they can recognize, such as being denied the opportunity to travel because they are mothers, much has gone underground. It takes the form of a working atmosphere that offers neither direct resistance nor the support traditionally afforded valued employees. Women are not starved of all resources to make their careers and programs flourish, but they are often given the organizational equivalent of bread and water and are expected to perform like champions. If they do not, those around them may comment on how thin they are, and how if they really cared about their careers they would gain some muscle so they could do the job right.

Discrimination is neither an accident in an otherwise fair and impartial hierarchy nor a calculated conspiracy implemented by men in penthouse offices using management by objectives. It is carried out by well-meaning people. At its most obvious, discrimination against women MBAs means incidents like having a male boss take credit for your work, being denied promotion or the opportunity to do special assignments that can lead to promotion, or being passed over for training and travel opportunities or visible projects that could give some exposure to upper management. In its more subtle forms, discrimination may mean anything from being set up to fail by being given inadequate information or resources to do a good job, to being excluded from social functions where male colleagues meet or having no feedback on your work outside required performance appraisals.

Formal or informal, conscious or unconscious, discrimination arises from a complex, invisible accord among men in the workplace that cannot be underestimated. It is that accord that women will never be able to reproduce exactly, even if they occasionally produce an acceptable substitute. Rather than male bonding, the basic patterns of relationships between women and men are fraught with sexuality, and social and power relationships. The scene between them is set fundamentally differently than the scene among men.

Isolation

Even where a specific series of overt acts against a woman's progress cannot be traced as it would be in a court case, at a subtler level a woman may feel isolated and unsupported. Anyone who has experienced social exclusion can imagine professional exclusion: it is a glance withdrawn, a telephone call not returned, a meeting that was never mentioned. Those conditions play themselves out directly in stalled careers: it is almost impossible for a woman who feels excluded to do her best work. She may even protect her sense of safety by not recognizing the times she is being isolated, except in retrospect.

Yet, over time, a pattern may become clear to her. The assistant business manager of a television station acutely feels the isolation of being one of the few women in her job:

> Men in a working situation want their team, and they don't want certain people to play on their team in the long run. The jury is still out on whether they want to have me there, but I tend to get the oddest feeling that I'm not really included, especially since there aren't many women involved in the financial area. In fact, there are none. Often, I must admit that I feel excluded from the information flow.

Isolation has other ramifications. Although there are certainly increased numbers of women MBAs in many workplaces, in many settings they are still "the only one" or "one of the few," especially once they have reached the middle level. Having only a tiny percentage of women at all levels can create an atmosphere in which even the crudest forms of sexist behavior are acceptable. For example, a woman who works with a defense contractor, with almost no other women, has her office in a building that surrounds the swimming pool in an apartment complex:

> In the summertime, all the guys are looking out at the women by the swimming pool, making comments and giving them little nicknames, like "Thunder thighs." It drives me crazy. I don't like it anyway, but I generally try and work. I go in and say, "Can you look at this," or, "I want to talk to you about that," and they're hanging out the window with their binoculars.

This illustrates more than the unwarranted distraction of sexist behavior in the workplace; it shows how an atmosphere is created in which women are denigrated and seen as the objects of a spectator sport. How could this woman expect to be taken seriously by the same men whose eyes have been glued to the window? Is it realistic for her to expect to be seen first as a professional and then as a woman? How can she object to their behavior, or discuss its implications for her career, without being seen as a prudish spoilsport, particularly if there are almost no other women who could support her?

Because most women are on the alert only for the most obvious forms of discrimination, they often miss signals that their careers are on the rocks. Most of the women I talked with were very reluctant to believe that their careers were affected by the broad discriminatory patterns working against them in the labor market. Unless they could point to one specific incident, they did not believe it. But the drama of discrimination is rarely a two-character play with one white male villain and one heroine. It is more likely to involve a multitude of bit actors, distracting subplots, and special effects that detract from the main scenario. At the end, the heroine may suddenly find herself in the background of a crowd scene instead of being crowned monarch as she had expected.

The Trap of Self-blame

If she is like most women, she is more likely to blame herself than to realize that she has been upstaged. She may well overlook the way other actors positioned themselves in front of her to attract more attention or their failure to push her forward at the appropriate moment. She is naive about their ambitions and tactics at her peril; she will never be the star, no matter what the written script says, if she does not wake up to the realities.

If a woman MBA pays attention to the experience of other women in the workplace (including perhaps those in her pre-MBA occupation), many of the trends affecting her are dishearteningly familiar. Women MBAs suffer from the same discrimination that affects all other white-collar women. Most of the warning signals will be yawningly ordinary to anyone who has informed herself about employment issues: not being taken seriously, being passed over for promotion and other opportunities, being patronized or sexually harassed. Although many women MBAs see themselves as having escaped traditional occupations, much of what they report is commonplace.

Detecting Career Blockage

Often the denial of real opportunity is not so much a series of deliberate, active moves against a woman as it is a series of non-events: the times she is not considered at all for a new assignment, when she is eliminated simply because she does not cross the minds of the next level of management. Sometimes a woman will be unaware that she has been stopped in her tracks. The invisible, soundless closing off of opportunities can occur when she is not offered a choice executive training course, not asked to give a talk at an influential professional meeting, or is cast in a conventional role as a minute taker or report writer.

The women I interviewed sometimes had not recognized what was happening to their careers until it was too late. When something went wrong, they tended to look inside themselves first for the reasons, rather than seeking external causes. It seemed that they would rather feel responsible for their own failures than feel helpless because their problems were the result of a chaos of uncontrollable outer forces. The corollary is that, when they succeed, they can believe that they rose only through their own merit.

Despite her years in the workplace, a mid-career executive accepted it quietly when the employees she supervised were taken away from her and her section was dissolved. She believed that cost cuts were necessary and they affected everybody; she had been brought into the area originally because there were problems, and had told the higher ups that she needed more technical persons to do the job right. Rather than commit the necessary personnel, the company decided to cut the area out. It sounded very straightforward.

It was not until the section was reestablished with the exact number of workers and other resources she had recommended, under the leadership of a less experienced man, that this MBA began to have doubts. When she did, she doubted herself: what had she done wrong?

> Now it looks as if a woman didn't know how to handle the situation, and I keep wondering. I talked to my husband about it. . . . He said, "They wouldn't have given you the personnel, they wouldn't even have loaned it to you." . . . It's irritating to see that happen, because it's a very subtle thing.

Some women, particularly the more experienced or isolated, are realistic about what has changed in the workplace—access to entry-level jobs—and what has not—access to upper management. They expect that there will be subtle attitudinal barriers as well as obvious ones (verbal remarks, sexist jokes or posters, etc.). They recognize that the context in which they are working has traditionally denied women opportunities. If they were to assume that everything had improved, they would naively and inevitably find themselves in stagnant positions.

Whatever a woman's qualifications may be, the most obvious fact about her to any passing stranger, her gender, determines the course of her daily working life and career. As long as women MBAs try to separate themselves from other white-collar women, very little is likely to improve for them as a group. While there are many possible points of connection, one of the most obvious similarities among all women workers is the way their careers are configured by traditional concepts of their purpose in life as females, which in turn shaped their personal context. Just as women MBAs experienced the same spectrum of discrimination as other women, even where it took different forms, the issues they face in integrating professional and personal life are similar, if not identical.

The Personal Context

Management jobs are traditionally structured for workers assumed to be married men with full-service wives, or undistracted bachelors. They are expected to work long hours, travel anywhere, be available on weekends, or cancel personal arrangements in favor of sudden assignments. Career commitment is defined in terms of hours worked and putting the job first.

Some women can and do fit into these expectations, and make the same sacrifices men have traditionally made. Most, however, do not fit the mold. All women, whether they are married or not, whether they are mothers or not, fulfill traditional expectations as care givers, which are not required of men. They are responsible for looking after relatives, friends, and partners, and maintaining church and community activities.

Among married women with children, a few said that their husbands were very cooperative in assisting with domestic chores, although none felt that men assumed equal responsibility for the household and parenting. Even where there was assistance, it was often inconsistent. Male partners rarely shouldered full and permanent responsibility for family chores. Even so, women who had helpful partners considered themselves lucky relative to other women. Because relatively little has changed in the division of domestic responsibilities, mothers and married women often had a whole chorus of demands to meet in addition to their jobs. The stress was most extreme for single mothers, who not only had no help but far fewer economic resources.

Mom as the Norm

On the whole, women experienced extreme difficulties in living up to both their traditional female identity as Mom and their identity as career women, difficulties that they considered normal and often did not even define as problems. Because most did not find it surprising to have no support from employers and male partners in coping with children, they often did not identify that lack as a barrier to their careers.

Of all the women I interviewed, only one was able to tell me about a concerted effort on the part of her employer to provide child care for anyone who needed it in a company-funded center. To her, nothing could be more important in allowing her to give her full attention to her career:

> If you know your child is safely cared for, then you can go off
> and beat down worlds. Having the responsibility of taking care
> of your child and not feeling like you are doing it very well, you
> can't do a very good job, either.

For the most part, though, women improvised their arrangements. Their experience reflects the reality that only about 2000 of the hundreds of thousands of employers[1] in the United States have made an effort to assist employees with child care by providing information, funding programs, allowing special time off, reimbursing expenses, or opening centers.

Even those who work for these more enlightened companies may find them less than ideal. An MBA in a corporation often cited as a model said that there was a big difference between theory and practice:

> Even now, I've found that you use any excuse but "I had to stay home with the kid." I just called in sick when I had to be home with Cindy. I would talk with the people I was working with and they would know, but not my boss. They don't want to know what your problems are or anything.

An organization with an overview of child care among United States employers from the perspective of women is New York-based Catalyst. Several years ago they held focus groups for women managers throughout the country about related concerns, and they have been collecting written information about the issues from a wide variety of sources. According to one woman who worked on the project, little is being done, although more is being said:

> A lot more is being written about it. At Catalyst, they started with only about 500 entries on the topic of dual career issues, now there are about 5,000. There's not a lot of action; there's a lot of verbal saying, "Yes, well, we ought to." In reality, it's still an individual case: "I've got a really super woman. I'm going to let her work at home, and plug into our computer terminal."

The significance of most employers' dealing with parenthood and child care issues on a case-by-case basis is many sided. It shows how far management is willing to go for individual women at higher levels rather than for the majority of women employees who have, after all, been having children for decades. Many of the weak efforts that have been made follow the entry of women en masse into beginning-level professional jobs. Employer inaction also assures that motherhood will continue to be an additional stress hampering women's careers. Wondering whether the babysitter will have to go home early or whether the child-care center will be open an extra five minutes drains women's energy and focuses them on daily coping rather than career strategy. Too often, women reported that the prevailing attitude was that children were a nuisance whose births, illnesses, graduations, and medical appointments needlessly interfere with an employee's effectiveness. More than one mother noticed that she was criticized for taking her child to the doctor, while her husband was lauded as a hero when he undertook it.

Doing it All

In their eagerness to show that they can function in the workplace, the women I talked with generally tried to take care of anything related to their children by themselves. Only a few even attempted to share responsibilities with male partners, much less reach beyond the traditional family unit to organize alternatives with other women employees. While the lack of child-care facilities is mainly the result of employer reluctance and regressive social policy, it is also discouraging but true that the women themselves had not pressed for better provisions.

The women I interviewed, and others they told me about, tended to cope with being parents one by one, cutting an individual deal for maternity leave and making private arrangements for child care when they came back. No one could cite a single example of women MBAs' working with other parents to press for change by proposing sick leave policies for children's illnesses, by negotiating for child-care benefits as part of all salary packages, or by approaching corporate boards to establish on-site centers.

Because the outcome of the multitude of individual arrangements is frequently unsatisfactory, some women weary of it. As long as their home identities remain unchanged, with or without an infant, there are simply not enough hours in the day for them to add on the requirements of a demanding job. If, like most women, their careers are stalled after a certain point, they may begin to wonder if the additional effort to attempt the next step is worth it.

> All of a sudden you get to a point where you are working as hard as your husband, maybe not the same salary, but maybe you haven't hit the same level of responsibility in the job. Not that you haven't worked as hard. There's still a difference, but you're still working double duty.
>
> Your husband can come home and sit around and talk about business all night, but you're sitting there worrying about, "How am I going to get this dinner on the table, listen to him, take care of kids who came home from school with a problem," and it's not such a glamorous situation.
>
> At this point, you make a decision: are you really willing to make the next leap? It's going to take an enormous amount of energy, a lot more than you were putting in when you thought you were working twice as hard as a man. You're going to have to work four times as hard as you did before, because those men are working that much harder also.

Women who are considering having children are deeply concerned about just such effects on their careers: the effect of taking time off, and the long-term stresses that are the inevitable accompaniment of women's trying to "do it all" in a climate in which that is expected of them. They may also find that their relationships change; one discovered that the same man who was delighted to have her bringing in a handsome income did an about-face when they had children. Suddenly, he wanted her to stay at home with the baby, MBA and all. She compromised and cut back to half-time.

Like her, some women do make career sacrifices as a result of having children. Helen Axel, an expert on work and family issues with the Conference Board, said:

> Women are realizing now that it's really not possible to have everything. There are trade-offs, and if you're going to have a family and raise them, there are going to be plateaus in your career. It's very difficult to get promotions and advancement when you are taking blocks of time off for your family life, or when you are part time. . . . That's bound to reflect ultimately on where you are going to go.

Retreating from the Fast Track

Women who agree with Axel's view may simply back down, especially if they are already stymied in their jobs. One Goldmine MBA told me she was convinced that some of her classmates decided to have children not so much as a positive goal but because the alternative was a frustrating career. A management consultant from a Generic school said as much when she was unemployed for months after getting her MBA: having a child was at least something to do with her life.

Even where women did not drop out of the paid workforce when they had children, they made compromises. A classic conflict emerged as I talked with one mother of two young tots. She holds a part-time management job, a real rarity:

> The job is meeting some goals. But I'm always in constant struggle with my commitment to the kids versus my commitment to my career. It's always on my mind.
>
> Q: How does it come up? What tends to trigger it [off]?
>
> Whenever I feel that I want to move on, I go through that, periodically when I feel I've got to get another job because this isn't what I want to be doing. Because it isn't—what was your question?
>
> Q: I was asking about the times when the conflict comes up.
>
> OK, so that—hi, Kyra [as the two-year-old stepped out onto

a precarious balcony]. Don't come out on that porch, OK?—
What's keeping me from making it is my kids, so it comes up
every time I get frustrated with my job.

It is understandable that some women beat a retreat from a system
that has not rewarded them and that puts insurmountable obstacles in their
paths if they choose to have children. Sometimes the crisis point is reached
after the second child is born, when a woman decides that she just cannot
keep up the pace. According to Dr. Joanna Mulholland of the Philadelphia
College of Textiles, women often begin their careers with inflated
expectations:

> I think they're naive in their perceptions. They expect that if they
> are nice and they get a good education, everybody is going to
> accept them with open arms. I don't think they realize the tre-
> mendous competition not only from people at their own level,
> but what they have to face with superiors. Two things can hap-
> pen. They can either survive it and become tougher and smarter
> because of it, or they can give up. They get married and stay
> home with children. They become burdened with all the prob-
> lems women have. They then go into menial jobs or try to change
> careers.

Overall, the issues raised by women's lives outside the workplace are
still unresolved. As more and more women have exactly the same educational and experiential qualifications as men, their traditional identity as
wives and mothers becomes a more common rationale for lack of progress
in management. Coupled with the decline of affirmative action is the push
throughout the industrialized countries to carry women back across the
threshold of the home. It is not surprising that, when all else fails, it is
argued that women cannot take on the duties of management, especially
at the top, because they have too many other responsibilities. That argument will hold as long as women accept their traditional roles as inevitable.
Until now, it is clear that they themselves have done the adjusting, one by
one, and that public policy, employers, and male partners have done little.
If women are to survive and thrive despite the climate and barriers, they
need strategies that take heed of their predicament.

Strategies

The notion that women need only improve their performance to have
successful careers is part of the myth of the egalitarian workplace, and
ignores the overarching realities of the paucity of women in top manage-

ment and the forces that maintain that situation. Women coped with the apparent intractability of the system in a number of ways, some more constructively than others. Some went in for self-improvement, such as assertiveness training, improving interviewing or speaking techniques, or gaining more organizational knowledge. These can all be valuable tools and may make women more confident and able to perform, although at best they affect only the individual.

Other women coped less constructively, by redefining success to suit the realities of what was possible for them. For example, women in the study of Stanford MBAs[2] adjusted their salary aspirations downward to reflect what they found in the workplace after they had been out for a few years. Among the women I interviewed, those with children were especially likely to trim their expectations to what they felt they could achieve while doing both a paid and an unpaid job. A few women dropped out of the system altogether as a means of coping with career blockage, sometimes to switch careers or spend more time at home, sometimes to start their own businesses.

For those who did stay in the conventional workplace, a few themes were repeated when I asked them for strategies that they would recommend to others, both as individuals and in networks. Although many more of them tried to advance one by one, those who did form networks found them a significant source of support and career strategy. They could improve tactics and performance, along with finding a healthy recognition that they were far from alone and could work effectively together. As with any other group sport, the best moves in career development always involve other players. Women can accomplish a lot working alone, and many do. But the most effective strategies involve support from others rather than isolating themselves, discussing ideas rather than muttering them in the tub, and acting in concert with others.

Pick a Good Boss

Having a boss who is well connected and respected in the organization makes a big difference in terms of one's future career, but even that is not enough. Finding someone who takes a genuine interest in developing subordinates and sees their growth as part of the job any manager should do is the ideal. An MBA in a huge bureaucratic organization in New York gave a useful definition of a good boss:

> A good boss is somebody who gives you the right opportunity, the right visibility, who's not threatened by you, who just lets you go and do your thing, gives you good assignments so you can prove yourself and is willing to reward you for it. It really

takes someone whose own career is not stalling. . . . Some feel like, "It took me ten years to get here, so why should I give it to you overnight?" A lot of guys are smart enough to know better, but they're still playing those games because they're insecure.

Positive support may not be forthcoming simply because the boss is a "nice person." More important is their willingness to recognize and tell a woman about her strengths and weaknesses, give her a chance to amplify the former and compensate for the latter, or whether they expect her to perform, and be seen and not heard. For women MBAs who are career changers and unfamiliar with the cultural norms of an organization, it is especially important to find someone who will give honest feedback. Compatibility of working style is essential: if you do your best when work flows across your desk at an even, orderly pace, think carefully before you choose a boss who thinks that working under the pressure of a last-minute deadline gets a better product.

How do you know if someone will be a good boss? Find out where your predecessors have gone and, if possible, talk with them. Rely on your own good judgment, but gather as much information as you can. It is surprising how easy it is to find out about the course of someone's career in an organization of any size, unless you are coming into a new geographic area and a new field totally cold. Knowing where your prospective boss fits into the organization and whether or not her or his star is likely to rise can give you an insight about your own future.

Spread Your Connections, Inside and Out

The more persons you know in different parts of an organization and in the community where you work (geographically and professionally), the more likely you are to be able to move on or up when you want to. It is risky to put your career into the hands of one boss and a narrow spectrum of people who know that you sit somewhere along the right-hand corridor. A woman who was eventually fired for political reasons learned the hard way:

> [Whether you advance or not] is usually in the hands of one person. It's very autocratic. . . . One of the warnings I would make is don't ever put yourself in a position where your fate is really being determined by the hands of one person who can get jealous of you.

Instead, she advises making sure that your work is visible to other people in the organization, so that one boss's description of who you are and what you have done does not become the last word on the subject. Looking at the work situation as a matrix and thinking about who above your boss knows about you is essential to protecting and developing your career. Finally, "You have to learn never to think that just doing your job is all it takes."

Finding allies and people with similar ideas and interests in an organization has saved many women, especially those playing nontraditional roles. Women need to spread their connections to keep from being isolated, both personally and organizationally, whether they are the only fifty-year-old in a room full of people in their thirties, the only black face in an executive dining room, or a closet lesbian. Feeling uncomfortable at a personal level nearly always translates into organizational ineffectiveness, and the strategy of isolating the token is only too efficient. Unless women develop their own strategies to combat it, they will become increasingly peripheral.

In an atmosphere where women still run into sexist attitudes, finding like-minded women and men to counteract them is especially affirming. A former teacher has resigned herself to the fact that there are still some unreconstructed men in the workplace, and finds that support from people she trusts is the best antidote:

> If you're going to run into guys who really are stubborn about women, who look at you as a woman and never ever see MBA clothing the outside, then you just have to hope that they're gone or that they'll stay out of your way. . . . If some believe that women don't belong in the workforce or in management positions, you're never going to change their minds; you're just going to outlive them. . . . You just have to try to find people in the organization at your level and above who are sympathetic—not to cry on their shoulder, but just to have those persons whom you trust.

Connections outside the organization are also important, especially when women need counsel about touchy situations that they would rather not discuss with another insider or that demand a perspective from someone not steeped in the prevailing history and values.

Use Direct Confrontation Wisely

For many women, including MBAs, direct confrontation is not part of their repertoire of behavior. If a boss is about to do something that would hurt a woman's career, she often thinks of a spectrum of behavior that begins with, "Excuse me, I was just wondering if maybe sometime we could have a little chat for just a few minutes about something that isn't very important," and ends up with complaining to her friends. Including confrontation as an option does not mean that it should be used every time. But when it is appropriate, it should not be ruled out simply because a woman is too ladylike or timid to use it.

Although she was able to handle many situations assertively, a consultant in a high-technology setting once regretted that she behaved like a good girl:

> My undergraduate degree was very varied liberal arts, but my graduate degree I did for a purpose, and took a lot of statistics, market research planning, and did very well in them. [An interviewer] said to me, "I see you've done statistics. What's regression?" I was extremely insulted. I should have said, "You know damn well what it is. Why are you asking me?" But I was brought up to be very polite, so I smiled and said what regression is.

Clearly, confrontation was not even on her list of possibilities in that situation.

Not so for a career changer who had put months of effort into a report form for the organization's president, interviewing many people about what it should contain and consolidating their ideas. Her boss wavered instead of pushing the project along, and finally she confronted him:

> My boss is quite an insecure man, and one day he thought my report form was good, the other day he thought it was bad. One day he just comes strolling by and says, "Well, we are going to have to figure out whether we just scrap those reports or use them." I said, "No, those reports are damn good. You've got to use them." The next day he came and said, "Finish them, they're going up to the president."
>
> Now, I don't know whether that has anything to do with my being female or whatever, [but if it had happened on a day when] . . . I wasn't so sure of myself, then all those months of work would have been gone.

Most women are socialized to be nice to other people and to defer to the needs and priorities of others, especially men's. Their role in families is often conciliatory and facilitating, so confrontation can be extremely uncomfortable to them. Many have gone a long way toward becoming assertive, self-sufficient individuals, but few feel completely confident about tackling a problem head-on rather than chipping away at it from an angle.

In the example cited above, confrontation was appropriate because the woman involved needed to protect her long-term interests, and she could see that if she did not initiate a discussion, events would overtake her. Confrontation was also the course chosen by a number of women who were offended by men's behavior in the office. A young woman with an MBA specialty in public accounting took a lot of abuse from clients who shouted at her, but said she had finally learned to handle it efficiently. I asked how, and she said, "I yell back."

Women who were among the first to enter a particular field or workplace also used confrontation effectively. One of the main anxieties men expressed in settings where they were unaccustomed to professional women was that they would no longer be able to swear. In an open plan office, an MBA who was a novelty to her male peers could not help overhearing their anxious whispers:

> The guys had a big conversation about what can they say, because sometimes they would use strong language. . . . So finally one day I said, "I don't want you guys to feel you have to do something that makes you uncomfortable, because we are all working together. If you feel uncomfortable with me, I'm not going to be effective. If profanity is wrong, you shouldn't be using it anyway. If it's OK, then it's OK."

When a woman finds herself in a situation where a "women's issue" is involved, a male ally can be helpful, especially if he is well placed in the organization. When a new woman MBA was told to type something by the end of the day herself, she refused and enlisted her male supervisor's backing. He took the incident so seriously that he discussed it with his own boss as well as his peer who had made the blunder. Again, confrontation paid off much better than gnashing teeth.

Dig in Immediately

Because many people expect MBAs to be unwilling to sully their hands with actual labor, a number of women, especially those from the Goldmine schools, found that it helped to jump right in as soon as they arrived. A young woman who had gone to business school straight from doing her undergraduate work found that her colleagues expected the worst of her, but she overcame her apprehensions:

> What usually works best is to show that you're willing to roll up your sleeves and dig into the nitty gritty. Ask, "Is there anything I can do to help? If you don't want to give me the numbers, show me where I can find them and I'll get them myself." And then they started working with you to show you. You have to show

that you're not just there to take their numbers and run off and get all the glory, but you're willing to do some of the work.

If you're not willing to do some of the work, you have to bluff them. Or sometimes dropping a name will scare them into being cooperative. In the extreme cases, you know you have to complain up the line and get to them that way, but that's really a last resort.

Deferring to the experience and knowledge of people who have been in an organization for years or who have some technical understanding that any MBA probably lacks can stand a new employee in very good stead. In the mid-1970s one woman who broke new ground in the auto industry found a vast contrast between the verdant campus of Goldmine and the car dealerships of the Midwest. She received a lot of advice about how to handle herself:

I learned that there is a world of difference between street smarts and book smarts. In the world of business, book smarts are nothing. They're nice, but they're not going to be any good. I had to be sure that the dealers understood that I was there to learn from them, because they all had street smarts.

My bosses had told me to let the dealers teach me my job. If you walk in there and tell them you know what you're doing, they'll wipe you up with Kleenex. They also told me . . . there were two topics of conversation that anybody in the world could get involved in. One was cars, and the other was sex. "Dammit, honey, you stick to cars."

By recognizing that they did not know everything and by trying to learn from the people around them, both women broke down many of the barriers that were inevitably present because they were MBAs in a setting where there were few others. Instead of being stand-offish, an understandable defensive reaction, or trying to display their intellectual wares, they worked along until, slowly, cooperation became more the rule than the exception.

Find Mentors, Traditional and New

According to Dr. Mary Anne Devanna, author of the study of Columbia women MBAs,[3] mentors are even more important in women's careers than in men's:

When we looked at the mentors, we found that the women were just as likely to have them as the men. But in the absence of mentors, the women were not going to make it, whereas some men without them did still manage to work their way through the system. The standardized career ladder works better for men than for women. The women still need somebody . . . preparing the way for them, convincing others that they are indeed capable of the next job.

The traditional image of a mentor is an older, wiser man in a high position in an organization, who picks up a young man like a pawn and places him in advantageous positions, teaching him what moves are possible and what the board he is playing on is really made of. In return, the pawn does more or less whatever is asked of him and reflects credit on his mentor.

One of the earliest MBAs I talked with was a Goldmine graduate whose career was nothing short of stellar up to the middle-management level. She attributed a great deal of her success to help by traditional mentors. She particularly credited them with their willingness to take risks and give her assignments that would strengthen her skills and confidence; they provided possibilities that simply would not have been there otherwise:

The breadth of experience I had, and the kind of fabulous assignments I had, were really very much because of my mentors. It had nothing to do with how good I was . . . accepting competence as a basic. It really had to do with the fact that they made sure that certain things happened.

Very few women have ever had the problem of being pushed too far too fast by a traditional mentor. Although several years ago it was all the rage to explain the consistently grim statistics about women in upper management by the fact that women lacked mentors, that view has become less popular. Some of the women I interviewed said that they had had mentors, but as they described them and as others talked about the kind of helping relationships they had in the workplace, it was clear to me that women had often moved beyond the traditional concept.

While both women and men acted as coaches, supporters, and inspirers (three of the most important ingredients in traditional mentoring), women gave each other the added dimension of understanding what it is like to be one of the first or one of the few to balance many different parts of a life that includes multiple identities and roles. They connected as friends in a social setting where there were rarely sexual overtones. The personal relationships between women in this new style of mentoring were often closer and more comfortable than they were with men. Because the particular obstacles women face at every level are similar, identifying and strategizing about them can act as an equalizer between women who may be in hierarchically separate spheres. One banker found that her female mentor helped others because of what she had been through herself as the first woman and youngest person to hold certain jobs:

> At one point I was up for manager of the clerical unit, and the man who would have been my superior said, "No way. She's just too young. They would never respect her authority." Mae more or less said, "She wants that job. You're not going to find anybody better than that. You command respect by your attitude, and age has nothing to do with it." . . . She really would go to bat for you. Certainly we [protegées] performed in kind. . . . She was very good about seeing that we got the visibility that we needed.

Because Mae knew what she had gone through herself, she was sensitive to the particular kind of sponsorship these young women needed to launch them successfully.

Certainly women who are in a hierarchical position to help an MBA have the power to create the kind of visibility, contacts, and projects that can advance her career. They may also be able to act as role models by showing how to combine caring responsibilities with managing a division or develop a management style that works equally well with blue-collar men and male managers. All these ingredients are very useful indeed, if not indispensable.

Other functions are usually associated with traditional mentors that are done just as well, if not better, by peers inside and outside the workplace. The point here is not to eliminate anyone—co-worker, friend, former classmate, or whatever—who might be able to give you the assistance that is traditionally thought to issue only from the magic wand of the mentor. For example, when work issues feel like personal crises, peers who are friends may be much more appropriate sounding boards for insecurities than a well-placed mentor who must continue to believe in your effectiveness.

Evaluate Organizational Games

Most of the women agreed that a certain amount of organizational game playing was necessary for them to develop their careers. Some of them found it as challenging as any other game, while others found it unsavory and even opted out of the business world because of it. No matter what kind of organization the MBAs worked for, they found that there were informal as well as formal rules, and the sooner they understood the unwritten laws the better off they were, regardless of whether or not they chose to abide by them. In some environments, informal social contact was an essential prerequisite for moving up; in others, it was cutting deals with allies in other departments that yielded the best results. Until a woman understood the culture in which she was operating, she could unknowingly fail to take full advantage of the opportunities or even violate the rules and offend people.

What they almost all discovered was that simply doing the job was not enough. A woman now in broadcasting, who used to work in an international accounting firm, said that evaluating the games is as important as the MBA itself:

> I find that even men who don't have MBAs are a lot better at playing the game that needs to be played to move up the corporate ladder. I was ill equipped to deal with these realities. . . .
> It's really impacting my process of deciding what I want to do with the rest of my life. I think women considering MBAs should realize that. Perhaps if they read about it first they'll know that there is a lot more to it than just the straightforward aspect of getting an education and getting competent. If they are unwilling to modify their own way of behaving, they might want to think twice about entering the whole corporate structure.

Women are often advised to play by the rules of the game as it has always been played by men, a different approach from learning what the rules are and formulating one's own strategy. Dubious as women may be about some of them, particularly the back stabbing that is the norm in some organizations, others may be quite useful, such as speaking up and taking care of one's own interests. By evaluating the games rather than simply buying into them, women can pick and choose the aspects they can live with ethically and develop other strategies that may build their careers in a different direction.

Don't Make Coffee

When I asked women MBAs for their advice to other women, coffee almost always came up in the conversation. It seems to have become a symbolic battleground where women are tested to see how far they can be pushed: are they hostile bra burners who won't even get a guy a cup of coffee, or are they sophisticates who have gone beyond all that and understand that you can catch more flies with honey than with vinegar? While no one liked to be asked again and again to make or get the coffee while men were not, most had developed their own ways of dealing with it. A woman who lets men open doors for her, which she says is simply a concession to the old world, brings coffee to men at meetings as long as she also brings it to women: in her view, setting the right tone at the beginning is essential. When I asked her what obstacles she thought might come up in a woman's first few weeks on the job, she said:

> The obvious one that, "We've hired another MBA, and the coffee machine is over there." Simply say, "Fine, I'd like a cup." You can't start off letting them get away with it. . . . I don't want someone out there saying, "You get the coffee" in my position.

Distinguishing between issues that are worth battling over and those that should be ignored was an area of real controversy. Some women felt it was vital to challenge behavior that offended them, such as being ordered to make coffee, while others, the vast majority, just ground their teeth over similar incidents. Where behavior is reciprocal, though, most were willing to be flexible, like this supervisor in a large firm:

> Women are certainly taken advantage of. But if my boss says, "I'm in a spot; will you make me a copy of this?" I always say sure. If the vice president asks me for a cup of coffee, I say sure, and chances are that half the time he's going to get me one.

Coffee assumes such large significance to women because to them it is symbolic of being treated as wives or as secretaries rather than being accorded the status and privileges of professionals. A number of women discussed the ambivalence they felt about their relationships with secretaries in their offices: on the one hand, they did not want to be confused with them in terms of their functions, but on the other hand they did not want to be alienated from women with whom they sometimes had much in common. Those who were especially isolated felt caught between two irreconcilable worlds where they could not fully be part of either side. Some reacted by doing their best to establish distance between themselves and the other women in the office through acting and dressing differently (as is often advised) and avoiding them socially and at lunch; others tried to find a middle ground of being in contact with everyone but basically adhering to the professional side of the aisle. Their choice was more conflicted and difficult to carry off successfully.

When women MBAs draw distinctions between themselves and other women workers to ingratiate themselves with the existing power structure, they ignore the common themes in the way all women are perceived and treated. A secretary whose application to become an accounting assistant is tossed out because of her background has a great deal in common with a woman MBA who is excluded from moving up because she does not have technical training, only experience. Mothers are in the same predicament; the only difference is that the MBA has more resources to buy an individual solution than does the secretary. The women who try to close themselves off from others pay a price not only in isolation, but in the possibilities for a more unified approach to the issues of concern to all women in the workplace. A policy against personal service like making coffee cannot stick unless all women take the same position about it.

Keep Asking

If women MBAs were only armed with one word as a strategy, it would be ASK—not only for feedback, but for visibility, special assignments, new jobs, budget, training, whatever. A theme that arose repeatedly in interviews was that no one else will be paying as much attention to your career as you are, unless you are very unusual and fortunate. The pattern of non-events will hold unless you counter it. It is up to you to let other people know what you plan and to ask for what you need to make it happen. If you are refused again and again, think twice about where you are working. One woman considered it part of her job to belong to professional groups and asked her boss to sponsor her as a member of an organization where she could meet other executives. Another shocked her supervisors by requesting a year's detail to a prestigious organization that had admitted men from her workplace before; they would never have considered her without prodding.

> I knew it was available, because I knew white males who had had it. I never knew any females or blacks.

Ultimately, her employer did sponsor her, since she clearly had the qualifications that the men before her had had, and more.

Being assertive carries risks, some of which are unavoidable. The same remark is heard differently depending on who is speaking; a male is heard differently from a female, a woman of color from a white woman, a woman who uses a wheelchair from one who is not disabled. People's perceptions may have little to do with the content of the remark, but may instead reflect their expectations of the person. A woman who asserts herself in one part of the country may be perceived as aggressive, whereas her behavior might be acceptable somewhere else.

When a woman does stand up for her opinion or asks for support in meeting her career development needs, she may be perceived as aggressive no matter how well she phrases what she says. Sometimes women are caught in a double bind, as this faculty member saw it:

> I think there are two extremes. In some sense you are always going to be accused of being too aggressive when you're asser-

tive, and you'll be accused of not asserting yourself enough. I've
been accused of all those things. I find it's more likely that females
are not as assertive. But when you are as assertive as the male,
you are still seen as overly aggressive. On the other hand, if there
is something you don't achieve because you didn't assert yourself,
then they say you didn't and the other guy did.

I'm not saying that you just ignore that. I think you have to
be aware of it. Look around and ask yourself, are my colleagues
being more assertive than I am?

Important as it is to be mindful of the possible dangers of being assertive, most women are far more conscious of the perils of that extreme
than those of not acting at all. Far more women are stuck in their careers
because they have not spoken up than because they said too much. While
being assertive does run certain risks, so does getting up in the morning;
and by staying in bed, many opportunities can pass by if one chooses not
to act.

Ask for Feedback

Because it is often hard for supervisors and others to give women the
feedback they need to help improve performance and image, it is important
to solicit it explicitly. Even if they do not like what they hear, they learn
where others think they could improve. Simply saying a few words can
give someone else the necessary opportunity: "I've been thinking about
how I could do better at my job and be more effective with my co-workers. I've noticed that it is sometimes hard for me to speak up in meetings
and get my point across. Does it seem that way to you? Is there anything
else that you can think of that might help me? I would really value your
opinion." Unless women ask, they are unlikely to find out how they are
perceived, particularly in terms of the stereotypes they want to avoid.

When women do receive criticism, they may find it difficult to evaluate it objectively and learn from it. An investment banker who switched
from another field noticed that the men in her office do not brood about
negative comments; they simply accept them and resolve to do better next
time. She herself, like other women I interviewed tends to dwell on what
she did wrong and is trying to learn to model herself more after her colleagues. The literature about women in management has stressed that they
personalize criticism easily. The banker agrees, and has found that revealing doubts and insecurities in her workplace can hurt her:

What's really important is not to personalize it. Certainly women
are much more socialized to want people to like them and take
criticism as an indication that, "I don't like you the way you are.
You're not good enough." Here you can't show any insecurity.

> You've got to exude confidence. People have to think that you
> think well of yourself. You can't wear your heart on your sleeve.
> If you're going to complain and worry, try not to do it in the
> workplace. Bring it home, and let your friends or lovers or what-
> ever deal with it. But not your colleagues.

She found that her reflexive desire to be open with people she likes can
work against her interests:

> Women are more willing to verbalize doubts and insecurities,
> emotions and feelings. It's a difficult task not to do that, not
> confide in people you like. There are a lot of wonderful people
> here, because they are interesting and friendly, but you still don't
> put yourself in the position of confiding in them your doubts or
> your insecurities. It's a very competitive environment and you
> have to be able to compete.

The pattern of women's taking criticism to heart rather than using it to
improve their performance and letting it go is common, as is revealing
negative feelings about oneself, which is appropriate in friendship but not
in many workplaces.

If women paid as much attention to positive as to negative feedback,
their career patterns might be quite different. Many discount others' point-
ing out accomplishments, strengths, and skills. They fail to build on what
has been said and to use that information as the basis of career goals and
strategies. Specifically asking others how to develop can help in establishing a sense of direction as well as build confidence. Women MBAs need
to learn not only to ask for feedback, but to use it constructively, whatever
it may be.

Ask for Promotion

One of women's primary concerns was that they were not thought of first
for new jobs and promotions. To combat that prevailing attitude, women
must keep tabs on what is going on in the organization and ask for what
they want. It will not always work, but it is more likely to be effective
than waiting on the sidelines to be discovered and offered the job of your
dreams. Asking to be considered for promotion or to have a new job
created for you is if anything even harder than asking for resources to do
a job well. A woman with a Generic school MBA who had been performing very well at an entry-level job in finance was pushed forward by her
boss. Even when she was doubtful herself he urged her to apply for a
position in another part of the company:

> My boss really helped me. He said, "Why don't you try for it?"
> I thought, there's no way. But I went to the vice president and I

said I would like to be considered for the position. And they gave
it to me. I was qualified, I knew the most about all the jobs in
the department, but if I hadn't said anything, I could not have
gotten the position. There are no bad feelings, because I asked in
the right way. I didn't say you must give it to me or whatever.
I didn't put them on the spot by saying if you don't give it to me
I'm unemployed.

Of course, simply notifying people of your interest is not enough:

If you feel you're qualified and there is a position open, let it be
known that you're interested. First of all, *they'll probably think
you're not interested,* and that's one of the things you'll have going
against you. Once they know that you're interested and you feel
confident that you can perform the job, and you have about twice
as many qualifications as any man there, you have a chance.

Tooting one's own horn is especially difficult for women who feel
that they need only perform well to be recognized. Self-promotion is one
area in which women are often less skilled than men. The same woman
who was quoted above, now a supervisor, told me that one of her female
subordinates had an aversion to taking credit for her work. In fact, the
supervisor had to initiate promotions for her:

I know how much work she does because I've done that job. She
gets upset because other people are promoted but I can't sell her
because nobody knows what she does. . . . If you give her
something to do, she'll do it, but you won't know if it's done or
not. Run into her on the elevator, and she'll say, "Oh yes, that
was done a long time ago."

Failing to promote one's own work and make it visible is still a woman's
affliction, although fortunately not everyone has such an extreme case.
Women need to speak up and make others aware not only of regular duties
well discharged, but of actual accomplishments completed over time.
Showing what one has done and the impact it has had is essential; in the
case above, the supervisor said that her employee had saved the accounting
area $5,000 by instituting new procedures, but had never either counted
the benefits or publicized them. If she did not do it herself, what is the
likelihood that someone else will?

Define Your Social Limits at Work

The question of how women handle themselves in social situations with
male colleagues is always complex. Some feel that to be included in the

professional world fully they must also become friendly with the men they work with. Others prefer to restrict their social contact to occasions that are specifically business related, such as lunches with clients. Because almost all relationships between women and men are sexualized in this culture, being friendly and civil without involving sexual overtones can be a real challenge. Often the lines are very blurry about when a woman can safely step outside her professional role. A telecommunications representative found herself in a real dilemma in a Peking hotel:

> I never felt so popular in my life. Everybody is saying, "Let's go have a drink," and I'm feeling the pressures of that environment myself, so I'm happy to go out for a drink. But there is one evening that I remember clearly. I wasn't out with clients, but with other businesspeople overseas. In this disco, I was *the* woman. I was sitting at a table with eight men. The band is playing. Here are these representatives of other major corporations.
>
> I'm still the woman. It would be kind of fun to dance, and they would love to get up and dance too. What do you do? I decided to go ahead and dance with a couple of people and I don't think there was anything wrong with it. It's having to think about it. How do you dance? Do you dance in a very promiscuous way, or what? I was much more reserved because, hell, you have to do business with these people.

Although not typical in its setting, the situation accurately describes the dilemmas many women feel as they attempt to get along with men without becoming "one of the boys."

On more routine occasions, women can feel excluded from conversations that revolve around sports, either literally or metaphorically. Those who make an effort to mingle may have to serve an apprenticeship and find that there is a price to be paid in terms of their own integrity. A Goldmine MBA was really alone as the only woman and the only single person in the group. She went through a rite of passage when one of them finally invited her out drinking with the boys after she had worked with them for a year. His peers gave him a lot of grief about why he invited her, since they said that she would tell their wives that they were off traveling and picking up other women (as in fact they were). She was being tested:

> I automatically gave the guys credibility, just because they were a group of guys with a woman. The girls they were meeting would look at me and say, "Are these guys OK?" And I would have to say yes.
>
> Q. Did you think they were?

I knew they were, but I also knew they were married and
not representing themselves as such. You have a moral conflict,
but then you have your working relationships and they are infinitely more important and you let that moral conflict go
away. . . . Sometimes that's how you have to prove yourself as
one of the guys, by doing things that as a woman you don't really
feel good about.

Because this behavior would be unacceptable to most of the women I
interviewed, some had chosen to avoid social contact with the men they
worked with almost altogether. There seemed to be very little middle
ground between opting out and immersing onself totally. Business lunches
and entertaining clients are an essential part of many women's jobs, however, and pose their own set of problems. When a woman is doing the
inviting, she has a lot of factors to consider: her status in relationship to
his, how he and others might interpret the invitation, what kind of place
to take him, and so on. A gesture that would feel quite appropriate from
another man—picking up the tab at lunch, suggesting a drink after work—
may be interpreted quite differently if it comes from a woman. If an invitation is issued in a businesslike way, making the purpose of the meeting
clear ("I'd like to have a chat about that new program you're running"),
there is less chance of misunderstanding. On the other hand, if your purpose is simply to get to know your colleague as a human being so that you
can work together more smoothly or exchange information more readily,
the limits you want must be set more subtly. You may do so through
nonverbal language that is neutral and open only to certain conversational
topics, as well as verbal language that keeps the discussion within certain
boundaries. About sexual relationships, a supervisor in Chicago had the
last word: "Don't sleep with anybody you work with or for or against."

A Note on Dress

Because the way women MBAs and other women in business dress has
been the subject of so much comment, choices about clothing have been
perceived as career strategies. Some of the women I interviewed read
everything they could on the subject, and slavishly followed whatever the
latest prescriptions were. Their theory was that they should look as much
as possible like the person, usually male, whose job they want. Others paid
no attention to the new commandments and wore what they thought appropriate. One MBA/CPA particularly objected to the imposition of the
male norm of wearing a suit:

I resented the fact that they defined professionalism in masculine
terms. Anything feminine was not professional. In most account-

ing firms, you have an evaluation after every client that includes dress, speech, everything on a scale of one to five. One time I got a very low mark for dress. I normally dress very well and spend a lot of money to look professional. . . . My supervisor commented that I wore dresses. Now we're talking about a navy blue silk dress with high collar and long sleeves, with a jacket over it, a strand of pearls, and usually my very thick glasses.

Considering the general emphasis placed on looking female in our culture, adopting male dress shows just how far many women are willing to go to be acceptable to the current power structure. There was never any question about women's adopting the uniform to impress themselves or each other; its purpose has always explicitly been to identify women in a certain way—as professionals—in male eyes and to make them less incongruous with the masculine image of the successful manager. The uniform reinforces and perpetuates that image.

When a significant number of women had obtained the qualifications that were supposed to be essential to do management jobs, explanations were needed for their continued lack of progress. Rather than focusing on the nature of the power structure that was impeding them, popular literature seized on the one aspect of corporate cultural analysis that could be readily applied to women. They might have obtained the proper degrees, but they were not dressed right. Once again, what a woman put on her body was more important than what she had in her head. Accustomed to following the dictates of fashion and eager to remove any needless obstacle from their paths, women flocked to exclusive shops to garb themselves as much like men as possible. It is interesting, however, that the one truly practical aspect of a man's suit—trousers that allow one to walk, sit, and climb up on chairs freely, and that keep unwanted eyes off one's legs—was eliminated from formal business wear for women.

Dress is certainly one of the least painful explanations for a blocked career. Once again, it is personal, near at hand, and within a woman's grasp. It does not involve questioning a whole organizational culture and the interlocking system behind it or analyzing the unhelpful behavior of people you may like very much. After telling me what a good environment her company is for women and how fairly she has been treated there, an MBA in Chicago told me:

I don't dress the part of a professional. I shouldn't run around in slacks but I do . . . maybe I should start dressing up. The director of my department hardly knows I'm there.

Others simply refused to conform, and take the consequences.

Teaching women how to dress can be an important, if unspoken, part of the business school agenda. When I asked one Goldmine administrator what she saw as the most important change in women from the time they entered until they left, she said that their hair was shorter and their wardrobes duller. Once inside the corporate world, dress norms are often strongly although informally reinforced. The new women on the scene, like anyone, want to conform and be accepted, and dress is the symbolic way to do it.

The pressures to conform can be fierce, but the MBA who gives up her individuality altogether pays a price, according to Dr. Myra Strober, author of the original study of Stanford women MBAs:

> I think some of that [imitation in dress] is very important. If you're so deviant that people just can't see you in the role at all, that's a problem, so it's a fine line. You need to be conformist enough so that you're accepted but you still need to maintain some individuality. Otherwise it takes a terrible personal toll. You almost have two personalities, one at work and one not at work, and that's tough. Your individuality, whether you are a man or a woman, can be to your advantage. It distinguishes you from other people.

Network Strategies

Network strategies are an indispensable part of every woman's career development, whether she is a corporate MBA or an independent entrepreneur, a secretary or a teacher trying to switch into a new field. A woman may pursue all kinds of individual approaches to self-improvement and organizational games, but as long as she is trying to run a solo Superwoman act she may be very isolated, and in the long run may undermine her career. Networks, formal and informal, provide more than support and relief from isolation, important as that is; they are also invaluable sources of information, ideas, and contacts, and provide an opportunity to build strategies based on the realities of others' experiences as well as one's own. Instead of feeling that she is the only woman in the world who has ever had this problem, a woman in a network can find others who have been swept along by the same tides and have developed steering mechanisms. Just as women helped each other significantly in groups at business school, they discovered that they could extend the same principles into the workplace.

Although friendship and family networks are the center of many women's lives, building networks for career development is also essential. For many women, the crossover between friendship and professional connections is a relatively new concept. They may have many personal friends, but these are not women they talk with about career issues. For one, volunteer work was the key:

> I'm just now starting to form a network of female friends who are job oriented. I did some work on a workshop to encourage high school students to take science and math courses. It was a really good experience to meet them and the others working on the project.

Personal friends can offer a great deal in terms of a woman's career as well as the rest of her life. Because they know her well in a different context, they may be able to pick up on qualities that she could exploit to good advantage in the workplace or be frank with her about areas on which she might improve.

A Goldmine graduate stresses that support from other women is as important to married as to single MBAs:

> I loved my all-women's college. I live by a very strong support group of women. Yes, I'm married and my husband is very close to me, but if I didn't have a couple of close women there, I wouldn't be who I am today.

Nevertheless, developing a network beyond personal friendships is important—especially to women who are isolated in a large organization where only men have done their jobs before. A highly successful banker who did not go to business school told me:

> Networks were my MBA. The bank had asked me to look into the possibility of setting up a new department. I knew zero about it and realized that I needed a support network to shortcut the time I would need to gain men's trust and confidence. I can find out whatever I need to know. There is still a creaming phenomenon because women have to be so good to make it. By having access to those women, the quality of my information and judgment is superior.

This woman did not wait for a network to come to her; she deliberately set out to create it, put a lot of energy into it, and has been reaping the benefits ever since.

A women's network within an organization can be an essential source of information and contacts. Even an informal and relatively infrequent meeting can help, as long as it is consistent. A dinner group of women in management jobs in the same corporation met every six weeks, to pass on what they were hearing about each other as well as devising strategies.

Although some women were initially reluctant to join the group because they feared being labeled, over time they found it very valuable.

Women's networks have particular advantages to offer: an opportunity to exercise leadership in the absence of the people who traditionally assume it; to discuss issues that they would feel uncomfortable raising in a mixed group; to pool their wisdom about surviving, even thriving, in a predominantly male profession or system; and to strategize together about effective ways to change their situations. Since organizational power is concentrated elsewhere, it is also important for women to participate in mixed networks, be they professional associations, alumni clubs, community organizations, or whatever.

I asked the women which networks they participated in, formally and informally, and selected a few to give a flavor of some organizations available to women MBAs, and how they have helped them cope with job problems and plan their careers. The spectrum is broad; the networks discussed here include a local group of women in commercial real estate; an alumnae network of University of Chicago MBAs; a general women's organization, the Philadelphia Women's Network; and a national professional women's association with local chapters, the American Society of Women Accountants. Each of these organizations has among its purposes sharing information, tactics, contacts, and support among women, but the context is different in each case.

Although many fields have become so open to women that they are a significant percentage in most workplaces, in a number of professions women still are a novelty. One of those is commercial real estate. A 40-year-old attorney and MBA who decided to enter the field was in for a jolt:

> I was so totally naive I thought sexism had gone by the bye. It's definitely a conservative holdout, and there is an enormous amount of antifemale feeling among the males in the business. There are only about 20 to 25 women in the commercial area out of 185 male brokers, so there aren't a lot of role models. The women who do it are a very exciting bunch of people to be around. They're very risk taking, gutsy people.

When she became aware of the realities of the field she was about to enter, this former housewife chose a firm that was relatively open to women. After a false start, she and four colleagues went to a network meeting for women in their profession:

> The women were professionals and had been trained to understand the different types of buildings and needs. You could say, "I have a client who needs 400 amps, six roll-ups for a 40-foot

truck, docking situations and 25 percent offices, and a clean room."
"Oh, I have somebody who can do that." You know you don't
have to describe exactly what all that is. It was challenging . . .
you want to be associated with people who have high standards
in their profession.

Because they could see the network's potential, two women organized
their own local group, which has been a forum for talking through some
career changes as well as for exchanging information.

The alumnae network of the University of Chicago similarly provides
both personal and professional connections for its members. It was formed
because women needed an organization to which they felt they belonged,
rather than being conspicuous, as they often were in business environments:

For me, and I think for many others, it was just [a need for]
identification. In our first meetings we generally attracted a fairly
good crowd of people, and it was just not being a freak any more.
You walked into a room where there were seventy or eighty
women all in business suits and who had all battled fairly hard to
get where they were. Granted there was a whole variety of people
and experience, but the common bond was that you had all made
it through the U of C. It was more a sense of identity, talking to
people.

The network has drawn specifically on the strengths of the Chicago area
and the university's connections, sponsoring programs with top executives
in the area. It serves a different function from the general alumni association:

I've always wanted to go, but just didn't want to walk into a
room with a million people you don't know. For some people,
that's easy to do, but for others of us it's not.

One way the network countered the impersonality of a large gathering was
to switch people from table to table between courses at its own dinner
meetings.

When it was first launched, the core group felt confident that it would
succeed, and they were right. In just a few years they had recruited more
than 300 members. With the advantage of hindsight, one of the organizers
feels that they expected it to work miracles in their careers and to do so
immediately. Networks seemed to be the magic thread that would bind
the elements necessary to women's success; they were portrayed as the
answer that would compensate for the failures of the past. Now, the organizers take a different view:

I think we had a very naive view of networking. I don't think it's
a quick thing that happens, but a long-term thing that takes a lot
of time. A lot of us who have been involved in the organization
for a long time have in fact seen some benefits. I don't think on
a short-term basis we really understood that. There was a very
great need for these women to associate with the group. I'm sure
everyone had their own particular reasons.

For all the value of the network as a source of needed strategies, skills,
data, ideas, and contacts, the most useful aspect for many women is much
harder to define and articulate:

Most of the purposes the network serves are really intangible ones.
I can't really say how important identity and reinforcement and
belonging are, but there is something I know, even in myself,
when I go to the monthly meetings, I walk away rejuvenated. I
can cope some more. For certain of us who have been around for
a while, I think we know that maybe the next generation will
make it a little further than we did, because we have created some
more pathways there for them.

Finding women with whom she feels comfortable as professionals as
well as women is of prime importance to an MBA on the board of the
Philadelphia Women's Network. When she moved to the area, she left a
situation in which she felt very isolated socially and was determined not
to let it happen again:

I set time aside when I first got back to look for a group of women
who, when I went to a meeting, I didn't feel that I had more fun
at home watching TV. That was how I settled on the network.
It was always worth it. I always ended up in a good conversation
with somebody, and that was enough.

Her increased participation in the Network's planning process has also given
her the basis for trying out the field of consulting as a volunteer, and she
even found a contact at one of the meetings with whom she can explore
particular possibilities.

On the other hand, the contact function of a network can be abused.
Sometimes the organization grows so large that women are no longer really
in touch with each other, and some are in it more for what they can extract
from others than for what they can contribute. As for the women from
the University of Chicago, it is the long-term connections that really count
and pay off, not only in the business sense but personally. Friends become
helpful in the professional sense and vice versa. To bring women together,

the Philadelphia Women's Network holds monthly meetings on topics of particular interest to its members. They enjoy not having to explain themselves to each other:

> It's the first time I have been able to find a group of women who have the range of interests. . . . In the Network I can find women where I can jump back and forth to any topic and I don't have to think to myself, "Will this person understand what I'm talking about?"

The American Society of Women Accountants, a national organization with 8,000 members including MBAs, focuses on women's contributions to the field and concerns with it. Christine Summers, the National Treasurer, spoke with me in Chicago. She advises women to belong to both women's and other professional groups. In addition to helping members with long-term career issues, the Society's local chapters provide a setting for discussion of daily issues and obstacles.

While professional information and exchange is still one of the Society's most important functions, being able to talk through the ramifications of personal choices is a close second. When a successful and ambitious woman decides to have a child, she must be very clear about how that might affect her career. Because of their diversity, members see a variety of possible career and personal decisions. For example:

> We also have some women in professions you wouldn't normally see. We have one woman who is controller of a construction company, and that's obviously going to be different from banking or accounting or any other private industry. It's that sharing and support that just get you to think about other options that makes the environment very stimulating.

Special credit for outreach goes to the annual effort to draw in bosses and expose them to what the organization is and does, rather than retreating into the comfortable shell of other women who agree with you. The reactions are gratifying.

> What I hear most frequently from people who attend is that they didn't realize that there were that many women in accounting, or "I didn't realize that you were such a professional organization." They expected the Girl Scouts.

While it is an important meeting ground for women and serves an educational purpose for their bosses, the Society also sees itself as having the power to make change:

With numbers of women coming together, we become more of
a force, in that we are an organization that represents 8,000 people.

One area where the force can be put to good use is in narrowing the wage
gap between women and men. Ms. Summers recommends that members
share information about their salaries to strengthen their negotiating positions with their own employers:

> Am I being paid what I'm worth? That is always such a very
> touchy thing. How comfortable do you really feel talking about
> where you are and where you should be? The only way we are
> going to make any progress is to open that and talk about, "This
> is what I'm getting for these kinds of functions . . . " There's a
> fear about being a little girl who says, "What if they're paying
> me all this money and I'm not really worth it?" That's just some-
> thing we have to work through.
>   A lot of it has to do with how comfortable you feel about
> what you are getting paid and standing on firm ground in terms
> of what you know about the market. Let others know that you
> are keeping up with the market and you know the value of jobs.

In her role as a national officer, Ms. Summers has had the opportunity to
assess the progress of women accountants over time. She is not fully satisfied, particularly in her own field of banking. Even where women have
advanced beyond middle management, they tend to be concentrated in the
administrative positions rather than the lending and funding areas, and are
often one of a kind:

> Although I recognize that a certain amount of time must elapse
> for women to develop the skills and be able to move, I think we
> are now reaching the point where women do have all the quali-
> fications. The recognition still isn't there. It's taking a lot more
> time to break into [the attitude that] you can't truly rely on a
> woman to do the job.

In her own career, Ms. Summers feels that she has benefited tremendously from being a national officer. By being in contact with many more
women and discussing their plans and ambitions, she began to clarify her
own strategies. Her involvement paid off; not only with her present employer, but because she has been approached by headhunters thanks to
articles in well-known business publications. Continental Bank, her employer, has been very supportive, especially as she has gained extensive
presentation skills as well as visibility. When her boss called on her to take

over a briefing for the senior vice presidents, she was ready, and did so well that she was invited back repeatedly.

In terms of her own career development, she sees her involvement with the Society as part of her commitment to herself:

> I am responsible personally to develop all the skills I am going to use. I have to pursue those. I can't just look at my boss and say, "Are you going to train me? What do you need for me to do?"

New Directions for Networks

Undoubtedly these networks provide their members with invaluable support, and help them cope with the business world in any number of ways. Most women can make use of programs that help them improve communications skills, rewrite résumés, dress more effectively, and keep a sharp eye out for mentors. But after they have gone through all the career development programs that networks can offer, after they have talked through the barriers they are encountering, what comes next?

Most networks focus strongly on self-improvement. After women have learned to play by the rules, what happens if they still do not advance? Not every woman, of course, will reach the top or anywhere near it, just as not every man will. The day has not arrived when women have an equal chance, a chance you can calculate by walking up and down the corridor on the top floor of an organization and counting up the senior managers' nametags. Until half of them are female, no one really knows that the top spots are just as possible for women as for men, no matter what they are told about pipelines and the necessary passage of time.

To be truly effective in changing the patterns of women's employment in management, networks must go beyond the stage of teaching women how to behave themselves and dress differently. They must also help women face and address the facts about the power structure and their careers within it, so that women enter those structures poised to develop their careers actively rather than waiting for others to choose and promote them. Rather than stopping at programs on how to dress or interview, networks should also educate women about the organizational structures and cultures they confront and ways for them to band together rather than fighting the system one by one; by sharing salary information as well as tactics, for example. If women understand initially that they are entering territory where they must struggle to succeed, no matter how friendly and comfortable it may seem, they can go beyond the appearances to adapt strategies to the underlying realities. At least equally important, they can help each other detect warning signs that their careers may be on the rocks.

What to Watch Out For

Significantly, the two most important warning signs of career blockage that women mentioned were not overt, like sports talk at board meetings or obvious sexual harassment. They were isolation and starvation of resources, and they underlie many of the specific trouble indicators discussed below. Isolation means withholding positive, active encouragement and support, including constructive criticism; starvation means being denied resources necessary to do the job right: information, money, or people. Women who expect these dynamics will be much more likely to counteract them than those who perceive their isolation or underfunding as a personal failure. Like meteorologists who understand that a wisp of cloud may mean a storm, they can be alert to warnings from the beginning.

The positive, active support that most women are denied means being singled out as a promising candidate for advancement, being given opportunities for assignments and training that one must have to move up, and getting honest feedback from both managers and peers. Ironically, one of the most positive signals that a woman is valued is being treated like male peers in terms of criticism as well as praise.

One of the first women and blacks to work in the headquarters of an auto company told me:

> They talked with me like they talked with the other guys, positive and negative. There, I felt I would get a fair shake on the deal. Too much of one or of the other—too negative or too positive, skirting around the edge of things—then I know you're not giving me the same deal that you're giving everybody else. . . . If they never criticize anything that you do or if they go out when they feel that they are on the verge of criticism, you're in trouble.

A recent career changer in her late thirties took the analysis one step farther, watching to see if she is being set up to succeed or to fail:

> I have men around me so that I can compare where they are moving up and where I am moving up. I know my strengths and my weaknesses, so I would know whether they are going to put me in a position where my strengths make a difference and where I either improve on my weaknesses or they are irrelevant. And I think at this point it is basically what kind of a possibility they are going to give me, and how they are going to reward me— whether they say, "We have to find something for her."

In other words, will she be set up to succeed by those who want to push her career forward, or will they view her as a capable workhorse but no more?

Is Nice Treatment Fair Treatment?

Although there are still some blatantly sexist men in the workplace, most have cleaned up their act to some extent. Many have learned to be pleasant and courteous to women professionals, although they may not behave the same way toward secretaries. They have learned not to interrupt women at meetings, not to ask them to get coffee or take notes. Some have learned that many women are capable colleagues and that, like men, they must be assessed one individual at a time rather than prejudged. Even when women feel that their accomplishments are recognized, however, they still may not be taken seriously in terms of career advancement. A publisher found that performance was a source of recognition, but not progress:

> Basically, the men where I work now will respect you if you're good. That doesn't mean that they'll think of you first, but if you're there, they'll respect you.

Being thought of first translates directly into pay and promotion. Is a woman the person who springs instantly to mind when a new job is being created or a trip to Japan is in the offing? Frequently it is the opportunities not offered—more non-events—that are a real measurement of how a woman has been either supported or blocked.

As employees move up, they are judged more and more on the basis of a manager's intuition about whether they can be trusted. While qualifications and performance enter in, much depends on how comfortable the higher-ups feel with a person, and that feeling depends on gender, race, age, and appearance, which are still the most striking human features to the naked eye. Everyone is affected by them. When a manager looks at a woman, what does he see? If he looks above to senior management, who is there? If he closes his eyes to imagine a CEO or if he leafs through his business magazine ads, the leader whose image leaps forth is a grey-haired but still youthful, distinguished white male in a business suit. If he instead imagines a woman, will she be a professional, or a housewife or sex symbol?

Whatever a woman may wear, say, or do, she is still a woman. The focus will probably be on her and her credentials in many situations, rather than the work at hand. A black female bank examiner was asked only one question after a long briefing to bank officials: they wanted to know her background and qualifications. If a woman is pregnant or a mother, those factors may well be her prime identity to upper-level managers. They may assume, for example, that she is unavailable for travel or for a year's special assignment. Everything that makes her different from that older white male is going to alienate her from a manager who cannot identify with her himself, let alone make her a leader. That distancing can undermine a woman's career just as much as actual harassment, as a black woman discovered:

> I had a supervisor who wasn't quite sure of himself and tried to sort of stay out of it. He was quite professional but clearly had never worked with females in this kind of position, and never with a black in any position. Even though he found there were no problems, he never ever was comfortable. Consequently, he wouldn't give me ideas that would be helpful. They're sitting there telling guys [what to do] . . . they look at them and they see themselves at a certain age. When they look at you, they don't see themselves.

Hiring decisions above the entry level are often made by the white males who have benefited from the system. Their ideal candidate is unlikely to be female. Even male managers who believe that women are as good as men (if not better at certain types of routine work) may not feel that women are equal to the demands of management. In their view, it requires breadth of vision and an air of authority that many men, especially the middle- and upper-class men who dominate most organizations, do not associate with women. All but the most unreconstructed have come to see that women have their uses as workhorses in entry-level jobs, especially since they are generally more qualified than men in the same jobs; however, it is another thing altogether to propose that they be moved into positions of power.

For example, a boss who allows a woman a lot of freedom to take on new tasks may be giving her a valuable basis for skills and visibility, but that does not mean that she will be supported fully in her career development.

> The man who hired me was helpful in throwing me into a lot of situations where I was instantly able to do the workshops. In retrospect, I think he did it because he needed to. He gave me the opportunity to learn, sent me off to observe things . . . so that was good. I needed that. Everybody was very friendly; if I asked questions, they would be answered, but nobody mentored me. I was perceived as an outsider.

While she felt that she earned her colleagues' respect eventually, there were no tangible signs that she was a valued employee being groomed for the next level up; training, raises, awards, or whatever. Although she had a strong goal in mind within the firm, although she performed well and had lots of rope from her boss, and although her co-workers respected her, this woman's career was blocked. In fact, in the end she was laid off because she was a part-time worker, and full-time, younger men hired after her were retained.

The Silent Treatment

The lack of appropriate feedback, positive or negative, is a certain signal that a woman is not getting real support for her career. When supervisors do not like something she has done, they are sometimes more reluctant to bring it up as directly as they could with many men. The result can be deadly, as it was for a woman who was given a poor job evaluation because of a series of failures to communicate about misunderstandings like this one:

> I went to a conference in North Jersey. I have a problem with driving because of my eyes, so my husband took me. I paid his part of the hotel bill. Weeks later I found out that my supervisor was furious because I was turning a meeting into a vacation. He said, "You're a big girl and you should drive yourself."

If the supervisor had been giving appropriate feedback, he would have raised this issue directly and immediately; constructive criticism is part of the support every employee needs. Another woman told me about a time she waited weeks for her supervisor's reaction to a piece of work that took months to prepare, only to find that he was considering dropping it, and did not have the courage to tell her. If she had known earlier, she could have defended her work far more effectively.

A number of women had similar experiences, indicating not so much deliberate acts of commission against them but much that was missing: a word of encouragement here or there, specific feedback about how they performed and where they could improve or build on a strength, a special assignment or training opportunity; whatever language the organization uses to say that it values employees, and wants to foster their careers to the highest level. A major word in that language is "resources," translated as information, budget, and personnel.

Lacking Vital Resources

Not getting the information they need to do the job right was a concern repeatedly expressed. Women told me they were left out of both formal and informal systems for circulating the news and the data that are the life blood of any organization. Reports never reached their desks, or women just were not there when the boys were gossiping in the hall. The assistant business manager of a television station was often left out of the system in her predominantly male working environment:

> I'm responsible for the payment of program licenses. We do a substantial cash outflow during the month. My boss is supposed to inform me when there are any significant contractual arrangements, and it tends to be an informal grapevine that comes through. If I don't know about it and I don't pay the distributor the right amount, it could fall back on me. I've found that in a couple of instances I wasn't informed, and I had to scramble at the last minute. I had the feeling that it was somewhat of an attempt to discredit me and make me look not so great in the eyes of the higher-ups in terms of having a handle on my area. It was all because I relied on the honesty of information from other people. They had not felt like telling me, for whatever reason, because they want general management to think that they were better at this sort of thing. . . . That happens quite frequently, and I know that it is a strategy and a tactic.

Women often saw in retrospect that "feelings" like these were invaluable indicators that something was organizationally amiss. Traditional games are often invisible and have the effect of unsettling the opponent. Like a fever, a feeling that something is wrong should be checked out through observation and seeking others' opinions and information.

Over time, women learned to keep their eyes open and their ears to the ground for signals that they were not being taken seriously. Because the younger women entered the workplace most hopefully, it was difficult for them to accept the fact that the system was not on their side or that the people who were so nice to them would eventually be the competitors who might undermine them. They had to be alert enough to sniff trouble out, which meant having an idea of what direction it might come from, without being obsessed by the negative possibilities.

Women often tried to make do on a shoestring. Anyone who has reviewed the budget of a women's organization will recognize the tendency. When women move into middle management, they may be so delighted to have an area of their own that they do not look closely enough at the resources supplied to see whether they are sufficient. In particular, the failure to make a woman a supervisor and provide subordinates when appropriate can be a warning signal. Several women told me that they had fought for supervisory titles and some had not managed to make the switch; one who "succeeded" found that the results were mixed at best:

> The first time they had the nerve to give me a subordinate, they gave me one who came in late and sat on the phone with personal

calls. I couldn't spur him into any action. He had a history like this. My supervisor ended up not letting me write a bad report about this man, so I stayed late at night to make up for him. I couldn't win, because if I ignored what he was doing I looked like a fool, but if I reported him I wasn't one of the boys.

Isolation by withholding positive support and starvation of resources underlay a host of other warning signals, many of which pointed in the same direction. Sometimes it took women months or years to unravel what had happened to them. Many signals were perceived only in hindsight by those who were so taken up with doing the best job and maintaining a traditional female identity that they overlooked their career path. Like passengers reading a book intently on a train, they did not notice that they were hurtling toward the wrong destination, perhaps, in fact, back to their point of departure. What follows are some signals they eventually saw, in hopes that other women can avoid them.

Early Signals Are Negative

The first reaction to a new woman employee can be very telling, whether it is spoken or not. Something is wrong if she is not introduced to the persons around her, placed in a reasonably comfortable or at least standard office, and approached informally as well as formally by colleagues who are trying to be friendly. A woman who had just gone to work for a major corporation could tell that she was not at all what her supervisor expected; they later overcame the barriers, but it was a rough start:

The very first day I told my husband, "Look at that supervisor of mine. You know he's thinking to himself, "Why do I get sent this problem?" Three or four months later he told me, "When you first came here, I didn't know what to expect or to do. I told them I wanted an MBA, and you're the MBA!"

Some women also found that their co-workers resented them because they were MBAs, with all the stereotypes that carries with it, and because they were paid more than some of the others in the office. Although I did not meet anyone who had encountered it personally, some women told me their friends found that people in settings where MBAs were a rarity sometimes expected miracles: simply because the magic three letters followed their names, they thought it would be possible to solve all the organization's problems overnight. When the MBA could not wave a diploma and make the problem disappear, others were very disappointed in her.

Sometimes, women knew immediately that they had made a mistake;

the setting just felt wrong to them. One with a Goldmine MBA who was one of the first women in her job in the auto industry discovered rapidly that she did not fit:

> If you're in a company where everybody is bowing down to Mecca and Mecca is Detroit, and you are bowing down to Mecca and Mecca is the East Coast, you've got a problem. All you have to do is check the direction of all the prayer rugs and you know you're an odd duck. Their incentive was that if you're good and you're wonderful, you will go to Detroit. For this they wanted me to suffer—for the privilege of going to Detroit? Who the hell wants to go to Detroit?

Unfortunately, she felt that she had to spend several years paying her dues before she could move; although she was successful, the price was high indeed.

Others Expect Little of You

Low expectations of women entering a new field can also be very undermining; if a woman lacks confidence at the beginning, she could easily fulfill the negative prophecies of those around her. She may just wait it out, however, as did an MBA attorney who was recently starting in the predominantly male field of commercial real estate:

> I think I would really like to become a hell raiser in another ten years. But I need money now, so I am doing the commercial real estate. I have taken a lot of flak. . . . For a while, I was set up. Everybody was waiting for me to fail. At every meeting, cracks would be made about me. They don't do that now, but they did for the first seven months.

When the people around you expect you to fail, they may well avoid investing time and effort into your development, since they do not expect your career to go anywhere. Whether a woman is perceived as overpaid or underpaid, her male colleagues may well keep her at a distance:

> There is even some lack of acceptance of me because I'm a woman and because I happen to have higher credentials than men who are paid twice as much as I am. . . . They want to keep me an outsider.

Their withdrawing can add to a woman's sense of isolation, play on her lack of confidence, and ultimately damage her performance, in much the same way that the practice of shunning in certain tribes eventually causes its victims to wander off and die.

You Are Oversupervised

Women in management are often watched more closely than their male counterparts. Dr. Betsy Jaffe, who has studied hundreds of careers, says:

> The women have more to prove. The ones I have interviewed say that their bosses are second-guessing them for the same project they will let a male run. They require checkpoints of the women that are not required of the men.

Oversupervision can take many different forms: bringing in collaborators where none are really needed, having every step reviewed at a higher level, checking with others to see how a woman is performing, and so on.

Unfortunately, having a female supervisor is not a guarantee against oversupervision; in fact, in organizations with few women in management, there may well be resentment against a new MBA who skips some of the first rungs of the ladder. For example, one woman was consistently undermined by the female boss who hired her:

> I immediately posed a threat even though she recognized that it made perfect sense that I should be there. She was insecure, and I can sympathize with that insecurity, because it's a man's world. . . . She was very personally critical of me, and overcautioned me rather than trusting my judgment. She wasn't really giving me advice and guidance, but was beating me down.

Eventually, this woman was able to move to a new field and situation where she found more supportive colleagues. Because she herself had organized women's networks at business school and earlier, she was aware of the need to counteract some of the hostility that organizations can foster among different groups of women. Although she knew that she was being oversupervised, she also had the perspective to understand the other woman's position and not to take the situation too personally.

Men Harass You

At the subtler level, women are asked on business trips about the impact of their traveling on husbands or boyfriends; or they are told not to work too late because the building is dangerous, rather than improve the conditions; or they are teased for not laughing at sexist jokes. However, at the

more serious end of the spectrum, women are still sexually pressured—
and are the subject of deliberate campaigns to undercut them. One woman
actually quit work as a result:

> I began finding harassing literature in my in basket. They kept
> telling me I was overreacting, but finally somebody put in an ad
> for Rely tampons (at the height of the toxic shock syndrome af-
> fair). That's when my supervisor and his superiors realized there
> was something bad going on. They investigated, and it turned
> out to be the man at the next desk. Finally they hired a new male
> secretary and I was the only woman out of seven. I began to
> wonder, is it for this that I get up every morning at 3:30 to catch
> the train? I decided to get out, sit out the company's reorganiza-
> tion, have kids, and then go back into a different department, or
> even switch to a different company.

In fact, she has been out of the workforce for several years doing voluntary
community work, and has not been able to bring herself to go back. While
not everyone reacts so strongly, one can only speculate about the damage
that similar experiences do in undermining women's confidence and performance. When women were the butt of harassment, they sometimes
took it doubly hard because they hoped things would be different for them
as MBAs.

The Odds Are Against You

Even where colleagues and bosses are compatible and perhaps supportive,
the statistics can be a warning signal that, if you want to move up, you
may well reach an impasse. A Goldmine MBA who has reached middle
management told me she had left a job just because the odds were so bad:

> It was a very complicated situation, because there were very few
> vacancies a year for promotion; maybe only two or three, and we
> had about a hundred people waiting in line. So the fact that you
> were number five [meant that] you may as well have been number
> fifty-five. Everybody except the top three knew that that was
> their situation. I was appreciative of the recognition I'd gotten,
> but I knew [promotion] just wasn't going to be coming around
> for me in a time frame that was reasonable. And that signal was
> very obvious. You'd have to be terribly naive not to see what the
> system was.

Women do, of course, take good advantage of positions in organizations
where the statistics are almost hopeless, to give them valuable background

and even experience at managing certain subject areas or projects. On the whole, though, they should treat bad statistics as a warning if they ultimately want to be promoted.

Your Job Level Does Not Match Your Tasks and Recognition

While it is sometimes obvious to women that their careers are stuck, more often it is difficult to assess whether or not they are moving in the right direction. Several women told me that they were doing work well above the level of their job titles, work they enjoyed, which let them expand their skills and show what they could do. That was not the whole story for a telephone company manager:

> Right now, I'm in an awkward—an interesting situation. I'm probably doing a job that's one or two levels higher than what I am, which is good and bad. I'm lucky to get a lot of really good challenging assignments. . . . They really needed people with the skills and abilities I have, and I am now recognized and respected. Most of the time I am dealing with people a few levels over my head, which is good. It means I can deal with some intelligent people, the work is more challenging, and I have more authority, which is great. But at the same time, I know if I were a man doing the same things with the same background and all that, I'd have been promoted by now.

Women welcome the opportunity to show they can do more responsible work, but there is a point beyond which it becomes exploitation.

A CPA/MBA at a Big Eight public accounting firm reached that point. She went through the process of pouring her energy into a project far beyond her job level without any reward, not once but twice:

> On both of these occasions I fully expected that I would skip levels, and they would of course give me the title in which I had worked for the last year. I didn't expect that they would give me the money, but I thought they would at least come a little bit close. In both cases, I didn't get it.
>
> In one case, it was because the manager who was supposed to promote me was up for partner . . . he said he couldn't stick his neck out for me that year, but he would promote me the next year. Not only that, but he said I'd done such a wonderful job that he was going to give me extra responsibility. "Now I don't want you to think we don't value you, so I'm going to give you

more work to do at a lower title and at lower pay [than it should
be]." . . . The second time the manager said, "But I can't tell
the partner that you did it, because that would reflect on me for
not staffing the job properly. I just can't do this."

As these examples show, hard work does not pay off for everyone. A
black MBA in a retail clothing business also developed a reputation as a
highly efficient workhorse. Her boss knew he could count on her to come
through:

> We had our disagreements and I knew he wasn't crazy about
> women, but when the projects came up they were mine because
> I could perform.

Although she did receive regular raises, she was passed over for the management job above hers time after time, usually for less qualified white
males:

> The man who hired me moved up to vice president, with two
> managers reporting to him. My area didn't have a manager, and
> I knew a number of people had moved up from my area [research]
> into marketing, or from analyst into manager roles. After a year,
> they created another management position, but they told me I
> didn't have the experience. They hired someone from the outside
> who stayed about a year and was finally fired. I applied again,
> and they told me five years' experience was required. By then I
> was in charge of the in-store work. The position was vacant for
> six months, and a colleague and I ran the department together,
> which worked out well.
>   They then brought in another person [white male] who was
> very capable. We hit it off from the beginning, but he only stayed
> three months. . . . He recommended me to take his spot when
> he left, but they hired another person [white male] who was a
> nice guy with a more limited background than mine and no grad-
> uate degree.

One of the classic elements of her experience is that although qualifications
were the excuse not to give her the job, the white males who were brought
in were less qualified—except for gender and race.

For some women, the problem is not being overloaded with responsibilities above their level, but receiving overinflated titles that do not reflect substantive responsibilities. Although titles may indicate that women
have gone far in some areas, a second look at the substance of their jobs
may reveal a different picture. Catalyst maintains a file of 1,200 women

whom they consider candidates for corporate boards. Dr. Betsy Jaffe reviewed their qualifications:

> They had impressive titles, but the content of the job sometimes had been cut out from under them, so there was less responsibility. Sometimes it was made up because we have to have a woman vice president, or a woman PR officer, or consumer relations or urban affairs. . . . Most of the women are in staff positions, and it is the line jobs which are more powerful.

(Line jobs, generally speaking, are those that provide services to clients in the outside world, while staff jobs provide internal advice, accounting, management, and other services. A line job may have more potential in the long run than a staff job, even if the level seems lower at first glance.)

Responding to Warnings

Sometimes women fail to heed clear warning signals because they are put off with excuses and reassurance. A Generic MBA ignored a whole series of non-events like having her reports overlooked because the head of the organization kept reassuring her. Ultimately, she was fired:

> Up until the day they threw me out, the president kept saying, "Hang in there. I'm going to make this work out for you and I have big plans for you, my dear." When I said, "What the hell is going on here?" he never looked up from his shoes.

Unfortunately, women sometimes respond to warning signals with self-defeating behavior. Rather than looking for patterns that are common to the careers of women in management, many of those I interviewed individualized their experience. They were like atoms denying that they were part of the organism that in turn interacts with an environment. Their repeated failure to recognize the events and non-events that affected their careers was partly the result of not looking for patterns. Some blamed themselves if they were not promoted or felt that they made it all on their own if they were. In fact, the truth is almost always more complex; the course of a career is determined by systems, interests, and games in an organization and economy, as well as by any individual's behavior.

As part of their denying that their careers were part of the overall pattern for women workers, they generally disassociated themselves from others in the workplace. Because their whole effort in earning the MBA had been to escape the dead-end jobs most women hold, they had a strong stake in focusing on the fact that they were paid better than most women rather than the strong commonalities. The MBAs did not speak up for other women consistently and tended to try to make individual arrangements with the power structure on issues such as maternity leave or sexual harassment rather than organizing to change policies for everyone. They often did their best to fade into the male woodwork, sometimes deploring women who gave the sex a bad name by being either "too emotional" on the one hand or "too aggressive" on the other. Essentially, some believed that they could erase their gender with a diploma, hard work, and a thousand small acts to distinguish themselves from "the girls."

All these responses to warning signals had serious career consequences. Women missed patterns they could have spotted early on, based on the experiences of others who had gone before them. By approaching every career event as though it were happening to her as an individual, a woman could ignore critical factors affecting her progress; she could fail to notice when someone was trying to do her in, when she needed help from a powerful ally and how to get it. She could hamper her career by neither giving support to nor receiving it from other women. She could cut herself off from being able to talk over her experience and strategize about it, and from feedback about her strengths and skills.

In pairs and groups, women can recognize what is happening to them— it was not an accident when he brushed against you or when the proposal did not arrive on time—and shatter myths about how much everything has changed. Recognizing undermining patterns of behavior and strategizing about them with even one other woman can make career planning more realistic, as well as give a woman the wherewithal to take action with others. The dramatic numbers of women entering business schools and management jobs are the result of just such collective action, not women wringing their hands one by one at their desks. Isolating themselves as if every career issue were individual is as futile as securing the furniture in one's cabin on a sinking ship.

Six

Beyond Gray Flannel: Starting a Business of One's Own

I had not expected to include a chapter on establishing an independent business in this book. It is so incongruous with my image of Ms. MBA: I saw her only in the corporate setting, perched in the heights of some vast skyscraper on Park Avenue. The idea of her leaving that environment to run her own show simply did not fit my idea of the organization woman.

By the time I had interviewed a number of women who were in the midst of playing career games, I could well understand why many were tempted to try out their own businesses. In fact, it was women MBAs themselves who suggested that this book address what happened to those who decided to leave the relative predictability of the conventional workplace.

At first, I thought it would be almost impossible to find MBAs who had gone into business for themselves. I expected that any woman who had decided on business school had by definition channeled herself into a career of working for someone else. As I talked with more women, though, I could see how wistful they were at the idea of a business of their own. The more they talked about what many had to put up with, not only daily, but with respect to their long-term prospects, the better I understood why the idea was so appealing. Three main reasons emerged: they were blocked in their careers (for women who had been out of school for more than a few years); they had had it with working in the system, especially in large corporations; or/and they needed more flexible schedules to carry out their additional unpaid work at home.

Fantasizing about their own businesses, women saw all kinds of advantages. At least they would be able to establish their own rules and put their effort into real work rather than catering to the irrational whims of bosses. Whatever they accomplished would be theirs, rather than being routed through a maze of organizational channels. They could act on bright ideas and try them out in the real world, rather than translate them into lengthy memoranda and selling them piece by piece up the chain of command, a process that could distort or destroy them.

At the same time, the countervailing pressures were strong. Despite their interest, the women I was interviewing had decided to stay in the fold, at least for the foreseeable future. There were all kinds of reasons for them to remain there, chiefly salary and security. The routine workplace had features that they did not like, but it did provide a regular paycheck, one substantially higher than most women workers'.

Moreover, starting one's own business is the ultimate professional risk. It means being totally exposed and vulnerable, financially and emotionally; it means not only being good enough at one's work to be competitive in a tough market, but selling oneself expertly over and over again. For most, it means going it alone, at least in the beginning, and being solely responsible for one's destiny, no matter who else may be in a helping role. What could be more contrary to most women's upbringing than opting for risk over security, the spotlight over the background, and isolation over community?

I became increasingly curious about the women who had decided to create their own working environments rather than settle for the status quo. As I began to look for MBAs with their own businesses, I discovered that my preconception was wrong: although I could more easily find women entrepreneurs who did not have graduate degrees, women MBAs who had set up independently were not scarce. I wondered if they would be different from the women I had already interviewed. Most of all, I wanted to know what had motivated them so strongly that they had overcome the multiple obstacles that kept most MBAs in more traditional careers. Did they have access to more money, or did they just assess the risks differently?

Beyond the question of motivation, I was intrigued to know what these women actually did: where had they found the skills they needed to create and maintain their enterprises? Had the MBA helped? How well had their decisions stood the test of time? Were they more satisfied than they had been in a more predictable working environment? I hoped that hearing about the advantages and disadvantages they discovered, and their advice, would help other women MBAs decide if starting a business on their own was really a possibility.

Because I wanted to explore those questions in depth, I decided to interview three women with quite different histories and present each as a case study to show how she and her business developed. This chapter focuses on their accounts: Janet, who runs a financial planning service; Kate, who has a real estate development consulting firm; and Judy, who created a tax and advisory service for small businesses and others, combined with a newsletter publishing operation.

Financial Planning on a Shoestring

I especially looked forward to interviewing Janet because she had gone to business school with the specific intention of going off on her own one day, having already tasted the possibilities within other people's organizations. The woman who helped me find her is a strong feminist, so I was not surprised to find that Janet had a support network of woman friends who sustained her through the first years of establishing her financial planning business. Virtually every minute of her day was booked, but she made time to talk with me at 8:00 one morning in her office. When I arrived, somewhat bleary eyed, she was already making her way through well-organized piles of paper. She led me into the library of the law firm where she rents office space. The elegant surroundings were a real contrast to the struggle she described in establishing herself.

Janet is a single woman in her thirties who is accustomed to talking about herself and her development. She was unusually open about the personal aspects of starting her business, as well as the mechanics. Her road to business school began, like that of many other women, with her realization that her career at an academic research center was blocked:

> I had a major emotional career crisis at about age twenty eight, and did not know what I was going to be doing: I saw that women and men who had just received their Ph.D.s, who were twenty four and twenty five, were coming in to be my boss. I really felt that I needed to have more control over my work life, so I spent a lot of time in a women's group, figuring out what I was going to do.
>
> I decided I would pursue something that they felt I was leaning toward, which was to write a business plan . . . on the whole concept of an old girls' network. I took my finished product to the Small Business Club at the local business school. The president of the club thought it was a terrific idea, and he said, "Why don't you do this?" I looked at the bottom line, and it said, "You have to raise a million dollars."
>
> I just freaked out; I didn't know what to do, and said, "If I really want to do this kind of thing, I should be trained to do it," and decided to go to business school first.

Janet applied to a range of schools and was somewhat disappointed that she ended up going full time in a Generic evening program, but she knew that it was the skills she was after rather than a fancy package. Soon, as she took more courses and was exposed to a wide range of people and careers, she began to clarify her direction:

> At that point, I decided to really do some searching as to where I wanted to be. I decided that personal financial planning was a new career opportunity, a new field and industry, and there were tremendous opportunities in it. I think that I have always wanted to start my own business; it just always came up when I began

to do goal setting and things of that nature, which I had found
very helpful—[take a look at] where I want to be in a year, five
years, and ten years.

That kept coming up as an objective, to control my own life,
to make as much money as I could make.

To achieve that long-term goal, Janet knew that she needed certain
skills. Business school provided some of them: marketing, reading financial
statements, doing taxes, and so forth. Since she did not receive direct training in financial planning (although it is available), she apprenticed herself
to a company in which she felt she could learn the specifics of her trade:

While I was in business school I was just an administrative assistant, but I was in on the ground level and saw what was going
on, how they did their work, and really established some of my
basic concepts of how to do my own business.

After completing the MBA, she moved to the East Coast and began
looking for a suitable place to enhance her skills further. She checked employers out very carefully:

I always felt that I wasn't just going to be contributing a specific
skill as a piece of a puzzle into an organization, but that I was
going to have an effect in a broader sense. . . . I really sought
out firms for training, worked with one for a year, and then
started my own business.

In the area where she chose to live, Janet could not find an employer
who fully met her requirements. What she had sought was training; instead
she was asked to create a new financial planning department on the basis
of three or four months' experience. But she was willing to try:

One thing I learned in business school was that the dumbest men
become very rich and very successful people, through their bum-
bling idiocy, and I thought, "Gee, I have a little smarts, I can
probably do as well if not better."

My business school experience taught me that you take the
risk to do this kind of thing; otherwise you're not going to get
anywhere. So I took it, spent a year at it, and realized I could
really do even better in my own business. That's why I started a
business.

There were all kinds of good reasons for Janet not to launch out on her
own at that time. One was lack of money. Contrary to my speculation

that women who took the step outside the conventional workplace had more financial resources than others, she started with almost nothing. Impossible as it seemed, she was impelled to give it a shot:

> I thought, "I've always wanted to do this; I might as well start now, and go out and do it." It was crazy: it was the craziest thing I'd ever done, because I didn't really have the capital to start a business. I had a lot of emotional support from friends, which was really crucial. There were many, many days when I was literally just crying in the morning, saying, "I don't know how this is going to work." I thought I would be a bag lady for sure.
>
> I wouldn't recommend the way I started my business. On the other hand, the fear I had to go through was very important to make me get things done that I was having trouble doing.

Janet found that the diversity of skills required of a business owner was even greater than she had supposed, and her fear pushed her through the ones she had not already developed, especially marketing. Keeping her confidence up was a major problem, as it is for others:

> I don't care how many degrees women have, sometimes you get out there and it's just hard to be confident in yourself. That's been a real battle for me the whole time. But the fear has led me to say, "I have to go and sell. I have to do it. Otherwise, I'm not going to have any customers." . . . In a way, I'm pleased that I didn't have tons of capital behind me to let me languish and sit around, and figure out what I was going to do next for months.

Although clearly the main hindrance to women starting their own businesses is lack of money, the observance of traditional roles is a close second. Being afraid to depend totally on oneself and one's own resources is a logical outcome of women's upbringing and reflects a generally accurate view of their economic predicament. When I asked Janet how she coped with her fears, particularly as a single woman, she had some very practical techniques to offer. She did not dismiss or gloss over how terrified she was, but developed some specific ways to overcome it:

> In the morning, I would think through the clients I had really helped, who were happy with my services, and I'd say, "That person was happy. Now what would happen if I went out of business?" . . . I had to continually reinforce, but when I had a setback—some client calls complaining about something—it would just devastate me. I would take it personally.
>
> I had all sorts of little techniques. I would leave these three-

by-five cards up in the mirror in the bathroom that said, "I am a good financial planner," or whatever, and all sorts of confidence-building things. It sounds crazy, but you have to do this. There was one poem somebody gave me from the Sisters of Hope . . . about pushing on when the chips are down. . . . I tried to keep looking ahead instead of backwards, "What do I have to accomplish?"

Even so, there were times when the fear got out of hand, when even the best techniques did not work. Janet kept at it anyway:

I got to the point where I would sometimes be immobilized by fear. I'd sit at my desk, all alone in a room, with just a phone. I'd say, "What do I do now?" And I would force myself to do things everyday, like call three people that I needed to contact, or have three in-person meetings a week. I set goals; sometimes I lived up to them and sometimes I had trouble meeting them.

Although Janet feels free of many of the fears and issues that plagued her at the beginning, she sees working through them as essential to any businessperson's establishing a new enterprise. A woman who decides to move outside the conventional workplace must be ready to be introspective and to fight her way through some inevitable rough times when she will feel totally unequal to the task. For Janet, one key in making her way through was the support of other women:

I would meet and have lunch with a couple of key women. I would share all my troubles and tribulations, and they would share theirs. I would give them advice when they were having trouble, and they would turn around and give it to me. We were just both telling each other the same stuff, that we couldn't tell ourselves. A lot of emotional stuff influenced my performance, my ability to be at my best, and if you can't clear that away, it'll be really tough.

I could tell by the way Janet was talking that she had taken enormous personal risks to start her business. Until we mentioned actual amounts of money, though, I did not fully appreciate the extent of what she had done. Here is what Janet started with:

I was all on my own. I had seven thousand dollars in the bank. I did not have another job. I lived with a roommate who paid a lot of the grocery bills for a while. . . . I ran through the seven thousand. I think at my lowest point I had two thousand dollars,

or a thousand dollars in the bank. I had to buy a computer, I had
to do lots of things; it got pretty scary. . . . I learned how to
minimize my lifestyle, and it was a good experience.

The contrast with her expectations from business school, often focused on
management with staff to run about and perform specialized functions,
was sometimes uncomfortable. Because Janet is personally responsible for
almost everything that happens, she must avoid being overly meticulous
about time-eating administrative details.

Although she can see that many successful people have managed beau-
tifully without MBAs, Janet has found her training helpful as her business
has grown. At the same time, many of the skills she is applying have
nothing to do with the degree. They draw more on the particular strengths
women have in starting their own businesses. In her view:

> Women have a very unique opportunity in business because . . .
> they can think through and understand what they're doing for
> people on a psychological level. If you can identify that and mar-
> ket to that, the world is yours. Nobody can touch you. I think
> that's why financial planning in particular is highly woman ori-
> ented right now, because there's so much psychological need.
>
> You get people who walk in and they're crying because their
> finances are such a mess and they can't deal with them. . . . The
> funny thing is that business school is so numbers oriented, and
> yet you can't be successful in business unless you are people
> oriented.

When I asked Janet for an example of a client who had come to her
with both human and financial needs, she told me about a woman whose
lawyer husband recently had died intestate:

> The amount she would have inherited from the law firm would
> have been cut in half by her tax bill. I worked with her, and saw
> her go from being . . . really attached to her old married life
> with her husband, to blossoming as a woman on her own. She's
> . . . probably going to retire early, and set up her own business
> in communications and development. I've helped her understand
> and not be intimidated by taxes, but also I saved her probably
> thirty or forty thousand.

Janet's firm has developed several areas of specialty: managing cash
(where the paycheck goes); budgets; retirement planning; investments
(where they are and how you move them around); tax planning; and estate
planning. She and her newly acquired partner see their role as financial

planners as a continuing relationship with their clients whose lives and needs are constantly changing.

When I asked Janet how long she had been in business for herself, she could hardly believe that the time was so short:

> Two years, is that all? I have really come a long way, and part of it is because I was starting on such a shoestring. I just had to move quickly and go through.

She feels that her business gives her a way to influence the world to be the way she wants it to be, allowing her to help people take more control of their lives. I was impressed by how deliberate she had been in her own career planning, even when she decided to take such a major leap. She had assembled the necessary skills and support like the pieces of a puzzle.

Reentering Business School—and Cracking the Market

Nothing could have been a greater contrast to Kate's situation. She fell into her own business. We must have scheduled three appointments to talk before I finally reached her in the hubbub of her office, and she sandwiched our conversation between projects related to her real estate development consulting firm. A married woman with three teenaged children, she had taken a crack at business school long before women were represented there in any numbers. In 1964, Goldmine was intolerable to her, and she dropped out:

> I started when there were only two women in the entire business school, and a lot of discrimination against women. I was not strong enough or motivated enough to handle it. I majored in marketing, took all the requisite courses, but didn't complete my thesis.

Regardless of how strong or motivated she might have been, it is easy to understand why Kate felt out of place and unable to perform. She dropped out and went on to have three children with no particular thoughts of returning to school. Then she had an unexpected phone call one morning:

> When the third child was three, the dean of the business school called me to ask me about some research I had done. . . . I told him I wanted to come back and take the courses in my specialty, this time in real estate. I had no plans to say that; I didn't know he was going to call. . . . My husband was very supportive when

we discussed my reentry. I was accepted, and when I went back to school in 1975, it was eleven years later and the climate was entirely different.

Men were not nearly as overtly oppressive in the classroom, although she was still the only woman in some of her classes:

I found that my first reaction was to defer to men for about 30 seconds, and then I realized that no one gives a damn if I'm a man or a woman in this place. The whole attitude had changed remarkably. There were far more women, though not that many. In most of my classes I was still the only woman, but I saw that there were other women around taking classes. They just didn't happen to be in real estate.

Kate herself had changed, but she recognized that changes in wider society made her accomplishments possible. Despite those changes, she had no one to identify with as a reentry mother in business school. Nevertheless, her experience the second time around was overwhelmingly positive:

It was a tremendous experience from several standpoints. It gave me a perspective on the industry that I wouldn't have had otherwise, and much more than if I had just gone to work . . . in terms of interest and ability, it gave me confidence. When I entered, my confidence was not very high. All my friends were successful—at least their husbands were successful—and I was terrified that [I would] go back and fail.

Being a reentry woman meant that she had some particular pleasures in store after spending several years at home:

The reentry woman has a treat that's different because it opens up a world that is so intellectually stimulating, especially after staying home with small children. It gives you the tools, the union card. It's more than just a union card. It gives you the perspective that's different from someone who just has an undergraduate degree. The experience also gives you confidence that you can compete. My self-esteem improved tremendously from receiving high grades and respect from both faculty and students. I really cherish that decision to go back.

Unlike Janet, Kate did not think immediately of setting up her own business. She became one of two professionals on the staff of a redevelopment project, working on a part-time basis because she felt guilty about leaving her children. After finding that only her salary, not her hours, was truly part time, she switched to full time. Yet she was sure that she did not want to stay in the public sector forever, especially as cuts were clearly in store, but she did not consider her own business as an option. Over the summer, while her children were out of school, she took some time to obtain her real estate broker's license. Before she knew it, people were approaching her:

> People kept saying, "While you aren't doing anything, would you do this for me?" My husband informed me that I was consulting, and encouraged me to continue.

Kate did her best to ignore the fact that she was running her own business. Even as it threatened to take over her home, it did not seem real to her:

> I started in May or June, and I was working out of my house because it never occurred to me that I could have an office. The kids were off from school and there was no summer school that year, so it was really getting to be pretty much of a nightmare.
>   A friend of mine said, "You really should rent an office." I said to him, "How do I know what business I'll have next month?" He said a man can get away with working at home, but when a woman does, everyone thinks she's cooking. I rented an office the next day.

From that modest beginning, with an office that rented for $100 a month, Kate has built an eight-person firm, which she considers just about the right size, that specializes in the interaction between public and private sectors in the economics of land development. It has taken about six years to reach this point, thanks to her being in the right place at the right time.

The MBA helped Kate in specific ways: the financial and marketing courses were indispensable to creating the service her firm provides and to establishing the business and planning for it to succeed. She has used her business school experience as a complement to her technical expertise in restoration and development, bringing both financial and earlier skills into play. In reflecting on the advantages and disadvantages of having her own business, the diversity is the first factor Kate mentions:

> One of the real pleasures about working for oneself is that there is so much variety. . . . I wish I'd worked first for someone else in something like this before I tried doing it. It's a learning experience every day, but it would have been easier if I'd had a model. There are times that I would rather do the work than

spend the time on administration. There are times when I would like to know that somebody else has the responsibility of the payroll, not me. Or times when I want a partner. But I wouldn't trade.

Nevertheless, there are moments when she is afflicted by the unpredictability, even though the firm has always had work. She suggests that women who are considering going into business for themselves think seriously about what that means, especially in its impacts on their personal lives:

> The time commitment's much greater than if you work for someone else. . . . I had some idea that I would have some flexibility. Being self-employed gives you the flexibility of working weekends. . . . It's stressful on personal relationships, or can be, and you need a lot of support at home: emotional support as much as any other kind, because there are probably greater ups and downs. On the other hand, generally people who have their own business tend to be dynamic, energetic people, or had better be. You have to develop it if you don't start out with it.

In Kate's view, establishing a business of one's own may be an especially appropriate option for older women whose accomplishments are rarely recognized in the conventional workplace. As new MBAs, they almost never have opportunities that really take full advantage of their backgrounds. Like Janet, Kate feels that women have a great deal to offer and have a better chance of contributing everything they can if they set up a structure for themselves rather than trying to fit into someone else's.

Although Kate is fundamentally pleased with her choices and recommends them to older women, they do have a cost:

> It's very lonely. That's probably the other thing I would say, even when you have a lot of friends. There are certain aspects . . . of running your own business—you're always working, you're always "on" in one way or another, the unpredictability. It means that friends have to be very understanding. It also means that sometimes you have to pull out of things you said you would do, sometimes at the last minute. I think it's very difficult for people with regular jobs to identify with the pressures and commitments that a more independent life implies.
> More independent—I just realized the irony of that.

Inventing a Career in Business and Law

It was that desire for independence that drew Judy, a former French teacher who holds both law and business degrees from a sound Generic school, to

start her own business at age forty. Although we were unable to arrange
a meeting in her home city, she talked with me while she was in Boston
to sell a successful small business she created to a large publishing concern,
only one of a number of balls she has in the air, in addition to her tax and
advisory services. Judy spent her twenties doing what was expected of
many women: she married young and trained as a teacher. Eventually, her
marriage broke up. She became thoroughly bored with the teaching profession and decided that she wanted to go to law school.

Lack of money might have held Judy back, but her mother helped her
by giving her enough to apply to schools. Her mother's optimism proved
to be well founded. Judy remarried a truly helpful partner. He provided
the financial, psychological, and moral support she needed, as many wives
do for husbands in professional school, and has shared household responsibilities fully. While every aspect of that support is important and, according to other women I interviewed, rare, the financial part was critical.
Since women still earn only about three-fifths of what men earn, access to
their money can make a woman's education possible. Women who do not
have that access must turn to other, more limited resources.

Entering a Generic law school in her thirties was terrifying, but Judy
quickly discovered that what she really liked in her coursework were con-
tracts and the business aspects, so she made the leap to a joint MBA/JD.
Although she later saw her husband through a business school with a fan-
cier reputation, she feels completely positive about the quality of education
she received, and found it in many ways more practical and applicable than
his.

After a stint in a huge commercial bank as a tax lawyer, Judy went to
work for a large Ivy League university to arrange gifts from wealthy do-
nors, and worked for a law firm. She wrote articles, spoke, and made
herself visible. Before she decided to start her own business, she spent
months thinking through what it would mean for her:

> I wish someone had told me this when I was twenty two. . . .
> I started doing some real introspection and saying, "Can I do it?
> What happens if I don't succeed? Will I be able to face failure?
> Will failure mean that I have failed in all aspects of my life? Or
> will failure spur me on to a different thing that will be a success?
> Do I want to even try?"
> If you can't face failure, then you'd better not try a small
> business.

Asking those questions made her begin reflecting about different aspects
of herself and how each one might lead her in a different career direction.
Ultimately, practicality won out. Although Judy wished that she had gone
through this soul searching at twenty rather than forty, she didn't. Taking

into account the feeling, thinking, and doing aspects of herself, she opted to work with numbers.

Having consulted her own inclinations and experience, Judy finally decided to take the plunge and start her own business. When I asked her what finally moved her, she said, "An overinflated ego and an inability to accept other people's authority." Judy was prepared for what life as a small businessperson would really be like, both the rigors and the pleasures. When she and her sister were eleven and twelve years old, their parents owned a fish market, one of a series of small businesses. Often the girls were left in charge for periods of four or five hours, making sure that everything was clean and properly arranged, and waiting on customers. Sometimes they even opened and closed the store. Although Judy described it as being hard for her at that age, she also said that it gave her a foundation for what she does now, not only in her own business but in advising others.

Judy's MBA gave her the knowledge of business to complement her background in law, so she has been able to integrate both perspectives in her service. While she could probably have acquired some of the same information and skills through experience, the MBA has helped her provide clients with advice that takes account of both commercial and legal factors. The long-term planning she has done for the several businesses she ultimately created rests partly on her training at business school. At the beginning, though, she had quite a struggle.

Although she did not have to worry about food on the table and a roof over her head, Judy started her business on a shoestring $5,000. When she first went out to buy office supplies, she spent fifty dollars on everything she could think of. She returned to her office, sat at her desk, and reached for the ruler that was not there. Then she tried to roll her chair closer to the desk, and discovered that she was immobilized on the carpet. Before she had always requisitioned such furnishings from a giant central supply. It was the first of many adjustments.

Judy made a couple of mistakes that other women could learn from. First, she took on too much at once: she started her law practice and a small publishing business at the same time. Her practice draws heavily on what she learned at business school: she handles advice to small businesses (creating and running them) from cookie and muffin shops to more staid enterprises; estate planning; and many aspects of financing and managing charitable organizations. The publishing company, just sold to a major firm, printed a newsletter related to her practice. Starting both the practice and the company simultaneously seems insane to her now. She did not sleep for four months.

Second, despite her best efforts, Judy was soon running out of money. She decided to ask her bank for a line of credit, anticipated all her expenses, and came up with a request for $5,000. The day she went to the bank, luck was on her side; some writing she had done earlier paid off. As the loan officer was interviewing her, a nearby secretary overheard the conversation. She came over immediately. "Are you Judy Stone? Didn't you do a chapter in my law book? Would you sign it for me? I've got it right here!" A few days later, the bank came through with five times the amount Judy had requested, telling her she would need it all. As it turned out, she did use most of the money, with some in her checking account as a valuable cushion.

Although she had always carefully advised clients to prepare in advance before setting up a business, Judy feels that she herself did not do enough. It is not surprising that the first thing she tells her new small-business clients to do is set up a proper bookkeeping system. Then, she urges them to check out whether people really want their product or service, a seemingly obvious point, but most small businesses fail, often because the creators are so convinced their idea is right that they do not bother to check it out with anybody else.

Setting specific goals is the third point Judy stresses to new clients. She herself decided that she wanted to reach a certain level of billing each month during her first year, building from zero to an optimistic amount. She came very close, and actually had a good year in her first year, which is unusual in a new business.

To her, the disadvantages of vulnerability and unpredictability are more than outweighed by the freedom she has. At the end of last year, Judy and her secretary were exhausted after the push that always comes at that time. On December 30, two prospective clients called wanting crash jobs that would have brought in several thousand dollars. Judy said, "No. We're going home." She realized that she really could shut down the whole show for five days until she recovered. To her, it was worth it.

Judy has put a lot of effort into making herself visible both in her community and nationally, by speaking, writing, and participating in professional organizations. It has paid off in making her a woman to be reckoned with in her field. She made an important contribution to higher education by devising a new way to finance college educations, resulting in the establishment of a number of scholarships across the country.

In planning for later years, Judy sees herself juggling a whole series of businesses over time rather than sticking to any single venture. Unlike some of the other women I spoke with, who are sure they want to stay with what they have, Judy loves variety:

There's a part of me that says businesses are made to be sold. That's my approach. I love to create and organize businesses. Unless I can make a million dollars a year out of it, I see no reason to keep it. I want to create it, build it to a certain point, sell it, get out and start over.

Now she is approaching more decisions, much like the ones she had to make in getting out of her secure job at a law firm before. She is not sure yet which way she will turn, but she feels generally optimistic about her direction, as do her clients:

> To some degree, women and minorities are still locked out of many of the positions, and I find [people in] both of those categories becoming my small business clients. For the most part, they are very pleased to do it. It's a struggle and it's hard, but they see a tremendous upside potential in doing it. The more upside potential, the more downside potential, but they're ready to face that.
>
> If a woman wants to start a business and she's forty or forty five, I think she has to talk to herself and say, "What do I think of myself? Can I stand it if I fail?" If you need that even keel, don't do it. But if they can work real hard and be persistent, then I think it's a great opportunity.

For those who are trying to make up their minds about whether to leave the structured workplace behind, Judy warns that anyone with an additional strike against them, such as age, is particularly vulnerable to career blockage:

> Then you have to decide whether you want to take that leap into the dark abyss of no paycheck. "No pots, no food," as my friend the self-employed potter says. If you make that decision, you have to look at issues like whether you have the health and the energy to put in lots of hours.

For all her experience in advising other small-businesspersons about every phase of their management from creation to planning the estates of the partners, Judy feels that it is her first-hand knowledge that really enables her to assist others:

> It wasn't until I went into my own business that any of those words had any real meaning. I thought they had meaning before, but now I know.

Not everyone could go through the rigors of the early planning and research that Judy recommends, much less the personal testing that all three women reported. As I talked with them, it became clearer that their preparations and projections of income, markets, and sources of funding were the crucial factors that led them to their present situations. The MBA was unquestionably useful at that early phase. Each woman had the advantage of training in many of the technical skills entrepreneurs need: marketing, accounting, and finance; they knew how to pull together the detailed business plans needed for seeking funding and overall management. (Of course, many people do them highly successfully without MBAs.) Just as in the conventional marketplace, it can give them an edge on the competition, particularly in seeking the visibility that is necessary to any successful business. An MBA still carries some weight with potential clients.

All three women were thrown back on their personal resources in ways they had not expected, forcing them to develop qualities and skills they had lacked before, such as presentation and marketing techniques as well as technical expertise. Becoming totally responsible for one's income is an exercise in self-reliance and risk taking that most women must push themselves to undertake; for example, Janet, a single woman, had her economic survival on the line.

What motivated these three women—the desire for independence, and unlimited prospects and income—holds true for many other MBAs I interviewed. Some feel that they must step outside the conventional job market if they want to progress. One woman I heard about did a complete turnaround: in the late 1970s she firmly believed that the sky was the limit in her corporate career; a few years ago, she established her own consulting firm specifically to help other women start small businesses, which she now sees as the route to more economic power.

While the trend for women in large organizations, including MBAs, to abandon hope and create their own alternatives may not be statistically significant, knowledgeable persons did mention the phenomenon again and again. Helen Axel of the Conference Board pointed out that sheer statistics—never mind possible discrimination—drive some women out. The competitive odds are just too great:

> Women get to a certain level in the company and they leave, because they see nothing else there beyond for them. They start businesses of their own. They are moving out of the corporate community. . . . I've seen it happen in banks where women are made senior vice presidents and see that they are not going anywhere else in the bank. There are too many men. They are a relatively small number of women at that level, so there is going to be a fierce competition with an unlikely prospect. The alternative is to stay at that level.

More immediate frustrations may also motivate some to make the change. People in large organizations feel exasperated with bureaucratic demands, the need to conform with norms that may be personally uncomfortable, and the decisions of superiors with unreliable judgment. Women are under all these stresses, just as men are.

At first glance, it may be difficult to understand why hordes of women MBAs are not setting up businesses on every street corner. If the conventional workplace, and corporations in particular, are not ready to let them grow to their full potential for whatever reasons, then why not simply go outside it? Money is the obvious answer: women still have remarkably little actual wealth at their disposal to provide capital. Until quite recently, the idea of a woman-owned business was almost a contradiction in terms, except where inherited wealth was involved. But the three women whose careers are related here, although they had support from friends and husbands, began with very little in the way of capital. In addition, women's roles as care-givers held them back.

Among the women I interviewed, those who least fit the standard model of a career man were most interested in creating a workplace for themselves, rather than conforming to rigid situations designed for a married male. The mother of two small children described a dream she had with several friends:

> Three of us were sitting around one night saying, "Let's do something on our own." We knew there was this tremendous demand on one side [of women wanting more flexible and part time jobs], but is there a real need on the other to employ women in them? We thought we could make a bundle of money somehow, finding a place for these women to get into positions. They'd do anything for part time. Sometimes I feel that I am not into my career and I'm not into my kids because I'm doing both. That's been very frustrating to me.

Sensible and potentially lucrative as this idea may be, none of these women had the extra time and energy that would be needed to pursue it seriously.

In contrast, some mothers of small children do manage to set up their own businesses. I interviewed a woman with a Generic MBA who had looked for a job for nine months when she finally connected, through a deliberate network, with another mother who had established a consulting firm with very flexible policies. For her, it is an ideal working environment while her son is still a toddler. The business has been kept to a size that is manageable while the founder's own children are at home.

Women's need for security and predictability often keeps them in the conventional workplace. When I interviewed a telephone company MBA, for example, she first spoke longingly of a friend who went into the sushi kit business after fifteen years at two major corporations. She said, "It's nice to see something like that, because for once somebody got disgusted and went out on their own and made it." But she backed off when I asked her if she might follow her friend's example some day:

I probably won't do what Joanna did, to tell you the truth. . . .
The upside of large organizations is that I can go on vacation, and
everybody's still going to get a dial tone when they pick up the
telephone. The company's still going to be here when I get back.
I don't think I want the around-the-clock responsibility of owning
a business. My father has his own, and he hardly ever gets away
from it all.

Being self-employed requires a degree of dedication that she shrinks
from. In addition, a large organization offers variety rather than the homogeneity of having the same business for years. Women may also be
deterred by the fact that the entrepreneurial route does not work out for
everyone who tries it. A woman with combined CPA/MBA credentials
was at her wits' end after trying to make it on her own, when a client
offered her a job:

I was definitely burnt out by the politics and by getting nicked
since I didn't know about certain of the games that were going
on. . . . After three months of working almost full time here,
when they offered me a job I realized that I was going to have a
hard time indeed keeping my consulting practice at the level I
wanted for the short term. I chose this job mainly because it was
a sure thing in terms of income, and it did have some projects
that were really challenging to my background.

The relative stability of income, combined with the work itself, won over
the possible hazards of the new venture.

Women who are considering setting up their own business must assess
personal and financial factors, and above all, must be clear about what field
to enter. When I sought a variety of women who owned businesses, I
learned that they took very different approaches. Some took a logical next
step, such as going independent to provide their old employer with a service that could be contracted out. Others made a 180-degree turn. Illus-
trating the extremes, a business school professor used her academic affiliation
to win a government contract, while a newly remarried MBA in her mid-
thirties ditched her management job and became the self-employed writer
she had always wanted to be.

The MBA is by no means a prerequisite for a successful business and
should be weighed skeptically as optimal preparation for entrepreneurship,
except in specialized areas like financial planning. Courses directed at people who want to start their own businesses may well provide adequate and
less costly background. Women who already have the MBA will probably
find it useful, however, in skills and knowledge as well as possible contacts.
Starting a business of one's own is not the answer for everyone, and clearly

there are trade-offs. The risks are high: about half of small businesses fail and at best, self-employment is an utterly demanding way of life. There is no time off, no sick leave, no moment when one should not be working. On the other hand, for these women and many others, the freedom is worth it. They have a level of responsibility and control over their lives that generally could not be attained for years with another employer. As long as the conventional workplace limits upward mobility for women and fails to adjust to their career patterns and schedules, forming a business of one's own will continue to attract some very talented women MBAs.

Seven

Evaluating the MBA for Women

By the time I interviewed women all over the country, my image of Ms. MBA was irrevocably changed. I had envisioned a youthful woman, dressed for success, gracefully climbing the organizational ladder, having gained income, prospects, and the all-important credibility with her Goldmine degree. She orchestrated her personal life as smoothly as her career, so she was never rattled by conflicting demands or disruptive family events.

Almost no one I met fit the image: some were too old or they went to the wrong schools. Others had problematic family lives or wore commonplace clothes instead of three-piece suits from a conservative clothier; a number preferred novels to the *Wall Street Journal*. Throughout our conversations I asked these women what they thought they had gained from the degree, as opposed to what the myth of Ms. MBA had led them to expect. I wanted to know what they had achieved with the degree, not only in terms of income and opportunities, but also with respect to their self-image and how satisfied they were with the results. To put their workplace experiences in a larger context, I went back not only to my own starting point, the evidence from earlier studies of women MBAs from particular schools, but also to data about broader trends in women's employment.

Often, there were discrepancies between the reality of the workplace depicted by that information, and women's fundamental orientations to their careers. Even as their own lives challenged many of the myths about Ms. MBA and the egalitarian workplace, most women undermined their careers by planning and conducting them without recognizing and allowing for the broader context of their individual situations. For example, they blamed themselves for being passed over for promotion, rather than looking objectively at the games and structural factors that affect women in particular (as well as some that affect everyone). By basing their careers on an overly narrow and individualistic view of their predicament, women limited their careers. The overall progress of women in management will be hindered if they do not look beyond their personal situations to develop realistic strategies, both for themselves and for women as a group. Specific suggestions about career planning and action based on the experience of women I interviewed, and the implications of their behavior, deserve the attention of both women MBAs and those who are considering it.

What Women Gained: Money, Skills, Perspective, Jargon

Most women earned more money after they had the MBA than they did before, when working in traditional female occupations. The exceptions were all women with Generic degrees who did not fit the organizational mold because of age, race, having a small child, or already being too high up in a prior occupation to match salary and level of responsibility.

In addition to dollars, most women thought that the MBA had offered them an overview of how the business world operates and had given them some specific skills to help them operate within it. They learned to understand other people's jobs better. Because of the new breadth of the perspective, many felt that they could apply the degree in many settings. A faculty member told me that, since everything from the local museum to a child-care center or corporation has to be managed, the skills women learn in business school are almost universal:

> It gives you a way of thinking about processes which can cut through to the problem. You have to be careful sometimes because you can get myopic, but you have a mission, you learn to ask certain questions, you learn to think in a certain way.

Valuable as the perspective and skills may be, it is important to note that not every woman used what she learned at work; one woman who had been looking for a job for months said:

> I haven't been able to use [the MBA]. I didn't enjoy [school] while I was there, and I'm not particularly proud of it. . . . It wasn't an achievement for me, and I don't know what it's getting me now.

Even she, however, felt that mastering the jargon of business was helpful. A number of women compared their experience to learning a new language in a foreign country. Often they had to understand a whole new culture.

Overall, women said that they understood the economic world better when they left business school. One had always thought of interest rates as fixed like the stars, and it was a great revelation when she learned how and why they were manipulated, and by whom. Many read different books and articles than they had before, and enjoyed feeling on top of subjects that had previously alienated and intimidated them.

Credibility

Learning a new language and mastering some business techniques were, women hoped, the key to establishing credibility in the workplace. They sought not only to impress others with their newfound competence, but to build their own confidence. Many sensed that they needed something extra to ingratiate themselves with organizations to which they sought access. Some realized that being skilled and bright, or full of ideas, was not enough. Even though a few men seem to have slipped through the cracks in the past, women rarely do. Men generally need only prove that they will be an asset to an organization, while women often must prove that they will not be a liability.

Some women did find that having a piece of paper gave them credibility, even when the job for which they were applying did not require the knowledge and skills an MBA can represent. The degree sometimes served more to legitimize experience they already had, rather than giving them new tools. A woman who made a major career switch said that the value of her degree was mostly symbolic:

> What I'm using at this point is the fact that I'm thirty eight and have organizational skills, because I ran a small library. [The MBA] gives you credibility. I wouldn't arbitrarily say do it; only if it would help your job opportunities, or if your employer would pay for it.

Although several thought that they could have learned independently much of what was taught at business school, they were sure that employers would not have responded positively to them without the degree itself. For women who came from top schools, credibility seemed to come somewhat more easily than it did for others. Although some expressed annoyance that the top degrees carried such weight, they all agreed that they did. A Generic graduate felt that a Goldmine credential has an impact on male bosses and colleagues:

> The one thing that the top business schools will do is get guys to stand up and pay attention, because that woman did something they couldn't. That's where the value lies, because . . . they say, "I could have gotten that, too" [about a Generic MBA]. But they know damn well they're not going to get into Goldmine.

Because it implies a certain weeding-out process, the Goldmine degree gives some women latitude to make mistakes that they might not otherwise have. One MBA found that it made a big difference to employers when she was trying to escape an unfavorable job:

> They believed I had transferable skills from one industry to another, and that if I didn't know what they wanted me to know, I was educable. Most people don't get that benefit of the doubt.

A former schoolteacher with a disability was sure that her 1984 Goldmine degree had helped her immensely, although she was not sure that it would have mattered so much to a woman with more business skills.

Building Confidence

Aside from credibility in the eyes of others, one of the common benefits women mentioned was building self-confidence. Having the MBA encouraged some to speak up more. They felt as though no one could say, "She doesn't know what she is talking about," since they had earned the qualifications to discuss business subjects. A typical comment came from an MBA who had made a total switch:

> I didn't go to a big name school. I was older and I still had the stigma of being a flight attendant. More than anything, it gave me the confidence that I could do something else.

In terms of their own development and how they felt about themselves, women's confidence grew as they progressively crossed the boundaries of what was supposed to be impossible for them, particularly if they were among those for whom business had been taboo. Even someone who was miserable in a Generic program and was unable to find a job in her field said that the degree had helped her feel better about herself:

> I love it now when I look on my résumé and see MBA. I just think, "Wow, I never thought I could do that." Even if I never end up working in business, I don't regret it.

Many women were venturing into new subjects by getting the MBA, for example, they all had to attain competence in mathematics. They explicitly stepped onto male territory by enrolling in business school, although some were more conscious of pioneering than others. They took over jobs that were traditionally male, and saw themselves as career oriented and able to take responsibility in stride. They were capable of making complex decisions promptly and handling the pressures of business school as well as those of the workplace.

Once they had actually graduated, particularly from Goldmine, a number of women said they felt invulnerable to intimidation by someone else's degree or status in life. One was blunt enough to say, "There were enough turkeys from there that you know a degree from Goldmine ain't telling you a damn thing." Even those who were angered by aspects of their business education felt proud that they had made it through.

The MBA catapulted some women out of traditional female job categories. An advertising executive who had floundered from one pleasant but dead-end job to another before she got her MBA said:

> I never thought that in five years I would be so pleased with myself and what has happened to my career. I feel much more like I'm in the right place.

While not everyone was so fully satisfied, most did succeed in leaving their old jobs, such as nurses, secretaries, social workers, and teachers.

Satisfaction with the MBA

Almost everyone took some satisfaction in what she had gained at business school. The majority, whose incomes rose, were pleased with the financial results of the degree. On the whole, the most satisfied women fell into four categories: those in entry-level jobs; middle-level managers who wanted to stay there; women with their own businesses; and the few who had made it to senior positions. Although those in the first three categories came from all kinds of schools, those in the last predictably were from Goldmine.

Entry-level women were by far the largest group. Except in extreme situations, they were so delighted to have made it onto the ground floor that long-term career prospects were not pressing issues for them. Some middle-level managers were very satisfied because they had advanced beyond the point they expected. They did not want to go farther because they liked having a life outside and did not want to sacrifice it, and/or because they had care-giving responsibilities to fulfill. Women with their own businesses had a sense of control over their lives that they preferred to the confinement of working for other people. Finally, the few women who had made it to senior management were gratified by their success. One had just been named one of the first women partners in her prominent accounting firm; because she sees herself as an exception and feels that many other equally good women have been held back, she is making the most of her position to be helpful to other women.

Disappointment with the MBA

At the other extreme were the disappointed women who did not even benefit financially, much less in terms of their overall careers:

- A mother in her thirties could not find a part-time or flexible full-time job, and was deeply in debt from business school.

- A middle-level administrator in a nonprofit organization could not persuade the business world to take her on, even at a substantial cut in pay, because she was too experienced (and also seriously in debt).

- Two women in their fifties had to return to their old careers in government and public relations—careers they sought to escape by going to business school.

- A black woman had to turn to high school teaching; she could not find another business job after being laid off after six years with one company.

Apart from financial outcomes, women were dissatisfied when they had to take jobs for which they were overqualified. They felt that their educations were going to waste. One went so far as to say that a high school graduate could have done her job; another could see that she had more education than most others doing her job. After their investment of time and effort in the MBA, women had difficulty accepting such letdowns. Similarly, those whose careers halted at the brick ceiling of middle management after seven or eight years in the workplace felt restless and ready to make a change, but were not sure what strategies to use. They discovered that the MBA only went so far, like this woman with a Generic school MBA:

> There's no question that it opens the door, but I think that's as far as it goes. Every individual has to decide from there on where they want to chart their course. That was something I was totally unaware of at the time I got my MBA.

A few reacted to their dissatisfaction by dropping out of the business world altogether, like a newly remarried and pregnant woman who had used the MBA to earn a decent income as a single parent:

> I had a good job and I bought this house. I tried for us not to have to lead a marginal life of struggling . . . that mattered a lot to me. No, I'm real dissatisfied. I don't know what I want to do. Now I'm having a baby by choice, and that's nice, but it certainly prevents me from reentering the work world for a long time.

Despite the range of their views, most of the women I interviewed felt that their careers would be better with the MBA than they would have been without it. Their opinions varied about not only how satisfied they were, but how far they would really be able to advance.

The Myths Persist

Even as their own experience contradicted the myths of Ms. MBA and the egalitarian workplace, many women still based their interpretations of their careers and consequently their strategies on those myths. Dr. Phyllis Schlesinger, who has taught women MBAs and studied middle-level women managers, was one of a number of observers who confirmed my findings:

> They don't anticipate any problems. . . . They feel very well trained, that they can leap tall buildings with single bounds. They think that they are really going to be judged on their merits— performance rather than personal skills, political skills. They haven't been in the workforce long enough to know that there is a lot that goes into making performance happen.

Several told me that their employers were very fair to women or that their working environments were supportive. But they could cite little substantiating evidence, such as the presence of more than a token number of women in top jobs, equal access to special training programs or assignments, provisions for child care, or management focus on women's contributions and concerns. They were often surprised to hear the results of studies comparing male and female MBAs' career patterns.

Women MBAs are trained to seek out and analyze data, but almost none of them had done any research concerning their own probable career pattern. The material would probably be just as surprising to many faculty members and administrators as it was to women themselves. Not only were the women I interviewed unfamiliar with the data that could help them assess their futures; in some cases they were often actively averse to that information.

Because the power structure in the organizations where most worked is clearly male dominated, they did not see what could be gained by associating themselves with other relatively powerless women. They cast their lot with the system in the expectation that it would treat them well, rather than recognizing themselves as outsiders who need each other's insights, information, and support.

Few have male MBAs working side by side where comparisons are possible. They match themselves instead against other women, and see that they are making more money. They observe a large volume of women at the entry level, which encourages them, and just enough token women farther up to give them hope. They see all the events around them as single, random happenings with no past or present context. They read success stories that feed their aspirations. For these women, who have no faith in strategies to change the system, the alternative to the myth of the egalitarian workplace is despair.

More Pessimistic Orientations

In contrast to those who clung to the fond hope that everything had changed for women in the egalitarian workplace, some women held a more pessimistic view. They did not suppose that the men in power in the workplace would give women a boost up the ladder. They had learned to expect resistance. These women made the best of what they saw as a difficult, if not impossible, situation using three major orientations: being thankful for what they had, curtailing their aspirations to fit what was possible, and putting their energy into traditional female caring identities. They saw the situation with a jaundiced eye and found ways to feel successful and competent despite limited opportunities.

Some women were simply thankful for what they had achieved, rather than aspiring to further career development. Compared to other women, they felt that they were doing well. Some had gone considerably beyond the boundaries of what they had thought would be possible for them, attaining management positions rather than being stuck in secretarial or other lower-paid roles.

A woman whose mother worked in a textile factory for nonunion wages may well be satisfied with a low-paid clerical job: it is clean, the conditions are better, the pay is higher and includes Social Security. Similarly, women with MBAs who expected their lives to follow the traditional pattern may be thankful indeed to be independent and making more than $20,000 a year. It is difficult to sustain a sense of injustice when you are in the top percentages of employed women in terms of income.

Some women also coped by deflating their concept of success to what they perceived as possible. One who doubts whether she will ever be able to get past a certain point can either live with perpetual discontent or decide that she has gone as far as she wants to. In taking the latter course, she can simply declare victory and celebrate rather than wring her hands over her long-term career goals and try to fight the system.

Back to the Home

The most surprising orientation to me was the reassertion of women's traditional identities. Some women MBAs who saw the system as intractable retreated into the sphere where they knew they could be successful. In caring for others they not only had more power than they had in organizations, but they were often more appreciated and admired in society. Rather than continue to play a game they could not win, they looked for satisfaction in the same places where women have traditionally been permitted to excel.

Unchanged roles outside the workplace directly stall women's careers. Listen to this woman, talking in her backyard on a sunny fall morning with her two small children playing nearby:

> Maybe we got caught up in being successful and having careers so we did our thing until we had children—and then it's so clear to us what's important and what's not.

She went on to reveal something that may underlie other women's choices to put more energy into their families, a traditionally approved area where they can play a vital and responsible role:

> I have not met much failure in my career. I also have not been terribly committed to it. One way of not failing is not to be terribly committed, with all your eggs in one basket. I guess I've always felt that I could go as far as I wanted. Maybe because I don't think I ever want to go that far because of what it means giving up in my family and personal life.

How often does a sense of the possibility of career mobility rely on a woman's restricting her aspirations and pouring energy into the one arena where success is assured for her? Taken in the aggregate, individual and apparently private decisions about having children and caring for them in certain ways may reverse the trend toward higher aspirations for women. They may represent a return to more traditional female identity after a relatively short period of deviance.

To say that women choose to give priority to care-giving ignores the importance of conditioning from birth and the almost total lack of support from society at large to spread caring functions more evenly and collectively, as well as the minuscule changes that most fathers and other male partners have made in sharing responsibility for these tasks. All women's lives are influenced by the traditional roles and expectations, not just those of married women. This is not only because every woman is expected to care for others (be they parents, friends, lovers, or whomever), but because they measure themselves against Mom as well as Ms. MBA. It is not surprising that, in the face of a workplace where prospects are at best uncertain, women play the game they know they can win.

Only a Matter of Time—Or Is It?

Some women, then, were considerably more pessimistic about their career prospects than others. How did their assessments hold up to the realities?

Among those who believed the egalitarian workplace myths, some were conscious of sex discrimination in the past. They often believed that it had been eradicated by a well-meaning system as soon as the error of its ways was made apparent. According to that view, it is only a matter of time until women attain half of the highest positions in the land, since they are in the pipeline.

Unless there is a major cultural and historic upheaval, the overall impact of the MBA on women's careers and progress in management is predictable—and not encouraging. The evidence against the egalitarian workplace, and the pipeline theory that supports it, is both contemporary and historic. The experiences of women reported here, and the other studies of women MBAs speak for themselves. They reflect a reality that is illustrated in the popular press; for example, although women hold seats on the boards of less than 1 percent of all publicly held corporations, in 1982 the *Wall Street Journal* reported that firms were adding them more slowly than they had during the 1970s push for affirmative action.[1] Even where women are directors, often they do not hold influential posts on the boards to which they belong.[2]

Looking at less exalted roles in just one industry, purchasing, a 1983 survey of almost 6,000 people (919 women) showed that education was not the answer for women. It found that women MBAs made an average $30,000, the same as men without degrees, while male MBAs averaged $42,000.[3] Although banking is often thought of as a very receptive field for women, only 2 percent of senior-level bank executives are women, the same percentage as in 1953.[4] These and other statistical data toll the death knell of the hope and expectation that male colleagues would be increasingly accepting of women in new roles in the workplace as their numbers increased. Studies by Harlan and Weiss showed that resistance actually rose when women appeared in more than token numbers.[5]

Once they have moved up the ladder to a certain point, women take the possibility of discrimination more seriously. In a survey of 600 top women executives by Korn/Ferry International (a search firm), almost two in five felt that their sex was the greatest obstacle to their career advancement.[6] The tiny numbers of women being sponsored for executive MBA programs is an index of how their potential for senior management is rated: the Harvard Advanced Management Program included only 6 women out of 158 students in 1984.[7]

Results of Long-term Studies

The evidence presented in long-term studies of women MBAs' careers supports the apprehensions of the less satisfied women rather than the optimism of those who felt certain that their hard work would pay off in a top job one day. The findings of the few studies that exist comparing female and male MBAs' career patterns are discouragingly consistent. While a few others may have been completed by the time you read this book, the basic trends are unlikely to change. The current literature and the data being collected by business schools themselves reflect so little interest in gender issues that there is scant hope that better information will be collected and analyzed extensively over time. The research to date is the only actual evidence about what happens to women MBAs, as opposed to popular speculation that it is the key to success. Major studies conducted as of this writing involve MBAs from Harvard, Stanford, Columbia, Wharton, Temple, the University of Chicago, and a few other schools.

Dollars and Cents

While studies varied somewhat in methodology, they all explored differences in salary and advancement between women and men, and explanations for those differences.* Notwithstanding some contradictions among the findings, the overall pattern is clear. Even with the ultimate credential, the Harvard MBA, the gap in pay and responsibility between women and their male counterparts only widened over time.[8] Ten to fifteen years after earning the degree (enough time to reach upper middle management), Harvard women MBAs made 59¢ for every dollar a Harvard man made, about the same wage gap confronted by women in the general workforce. They also occupied jobs at lower hierarchical levels than their male counterparts.**

If the Harvard study documents that a Goldmine degree is no vaccination against discrimination, the Columbia data[9] on matched pairs of forty five women and forty five men graduates from 1969 to 1972 dispose of

---

*Salaries for MBAs depend on many factors. Some industries pay better than others; for example, consulting and investment banking rank far ahead of commercial banking and accounting firms (which are two of the top three employers of women MBAs). A glance at actual job functions also shows similar disparities between women's and men's salaries, with consulting and planning leading the pack. Certain parts of the country provide better salaries, with metropolitan areas paying more than rural locations. Comparisons among different schools always cause gnashing of teeth among the Generic graduates, who cannot expect the entry salary of $34,672 received by 1984 University of Chicago graduates.

**Women today might discredit these findings because they apply to women reared in a more traditional style, at a time when the workplace was less responsive to women in management. Those factors may well have been counterbalanced by the fact that women at that time must have been extraordinarily bright and motivated to go to Harvard at all, much less graduate.

several other myths: that women are paid less because they have less experience or education than men; that women are paid less because they choose different majors in business school than men; that women are paid just as well as men if they enter the same industries; and that women are less motivated or committed to their careers than men. What had emerged after a decade was a significant difference in the average salaries paid women and men in different industry sectors, plus a large wage gap between the sexes in manufacturing, the highest-paid sector. Thus as the study points out, women's choice of a particular industry did not cause them to be paid less; the problem was unequal treatment within that industry.

Similarly, the Stanford study[10] of 26 women and 150 men from the 1974 class documented the wage gap and eliminated another handful of fallacies about why women MBAs are paid less than men. It showed that school grades, job changes, training, travel, employees supervised, line rather than staff positions, and having mentors all failed to explain why women make less money. In addition to the difference in pay, a gap in responsibility was implied by the fact that more than three times as many men as women had the authority to approve expenditures over $100 (13 percent of women and 43 percent of men).

Sad to say, these women had learned to cut their aspirations down to the size of what they could expect. Right after graduation, the peak salary they hoped for was about 60 percent of what men hoped for. By 1978, after exposure to the realities of the workplace for four years, their salary aspirations had declined to 40 percent of men's. Their ambitions also show a gap: half of the men as opposed to only a quarter of the women expected to achieve a top management job (owner, partner, president, CEO).

A comparative look at 500 female and male graduates of Wharton (a Goldmine school) and Temple (a Generic school)[11] from 1976 to 1980 shows that 47.8 percent of the men earn $35,000 and up compared to 24.5 percent of the women. Just under one-half of all Wharton graduates make over $35,000 while just over one-fourth of all Temple graduates do. Thus gender differences approximate the well-documented contrast among Goldmine and Generic schools.

When researchers called ten graduates from each University of Western Ontario Business School class from 1976 to 1982, they found the same pattern as the other studies. Seventy-one women and 70 men were interviewed, and there were great disparities in the jobs they held. Thirty-nine percent of the women were still in "low" management levels, compared to only 11 percent of the men. At the other end of the scale, five times as many men as women had attained senior management posts (26% as opposed to 5%).[12]

Finally, only one study (in 1977) attempted to take both race and sex into account as explanations for the wage gap,[13] comparing a tiny sample of thirteen women MBAs to their male counterparts. Black women MBAs who went to predominantly black schools actually started work at less than $10,000 a year! They fell behind black men in all categories. The available research ignores class even more than race.

Unlike the data discussed so far, which pertain only to graduates of particular schools, the Association of MBA Executives' Career and Salary Survey[14] of 1980 graduates (the most recent complete information) casts a wider net. In twenty nine of thirty three industries they examined, men's starting salaries were higher than women's. In three of the four remaining fields, the annual difference was less than $150.[15] The widest gaps were in the instruments industry, where women made $3,668 less than men; in government and nonprofit organizations, where professional female employment is usually higher than in industry (a $3,435 difference); and in consulting firms ($3,053).[16]

There is some anomalous evidence from a few studies conducted on very specific groups. A study of University of Chicago graduates[17] from 1969 to 1976 deviates slightly. It showed that, although the mean starting salary for women rose steadily over that period, the overall effect of being female was to depress the level at which one was hired. The Business and Professional Women's Foundation studied recipients of their loan program that helps women attend business school[18] and found that women did gain financially compared to their earlier jobs, although no comparisons were made to male MBAs. The group selected for the loans was already earning significantly more than most women in the workplace, however, and they all attended top institutions because, as the program director told me, the foundation has to get its money back.

Finally, a study of graduates of the Sloan School at MIT, conducted by the eminent economist Dr. Phyllis Wallace, is less unpromising than most of the other evidence about women's salaries.[19] Comparing 62 women and 115 men over a five-year period after graduation, she and her collaborators found that factors other than sex accounted for the $2,700 difference between men's salaries and women's.[20] They hasten to point out, however, that women work longer hours and pay a higher personal cost to earn the same money.[21] Regardless of the dollar amount of compensation, "We have reason to doubt that females and males are treated the same at work."[22]

It is, of course, possible that these data are genuinely out of keeping with the earlier studies and that women graduating from Sloan from 1975–1979 are not seeing sex discrimination in their salaries. Other explanations are also possible: the women graduated in the heyday of affirmative action and may have launched their careers in a favorable time from one of the best possible bases. They were rare birds indeed when they graduated. No information is provided about their earlier fields of specialty, but it would be surprising if most did not have technical or engineering backgrounds, which would make them rarer still. Moreover, the percentage of women in the classes studied must have been small indeed; in 1975 they were just over 10 percent[23], which means that they would have to have been considerably more motivated and qualified than their male counterparts. Whatever the explanation, the finding that women have to work harder to end up with salaries only slightly below men's and are under more stress while doing it is hardly encouraging.

Women MBAs Are Still Women Workers

Overall, the studies of women MBAs fall in line with general patterns for professional women and current data about all women workers. No matter what their field or era, women earn less and occupy less responsible positions than men, regardless of training or length of service.

The well-publicized wage gap between women and men cuts across all occupations, with the result that women with five or more years of college make one dollar less a week than men who did not even graduate from high school. Whether they are engineers making $479 a week to men's $592, or managers and administrators making $309 to men's $507, women's predicament is the same.[24] Even if there were no studies specifically of women MBAs to show that they are paid less than men and occupy less responsible jobs, those trends could be predicted from the evidence about other women workers. The patterns for women MBAs are unlikely to be different, especially at a time when opportunities for everyone in management are constricting and when opportunities for women in particular are no longer being pushed.

As much as they may wish that their MBAs could give them immunity from wider market forces, women may have to pay attention to trends like the greater frequency of wage discrimination against young white women in 1980 than in 1970. The Census Bureau found that, although women's credentials were improving, more of the gap between the sexes than ever could be accounted for by discrimination.[25]

Looking at the history of women moving into male occupations in the past, it is clear that pay, recognition, and opportunities drop when women enter a field. Women were specifically recruited as teachers, for example, when school boards wanted to save money. As is generally the case in female-dominated occupations, men hold a disproportionate number of the administrative and other top posts to which teaching can lead; the low pay and recognition of teachers relative to other professionals is a commonplace. The history of secretaries and librarians is much the same. I was not able to find a single example of a male-dominated field becoming feminized that did not follow the classic pattern.

The Home Front

Even if women MBAs were the exception to the rules that govern other women workers historically and currently, and even if there were no evidence that they are not progressing as well as their male peers, their careers would be slowed because their identities outside the workplace are virtually unchanged. Unequal responsibilities outside the job hamper them more profoundly than simply subtracting a certain number of hours from their days. They also reinforce the notions that women are made for caring and sexual functions. The power structure of most organizations is heavily dominated by middle-class men, the bulk of whom are married and few of whom share domestic responsibilities. These men arrive in the workplace with certain expectations of women. A man whose clothing has been picked up from the dry-cleaner, whose toilet has been cleaned, and whose breakfast has been cooked can hardly be expected to have the same attitude toward female subordinates as he does toward other men for whom those things are done. The full-time secretary whose major purpose is to smooth his life at the office, as his wife does at home, reinforces the idea that women's purpose is to serve. Whatever qualifications they have, in his eyes they are women first.

In fact, even if men treated them identically in the office, women still would not have the same career course as men. As long as women continue to accept the pressures of traditional female roles and of the new demands to succeed in the workplace as well, they will put themselves under tremendous stresses that cannot help but affect their careers. Often, they find little time to plan and organize their futures because they are under the gun of the moment.

Some of the women I interviewed questioned the wisdom of trying to do it all, but only a few pressed partners and others to share their responsibilities. Instead, they changed their own schedules, cut some tasks out, or shifted gears to a lower-profile career. They considered taking time off when they had babies or switching to part-time work. It is unclear how women are affected in the workplace by such decisions, but it is difficult to believe that they are not hindered in comparison to the fully serviced males. Such men are perceived as 100 percent dedicated because they often spend more hours in the workplace, participate in social activities related to the job, and are freely available for travel and special assignments.

When women arrive in the workplace, most have already performed hours of unpaid work or arranged for another woman to do it. These responsibilities cannot be shed at the threshold of the office. Ironically, however, the myth of the egalitarian workplace maintains that all doors are open to women, as though the workplace existed in isolation from the rest of society. Women are told to pay their dues, that they cannot expect rewards without sacrifices. They are like farm horses who must plow from dawn until midnight, and are suddenly told to compete with racehorses who have been prepared and urged toward that goal every day of their lives. As long as their roles at home are intact, they are necessarily at a disadvantage compared to men, in organizations constructed to reward those whose lives are more one-dimensional.

How Women Coped with the Realities

Regardless of their orientations to their careers, women's behavior was remarkably similar in several ways. They rarely planned for the long haul, perceiving and seizing on opportunities as well as creating them; the optimists often expected the system to take care of them, and the more pessimistic had often given up on planning because they did not expect it to work. In their daily behavior, women fell into some common traps: they individualized their experience, believing that every event was happening only randomly and to them, with no current or past context; they personalized the events that affected them, believing that they were to blame or praise for everything that occurred; and they disassociated themselves from other women workers. Ms. MBA is often presented as a liberated woman—ambitious, with her own income, working with numbers, and occupying historically male jobs—but there are respects in which the women I interviewed fulfilled and even reinforced traditional stereotypes.

Women take a classically passive stance with respect to their careers when they either accept the rules as given and slavishly try to play by them, or when they opt out by declaring victory or putting their energy into being Mom or Mrs. Many women I interviewed were attempting to occupy a new spot in the workplace without substantially altering their identities outside it, whether they were married or not. By feeding historic expectations of women, they undermined the climate for all women to succeed within the workplace.

A Separate Peace

The exceptional successes of a few women who slipped through the system into senior posts reinforce the hope that a woman can make a separate peace with the hierarchy. Such examples encourage others to think that the way to get ahead is to ignore their basic predicament—historic, systemic discrimination that is not going to evaporate, combined with virtually unchanged responsibilities outside the workplace. Denying the commonality of their experience as women perpetuates fragmentation and prevents them from organizing some effective, positive strategies on behalf of themselves and others. When eighteen men and one woman are selected for management slots, there is little chance of change as long as each rejected individual is muttering and cursing only to herself, blaming herself, and trying to play by the rules. The rules that determine who has access to power were designed to forge certain bonds among particular men, relying not only on obvious links like going to the same schools, but on a wealth of common male experiences, including relating to women in certain ways. It is not surprising that the rules for men do not work for women: they were designed to keep everyone other than an exclusive group out.

Women emulate men at their peril. Unless a woman can look beyond the confines of her individual situation to see the larger forces at work and make use of the experiences of women who preceded her and who surround her, the dominant current of the labor market will probably sweep her away into stagnation. The hierarchy as it stands is firmly entrenched; women who attempt to establish themselves in it one by one are unlikely to succeed in more than token numbers. Their individualism is much more likely to serve the system's interests than their own. Far from challenging the system, women MBAs reinforce the current distribution of power in organizations when they pursue their careers individually, whether by playing by the rules or by opting out. At worst, their presence legitimizes the structure and gives the appearance of progress without the substance.

Admitting large numbers of women at entry is a new variation on tokenism: by flooding the bottom ranks with women, an employer can give a show of progress while changing very little. Flooding can benefit employers significantly, since they have access to a trained pool of women who are still more highly selected than their male counterparts. The net effect for the system is a supply of highly motivated, well-trained women who are willing to keep working in hopes of rewards one day or to settle for a career plateau. As long as even a few are promoted, the rest will be relatively undemanding if they continue to be persuaded that they can only make it on their own.

Women's presence in token numbers at the top and in profusion at the bottom lends credence to the idea that all other women workers have to do to succeed is to get more qualifications. The woman MBA is set up as a model for others to emulate, as though the fundamental problem were the lack of a degree rather than the system that has channeled them into certain jobs and roles. By feeding false hopes, the myth of Ms. MBA has a much more far-reaching effect than simply persuading some women to go to business school. It also inflates the aspirations of those who do not go. Because the system appears fairer than it used to, women may blame themselves more than ever for their lack of progress.

Is the MBA Right for You?

The experiences of the women described here and others who have been studied show that the MBA does not produce the same results for them as for men. Glib assurances that women will reach senior management if they just wait long enough are invalid whether they are weighed against history, statistics, or common sense about women's lives outside of work.

Where does this leave a woman who is trying to decide whether to earn an MBA? How does she know if it is right for her? There is no automatic answer. It is an appropriate degree for some women in some circumstances, but it is by no means right for everyone. The general statements about MBAs, when positive, usually apply less to women than to men; when negative (such as the evidence of a glut), they often apply more to women than to men. The MBA should only be sought by women who have reflected about themselves and who have researched the evidence that it would be a verifiably necessary step toward their particular career goal. Those who are unsure about what is next and want the degree to make their minds up for them are likely to be disappointed.

No matter how much the women I interviewed benefited from the degree, they found that it guaranteed nothing. Dean Maryann Billington of Northeastern University put it succinctly: "The MBA does not make the difference. You do. The MBA can help you make the difference." The degree provided knowledge, a perspective, and more or less credibility; however, it could not set a woman's goals for her or find her a job. It could clothe but not conceal her past experience, which might or might not be compatible with her new career goals. It did not set her on a predictable path to fame and fortune, nor did it protect her from working in routine jobs where she was underemployed, from being laid off or even fired, or from being passed over for promotion and other opportunitites.

What can you expect from the MBA? A foot in the door, maybe. Unfortunately, it might not be your best foot that you put forward, and the door might open into stagnation rather than opportunity. If you enter business school confused about your own goals and whether the MBA might help, you will come out stuffed with new facts and techniques, but you still may not know what to do with them. As an end in itself, the MBA can be a trap. But if you know what you want and calculate the pros and cons in advance, the MBA can be a useful, sometimes an indispensable, means to an end.

The best that the MBA can do for a woman is to provide her with some new knowledge and skills, and a perspective on organizational issues and structures that she can take with her wherever she goes. Learning the language of business and knowing how the game is played cannot help but stand her in good stead in a country where business is the major institution. She may well gain confidence from her degree, and if it comes from a legitimate school, it does give her more credibility in the eyes of some employers. Perhaps most important, the MBA gives access to the network of alumni from the same school, and particularly although not exclusively for Goldmine graduates, that can be a great asset. As discussed below, there are some jobs and situations for which the MBA is quite simply a prerequisite. Any woman who does not already have the background is bound to learn a lot from business school, and at the end she will have a degree everyone has at least heard of.

When Is the MBA Probably Appropriate?

An MBA is appropriate:

- To legitimize what a woman with business knowledge and experience already knows, but only if she is trying to move up in an environment where the competition has MBAs, and does not have her age working strongly against her.

- To aim high in the corporate world, if she is starting now and is working in industries where all the new promotions are to MBAs (as opposed to the founders, who may have no formal education at all).

- To provide access to entry-level jobs in certain fields or companies, especially if she has no business background.

It is worth considerable research to verify that the area you are interested in actually requires an MBA. While there is constant change regarding who requires which credentials, some of the fields that usually do demand the degree are corporate finance, health administration, investment banking, securities analysis, and management consulting. It seems to be less important in retail firms, insurance, advertising, sales, and commercial banking. Certain companies may require an MBA, while the majority of firms in the same industry do not; a Goldmine MBA discovered that the publishing firm where she wanted to work demanded not only the degree, but that it be earned from a particular school. For her and others, the most critical decision was whether to go to Generic or Goldmine.

How Do I Determine Whether to Go to Generic or Goldmine?

Should you go to a Generic or a Goldmine school? First, do not even consider most unaccredited programs, unless your purpose is purely to attain skills and you are convinced that the school can provide them. If you want to aim high in the business world, unquestionably you should go if possible to a Goldmine school to increase your odds, although it guarantees nothing. For everyone else, accredited Generic programs that fit the person and the situation can be an excellent choice when:

- They are specialized to meet the needs of a particular business community and have a good track record of placement.

- You plan to go into business for yourself and want skills together with three respectable but not stunning letters.

- Your employer is sponsoring you.

- You have a strong business background and are trying to use the degree to legitimize what you already know.

Do not assume that a Goldmine degree is automatically better than a Generic one. There are all kinds of reasons it might be unsuitable for you: the high pressure and exclusivity in some Goldmine schools, perhaps the necessity for a geographic move, or an intimidating atmosphere than can be particularly undermining to women. Be realistic about what you want: you do not have to accept the value system that says Goldmine is always superior to Generic. For you, with your particular personality, background, situation and goals, it may not be.

In terms of quality of education, a solid Generic program that is well suited to your purpose will probably do as well as or better than a Goldmine school. For all the mystique, much of the difference is labeling rather than substance. While Goldmine degrees may be rare in your circle of acquaintances, in the world of work they are remarkably commonplace. Thousands of persons already have them, and in the course of your working life the numbers will swell even more dramatically. Do not fall into the trap of thinking a Goldmine degree will make you unique: it won't. It will, however, connect you to a powerful network of alumni and, if you are an effective self-promoter, guarantee you a hearing in interviews you might not otherwise obtain. Some companies only consider Goldmine graduates.

It is tempting to say that women who least fit the MBA mold should get the "best" credentials they can, but it does not always work that way. For a woman with a strong sense of direction who has evaluated her situation and needs thoroughly, a Goldmine MBA may pay off. It may mitigate her race, age, class, sexual identity, or disability, but it does not alter the fundamental nature of the obstacles she faces or cancel them out, just as the MBA does not alter gender. It is no substitute for motivation, clearheadedness, and sound advance research. A woman with those strengths may well find that a Generic program will serve her purposes adequately.

Steps toward a Good Decision

In considering whether you should get an MBA, do not limit yourself because you think you cannot deal with numbers or business concepts. Allow for the fact that most women and girls are actively discouraged from cultivating those intellectual abilities from birth. It is surprising that some have slipped through the net to become so capable. If your left arm had been tied to your body all your life, it would not have grown; why should your math or business abilities be any different? Give yourself a chance to find out what you can do; approach it cautiously by taking one course at a time. If you really hate it, stop, but you may well surprise yourself, as many women before you have done.

Women who are averse to the world of business should not automatically eliminate the MBA, as so many programs apply to nonprofits, health care, arts, and other specialties. Most of the women I talked to had pursued their field, whatever it was, because of positive human values: a real desire to be of service in some way or to make people's lives better. They did not fit the stereotype of the hard-nosed, self-interested career woman at all.

Like any other major career decision, the MBA should be approached cautiously. Many small steps must be taken before a final decision is made: collecting information from printed sources and from other people (both MBA graduates and persons at business schools), doing research about financial aid, taking the GMATs, and so on. By observing the promptness with which you execute those steps and whether they feel like torture or a pleasure, you can begin to assess whether the MBA is a good choice. Informing yourself as widely as possible means talking both to those who enjoyed business school and those who hated it, those who went to a variety of programs, and those who succeeded in the fields by different routes. A certificate program takes less time and may serve your purpose.

You may find better ways to advance your career, especially if you have a start in business. A lawyer who had gone into commercial real estate with her MBA advised:

> I think a lot of women probably look at it in business journals and the newspapers, that the way to succeed is with the MBA. It's not always the case. It's not that it's not the way to succeed, it's just not always the most efficient or effective use of your time in your chosen field.

Women with well-established careers were often advised by those I interviewed not to bother with an MBA; they would probably be bored and find little of real benefit. One said:

> If you are already a woman who is at a salary matching those [MBA] entry-level salaries and are already in a good organization, what is the real benefit? Increased knowledge, certainly, but monetarily, will it make any difference to you? Money is not the only way you look at an education, but there is hard quantitative information that could be valuable.

Sometimes the more prestigious executive programs can give women what they need of the MBA coursework in a more painless form. Women at mid-career should examine the MBA particularly skeptically, whether they are changing fields or not. Some of the most frustrated women found that they could only get entry-level management jobs with their MBAs, despite significant prior experience. One said:

> I feel on the one hand that I've made a huge investment: five years and I haven't even counted up the money yet, but at least $20,000 or more. . . . I think being a mid-career person makes it much, much harder. . . . When you're older, I think you've got to think it through a lot more than I ever did. I hate to say it, but I think you do.

Credentials alone are not the answer, as the women I interviewed discovered time and again.

In addition to those in mid-career, others who should also approach the MBA with particular caution include those:

- Who lack a clear sense of career direction, and hope that the MBA will make their minds up for them. It may give you a display of the options, but no more.

- Who are trying to switch careers and have not tested the waters of business or the sphere they want to enter, either to see how they like it or how employers might react to their backgrounds.

- Who already have a solid undergraduate business degree and a start in their careers in a favorable environment.

- Who have a strike against them in addition to gender, particularly age.

Earning the MBA is a long, wearisome, expensive, and, for most women, stressful experience with an uncertain outcome. A woman with a Generic MBA with no prior business background expressed what some others had also told me:

> If you're like me, you're going to have to do so much work to get your foot in the door, even with the MBA, that you might as well do it without the MBA. You're going to have to do research, find out where your skills from the past fit into a major corporation, and get into that network.

Finally, do not assume that any MBA is better than none. A degree from an unaccredited program may actually do more harm than good: it puts you at the bottom of the pile of competing MBAs, whereas you might have been at the middle of the pile of entry-level businesspersons. If you are changing careers, the degree is nothing more than a launching pad, a blank staging area without the energy and everything else it takes to make things happen. A large-scale network effort and a few well-placed courses might well serve you better in the long run.

Test Your Interest

Testing your real interest in the subjects business schools teach can be approached in any number of ways: do not assume that you will find them fascinating. Read business periodicals and pages of the newspaper, browse in the local business school bookstore and library, and read through the curricula for some of the courses at schools you are interested in. If it does not excite you when you are dabbling in it, think how much worse it would be to spend years studying subjects you do not enjoy.

As you try to evaluate what good the MBA will do you, take a look at what you are expecting of yourself. Would you be trying to fulfill a traditional care-giving identity as well as taking on a full-time business school load, followed by a demanding job? How could some of your care-giving functions be shared with others, both inside and outside your household, to make the demands on you more reasonable? You may want to talk with some other women about how they have learned to delegate responsibilities.

No matter what you ultimately decide, you can only gain by building in support from other women who are going through the same process. You can help each other talk through the issues and help each other contend with the lack of confidence and direction that plague most women. Developing strategies to make decisions you can live with is an indispensable part of giving each other support.

Consider Alternatives

Looking for ways other than the MBA to meet your career goals can also be fruitful. The degree is a huge investment in many ways, and it should not be undertaken unless the alternatives have been thoroughly explored. If you intend to remain employed while going to school part time, the possible cost of neglecting your job may harm you more than the degree would help you, and you might do better to take on a new project at work or modify your job in some way. The MBA is not necessarily the best choice; if you are interested in some particular topic, try taking a course or two to see if that will fulfill your need.

For Those Who Have MBAs

What about women who already have MBAs? How should they approach their careers? To begin with, they should be fully informed about the realities of the workplace and about the myths that may still dominate their thinking. Working with others, they should not only exchange information and contacts, but establish realistic career goals and develop individual and joint strategies that can accomplish them. Rather than hoping that someone else will take care of their careers, they must plan a direction, building in a healthy recognition of the obstacles they will face, and a strategy to gain the support that can help to overcome them. Finally, women MBAs should challenge what they do not like about the way they are treated in the workplace, rather than assume that their careers will be better served if they behave themselves and play by the rules.

The importance of joint action cannot be overemphasized. Even social contact among women, the most innocuous connections, is indispensable in daily coping as well as in establishing and realizing long-term career goals. Making a vigorous commitment to helping women advance means more than a kind word here or there, important as that is. It also means attuning oneself in a serious way to the capabilities and aspirations another woman shows while she works and seeking areas where she might be able to develop herself. It means listening closely to her account of what is happening in her career and helping her dissect out the threads that may give her a clue to what can help her reach a new goal, or identify what that goal might be. While such support can always be exchanged in pairs, it is even more powerful when a larger group gets together, multiplying the information, contacts, and insights that are possible.

The process of career planning for women is made far more difficult because they have utterly confusing images behind and before them about what their career goals should be. On the one hand, they have the model of low-paid, dead-end jobs passed on by women of earlier generations. On the other they have the male model of success through a single-minded pursuit of career at all costs, made possible by a host of females providing services in the background. Before them is a fork in the road: one branch broad, cobbled, and worn by the footsteps of women over time; the other a narrow marble sidewalk with a border office where women must present their papers, swear that they will work ninety hours a week, and put work first, just like the men who have taken the same road. A few women can do just that and love it.

For most women, neither of these routes is appropriate. Those who try to smuggle babies past the customs officers are always found out eventually. On the other hand, the traditional route for women does not measure up to their rising expectations. They have been told that they can do anything they want, and if they do not take all the opportunities available to them, that is their fault. A few have succeeded in chopping out a path of their own that ultimately intersects with the marble route, but it is a risky business indeed. At best, it marks one woman's cleverness at slipping through, rather than an advance for all women.

Trying to plan careers in such a context challenges women's ingenuity. It is an art, not a science; if it is carried out with rigid exactitude it becomes a mechanical process that will probably be disappointing. The standard career-development formulas often do not fit women. Together, women can take into account the patterns they can expect their careers to take unless they make concerted efforts to the contrary.

While some compromise is necessary, some women go overboard and ignore their own values and priorities in favor of conforming to the organizational norms. Rather than accepting the system as it is as an absolute given and trying to work around it, women can and should find ways to challenge what they do not like. If the performance-appraisal system results in seven promotions for men and none for women who are well represented at the entry level, women should go beyond complaining to one another over a drink. Women MBAs, like other women, can only benefit from involving themselves in the broader women's movement. Who else can respond to the attacks on the laws and regulations that opened the doors of business school and management jobs to women? Only a concerted effort that cuts across occupational and other lines is likely to be successful. Many organizations already exist to work in that direction, and it is up to women MBAs to take an active role in them.

In addition to whatever other networks a woman forms, participation in professional organizations like those listed in the resources section is essential. They can help women build their professional expertise and challenge the underlying causes of some of their career dilemmas. Women in one organization may have found a way to influence company policy on sexual harassment, for example, while others may have initiated a new approach to career development training.

Whether they are entering organizations or being promoted within them, every woman should understand the context in which she is challenging the prevailing system by seeking fair pay. Knowing the overall patterns for women MBAs can motivate her to learn very specifically what others are being paid to do for her kind of work. Breaking the taboos and sharing information across organizations, as Chris Summers of the American Society of Women Accountants has suggested, is an essential first step. (Organizations like hers are listed in the resources section.) For women who do not belong to such clear professional groupings, exchanging information with classmates or with women and men in a broader network may be helpful. Professional newsletters can also compile information from members to help women evaluate where they are.

Beyond Negotiation

Knowing the trend of women MBAs' salaries and informing oneself about the situation in a particular field are important starting points. It does not help, though, unless a woman becomes confident that she actually deserves more pay and gets up the courage to ask for it firmly and effectively, neither of which can be done in isolation. While women can and should improve their negotiating skills, there are limits to that strategy. Women MBAs today do not have the encouragement of a favorable political and social climate. The return to traditional family values and attacks on women's gains in the workplace can only undermine an individual woman's career, no matter how exceptional she considers herself to be. Only as the tide becomes fully reversed will she realize that the miles she swam before were covered with powerful assistance.

Every woman MBA who is underpaid might equip herself with a full briefcase of facts supporting her case, perfect her communications skills, and deliver a dazzling performance in interviews and negotiations. Many would still not be hired at an appropriate level or be promoted in keeping with their abilities. Some would be, and all would have a better possibility than they would otherwise. But until women address the broader issues of employer attitudes and practices, and how those are permitted and encouraged by current national policies, any individual solutions to the wage gap can have only limited effects.

Women who try to ascend the ladder one by one can only aspire to become another exception, rather than changing the rules that apply to them all. Ironically, their very entry into business schools and management jobs is the result of just such basic changes, brought about by women working together after decades of trying to crack the system one by one. The result was a thin scattering of exceptional women at the bottom, until the civil rights and women's movements forced changes in law and social policy. The result is the tens of thousands of young women in entry-level management jobs today. Once again, many of them seem to be repeating the heritage of trying to make it as individuals, with the same results as women who tried to move into organizations on their own: a thin scattering of exceptional women at the top.

If women are to narrow the wage gap between themselves and men— and the gap in power and responsibility it represents—they can do so only by expanding their concerns beyond their individual careers. While a few women slip through to top management as exceptions, real change in women's access to senior as well as entry jobs must be affirmed by women who are organized and ready to support one another, challenge employers, and affect social policy. They must do more than just exchange business cards and telephone numbers. Paradoxically, individual career progress depends more than ever on women's ability to look beyond their own situations, see beneath the apparently benevolent surface of the workplace that calls itself egalitarian, and take action together, making way for women at the top, just as others made way for them at the bottom.

Eight

Postscript

What can those concerned about equal opportunity in the workplace learn from the experiences of women MBAs, and what should we do next? Whether we are scholars, activists, researchers, advocates, counselors, or others, we must assess the results of women's access to the MBA on the basis of more solid information about them. The outcomes for individual women have often, although not invariably, been financially rewarding, and a few have attained positions of real power. The structure of opportunities appears to have been changed little.

Whatever those realities are for women MBAs themselves, the myth of Ms. MBA reaches into the general population of women workers. It supports the notion that any woman who has not succeeded on her own, having armed herself with the necessary male credentials, has only herself to blame. In a larger sense, the myth feeds the illusion that there has been enormous progress for women in general. Because a minute proportion of the female population can attend Goldmine business schools, the opportunities available to them become the aspirations, even the standards, of the many. Generalizations about how far women have come are based on the exception rather than the rule. Overall, the focus on success stories of MBAs deflects attention from the plight of most women workers and supports the myth of the egalitarian workplace. The significance of access to the MBA for women as a group is also open to question because those who have earned it have not, by and large, allied themselves either with each other or with women workers generally.

Why has the movement of women into business schools had such mixed results for women as a group, whatever it may have done for individuals? The strategy of working toward equal opportunity for women, and hence redistribution of power in the workplace, by making women more qualified is fundamentally a conservative one. It takes the system at its word, that it will value, recognize, and promote women just like men if they get MBAs (or Ph.Ds, or some other credential). Thus the strategy is based on the fallacy that the system is basically fair. It also ignores the intricacy and rootedness of the systems maintaining gender differences in the workplace. Now that women are qualified but not advancing significantly, the informal systems and relationships that enforce those differences are becoming more apparent.

The charged relationships between the sexes, inside and outside the workplace, remain and deserve far more attention than they have had, by activists, researchers, and others, particularly in examining the interaction between the world outside the organization and that within it. Because of what women are off the job, there are qualifications that they cannot earn at school, no matter where they go and no matter what degree they pursue. The formula for equal opportunity must be far more complex and precise in its components and measures than most current approaches, attending to subtler aspects of the system. It must address a deeper level of power relationships between women and men, relationships that are configured outside the workplace as well as within it.

If there is one lesson to be relearned from the experience of the influx of women MBAs, it is the infinite adaptability of the existing power structure. Women have entered the system in great numbers, but find themselves as blocked as ever, albeit at a higher level. Once again, they are found wanting according to a male model of success. Failure is built in. While women are stymied by impossible demands, the existing system may actually be strengthened by their entry into its lower ranks.

Unfortunately, at least as striking as the power structure's flexibility are the new guises of socially induced feminine characteristics. Many MBAs I interviewed confound stereotypes about women as unmathematical, incapable of working in a high-pressured business environment, unambitious, or uninterested in the technical side of their jobs. Yet their individualistic orientation, self-blame, low self-esteem, and continued efforts to "do it all" were discouragingly familiar.

As a first step, real efforts must be made to make women in business school become more aware of what they will be up against, and to facilitate their initiating their own means of organizing to promote both awareness and action on specific barriers. Women's associations are an excellent starting point for mutual support and accountability. They must carry over into the workplace if women are to provide one another with a real alternative to allying themselves fully with the power structure.

Women MBAs have to develop and publicize ways to survive in an unsupportive organizational context, while challenging its values and seeking to transform them. Certainly those challenges should apply in obvious areas such as personnel policies toward child care, but they can reach issues like how to market to changing families or integrating a less driven model of the executive into the organizational culture. Unfortunately, women MBAs often see capitulation as their only choice. They need insight and strategy from those who are working toward equal opportunities, or they will probably continue to see no alternatives to the system as it stands. It is vital that they be educated to act on the broader issues for women in the workplace to see how their own careers are affected by them. Only on that basis will they become more active in supporting the overall social and political changes that make strategies in individual situations possible.

The larger question of female solidarity and how it can be fostered and maintained in an unsympathetic setting deserves much more attention than it has had thus far, as does the question of how women relate to one another across workplace roles and occupations. How can women be made accountable to one another in the context of a structure where they are relatively powerless, which they have entered specifically in order to gain power? Network programs cannot stop simply at teaching women to emulate men and telling them why they are not playing the game right; they must help women learn specifically how to support one another and find ways to change at least some of what they do not like in their working environments rather than simply accepting it.

The findings presented in this book, even taken in combination with all the prior work on women MBAs, are incomplete. They suggest far more areas of research that need to be explored. Among the most important are more data on the women themselves, an examination of the ones who are missing in business schools (both students who drop out and women who do not become faculty), and a description of the nature of discrimination in the workplace that calls itself egalitarian.

Data on Women MBAs

At best, the data on women MBAs are thin. Both qualitative and quantitative data are needed about a much fuller range of women than has usually been studied. In particular, information is needed about the work women are actually doing, and the ways they are being segregated. The MBA occupations are probably being reshaped as a result of women's entry in large numbers. They should be examined closely for the patterns that have occurred when other male fields have become feminized, to see where women are concentrated, and which functions they are performing more frequently than men. The lower status and recognition that accompany women's entry in numbers in any occupation should be investigated and, if appropriate, substantiated.

Women's impact on their workplaces has yet to be examined, especially in light of changing roles in entry-level management. In what ways are women conforming to organizational models and rules as they stand, and in what ways are they challenging these and bringing new issues to the fore? The efforts some women are making to manage differently require documentation, particularly those that involve new models of cooperation and employee development. A close look at how their entry in many capacities has affected the opportunity structure would draw out further information.

Missing Women in Business Schools

Much can be learned about the milieu of business schools by looking at the women who are absent as well as those who are present. I was told that a substantial fraction of women MBA candidates drop out, especially of the better-known programs. By asking why they decided to withdraw, researchers could get a better sense of the obstacles overcome by women who persisted, and the conditions they felt they had to accept.

The virtual absence of women faculty also bears investigation. The mechanisms by which women are excluded would probably be unsurprising in light of other studies of women faculty, but the particular pressures in business school would be worth exploring. Considering the advantages of university employment—flexible hours, summers off, and the lure of a traditional role in teaching—the forces pushing women in the opposite direction must be powerful indeed. Defining exactly what they are and how they operate would be a first step to overcoming them.

Discrimination in the Workplace

A full description of the nature of discrimination in the so-called egalitarian workplace is essential. Women knew what to look for when they were almost absent from the power structure, and when antiwoman behavior was rampant and obvious. Now, a typology of signals and invisible systems is needed to help them be as alert as possible. Descriptions are required of the ever more subtle ways that women are excluded and of effective tactics against them. Data are also essential to show how the level of discrimination is related to women MBAs' presence in both traditionally female industries and in areas in which they are more novel. Qualitative data would be useful to show the many ways they handle the disjuncture between the myths and their own lived reality.

Overarching these areas of possible strategy and research is the question of how identical treatment in admitting women to business school and to entry-level jobs came to be accepted as equal opportunity to progress. From the point of view of trying to change power relationships between the sexes in the workplace, the most basic questions are how have women become convinced that the battle against sex discrimination has already been won, so that collective action is unnecessary and inappropriate, and how can their resulting collusion with the present system be counteracted? If it is not, women in management will not only repeat the past, but will do so in the name of progress.

Notes

Chapter 1

1. Myra Strober, "The MBA: Same Passport to Success for Women and Men?" in *Women in the Workplace,* ed. Phyllis Wallace (Boston, Mass.: Auburn House Publishing Co., 1982), 25–44.
2. Elaine F. Weiss. "To B-School or Not to B-School?" *Savvy,* December 1983, 37.
3. Ibid.
4. David Clark Scott, "What Is the Worth of an MBA?" *Christian Science Monitor,* 4 September 1984, 25.
5. John A. Byrne, "The MBA Mills," *Forbes,* 19 November 1984, 316.
6. Thomas Petzinger, Jr., "MBA Recipients, Once Eagerly Sought, Now Eagerly Seek Jobs in Tighter Market," *Wall Street Journal,* 2 November 1979, 48.
7. Association of MBA Executives, *Career and Salary Survey,* 1980–81.
8. Susan Fraker, "Why Women Aren't Getting to the Top," *Fortune,* 16 April 1984, 40.
9. Interview with Helen Axel, U.S. Conference Board, September 1984.
10. Current Population Report Series P60, #149. "Money Income and Poverty Status of Families and Persons in the U.S., 1984 (Advance Report)," August 1985.
11. I am indebted for this concept to Jill Julius Matthews's outstanding book, *Good and Mad Women: The Historical Construction of Femininity in Twentieth Century Australia* (Sydney: George Allen & Unwin, 1984).

Chapter 3

1. John A. Byrne, "The MBA Mills," *Forbes,* 19 November 1984, 316.
2. Ibid., 322.
3. Photograph, *Golden Gate University Magazine,* November 1984, 16.
4. Michael Thomas, "Do Business Schools Teach Absolute Rot?" *Business and Society Review,* Winter 1981, 61–65.
5. Joanna Deluca Mulholland, "A Comparison of Perceived Career and Educational Influences of MBA Graduates for the Purposes of Counselling and Recruiting Women, with Implications for Marketing and Distributive Programs." Temple University, 1982.
6. Strober, "The MBA."
7. Elizabeth Jaffe, "Management Women in Transition." Summary available from Dr. Jaffe, President, Career Continuum, 7 W. 14 St., Suite 20F, New York, NY 10011.
8. Sandy Lee, Letter to the Editor, *Business Weekly,* 22 October 1984.

Chapter 4

1. Association of MBA Executives, Career and Salary Survey 1980–81, Exhibit 14, copyright 1985. Quoted courtesy of the Association of MBA Executives.
2. Ibid.
3. Ibid.
4. Ibid., 11.
5. Ibid., Exhibit 27.
6. Ibid., Exhibits 22 and 23.
7. Ibid., Exhibit 24.
8. Ibid., 10.

Chapter 5

1. Wendy Fox, "Companies Becoming Part of the Family," *Boston Globe,* April 21, 1985, 77.
2. Myra Strober, "The MBA," 1982, 25–44.
3. Mary Anne Devanna. *Male/Female Careers: The First Decade, A Study of MBAs.* New York: Center for Research in Career Development, Columbia University Graduate School of Business, 1984.

Chapter 7

1. "Firms Are Adding Female Directors More Slowly than During the Seventies," *Wall Street Journal,* 7 April 1982, 35.
2. J. Benjamin Forbes and James E. Piercy, "Rising to the Top: Executive Women in 1983 and Beyond," *Business Horizon,* September–October 1983, 39.
3. Ted E. Drozdowski, "Survey Proves Women Are Paid Less than Men," *Purchasing,* 22 December 1983, 14.
4. Marybeth Fidler Bernhardt, "The Female Contribution to Leadership Roles," *American Banker,* 11 September 1984, 22.
5. Glenna Collins, "Unforeseen Business Barriers for Women," *New York Times,* 31 May 1982, A14.
6. "Women Executives Face Obstacles," *MBA Executive,* May/June 1983, 3.
7. Lynda Gorov, "Masters of Career and Home," *Boston Globe,* 30 October 1984, 56.
8. Mariann Jelinek and Anne Harlan, "MBA Goals and Aspirations: Potential Predictors of Later Success Differences between Males and Females," Working Paper #19. Wellesley College, Center for Research on Women, December 1979, 3.
9. Mary Anne Devanna, "Male/Female Careers: The First Decade, A Study of MBAs." New York: Center for Research in Career Development, Columbia University Graduate School of Business, 1984, 1–6.
10. Myra Strober, "The MBA," 1982, 25–44.
11. Joanna Deluca Mulholland, "A Comparison," Temple University, 1982, 117.
12. Mikalachki, Dorothy Martin, and Mikalachki, Alexander. "Women in Business—Going for Broke." *Business Quarterly,* Summer 1985, 28.
13. Harold A. Brown, et al, "Exploratory Analysis of Discrimination in the Employment of Black MBA Graduates," *Journal of Applied Psychology* 62 (February 1977): 52.
14. Association of MBA Executives, Career and Salary Survey 1980–81. Copyright 1985. Quoted courtesy of the Association of MBA Executives.
15. Ibid., Exhibit 21.
16. Ibid., Exhibit 21.
17. M. Reder, "Analysis of a Small Closely Observed Labor Market: Starting Salaries for University of Chicago MBAs," *Journal of Business* 51 (April 1978): 263–97.
18. Business and Professional Women's Foundation, "A Profile of Success: The Tenth An-

niversary of the BPW/Sears-Roebuck Foundation Loan Fund for Women in Graduate Business Studies." BPW Foundation, Washington, D.C., 1984, 8.

19. Phyllis A. Wallace, Ming-Je Tang, and Cathleen R. Tilney, "Upward Mobility of Young Managers: Women on the Fast Track?" Sloan School of Management Working Paper #1690-85, August 1985. To be published in a book on the same subject by Ballinger Publishing Company.

20. Ibid., 13.

21. Ibid., 17.

22. Ibid., 13.

23. Ibid., 5.

24. Earl F. Mellor, "Investigating the differences in weekly earnings of women and men," *Monthly Labor Review,* June 1984, 20–22.

25. Robert Pear, "Wage Lag Is Found for White Women," *New York Times,* 16 January 1984, A1, B10.

References

Books and Reports

American Assembly of Collegiate Schools of Business. *Accreditation Policies, Procedures and Standards, 1984-5.* St. Louis, Mo.: 1984.

Association of MBA Executives. *MBA Employment Guide.* New York: Association of MBA Executives, various years.

Association of MBA Executives. *The 1984-85 MBA Career and Salary Census.* New York: Association of MBA Executives, 1985.

Berman, Eleanor. *Reentering: Successful Back-to-work Strategies for Women Seeking a Fresh Start.* New York: Crown Publishers, 1980.

Berry, Margaret. *Women in Educational Administration.* Washington, D.C.: National Association for Women Deans, Administrators and Counsellors, 1979.

Biklen, Sari Knopp, and Brannigan, Marilyn B. *Women and Educational Leadership.* Lexington, Mass.: Lexington Books, 1980.

Bird, Caroline, *Enterprising Women.* New York: Mentor Book, New American Library, 1976.

Brady, Mary Lou; Dyer, Lucinda; and Parriott, Sara. *Woman Power: A Woman's Guide to Making It on Top.* Los Angeles: J.P. Torcher, 1981.

Bronstein, Eugene, and Hisrich, Robert D. *The MBA Career: Moving on the Fast Track to Success.* Woodbury, N.Y.: Barron's Educational Series, 1983.

Brown, Linda Keller. *The Woman Manager in the U.S.: A Research Analysis and Bibliography.* Washington, D.C.: Business and Professional Women's Foundation, 1981.

Burrow, Martha G. *Women: A Worldwide View of Their Development Needs.* New York: AMACOM, 1976.

Business and Professional Women. *Women in Management: A Survey of Recipients of the BPW/Sears-Roebuck Foundation Loan Fund for Women in Graduate Business Studies.* Washington, D.C.: Business and Professional Women's Foundation, 1979.

Careers and the MBA. Brighton, Mass.: Bob Adams, 1983.

Catalyst. *Making the Most of Your First Job.* New York: G.P. Putnam's Sons, 1981.

Catalyst. *Upward Mobility: A Comprehensive Career Advancement Plan for Women Determined to Succeed in the Working World.* New York: Holt, Rinehart & Winston, 1981.

Catalyst. *When Can You Start: The Complete Job Search Guide for Women of All Ages.* New York: Macmillan, 1981.

Chastain, Sherry. *Winning the Salary Game: Salary Negotiations for Women.* New York: John Wiley and Sons, 1980.

217

Cohen, Peter. *The Gospel According to the Harvard Business School.* Garden City, New York: Doubleday and Co., 1973.

Collins, Nancy W. *Professional Women and Their Mentors: A Practical Guide to Mentoring for the Woman Who Wants To Get Ahead.* Englewood Cliffs, N.J.: Prentice-Hall, 1983.

Crain, Sharie. *Taking Stock: A Woman's Guide to Corporate Success.* Chicago: Henry Regnery Co., 1977.

Crosby, Faye J. *Relative Deprivation and Working Women.* New York: Oxford University Press, 1982.

Devanna, Mary Anne. *Male/Female Careers: The First Decade, A Study of MBAs.* New York: Center for Research in Career Development, Columbia University Graduate School of Business, 1984.

Easton, Susan. *Equal to the Task: How Working Women Are Managing in Corporate America.* New York: Seaview Books, 1982.

Echternacht, Gary J., and Hussein, Ann L. *Survey of Women Interested in Management.* Santa Monica, Calif.: Graduate Business Admissions Council, May 1974.

Editors of Working Woman Magazine. *The Working Woman Success Book.* New York: Ace Books, 1981.

Editors of Working Woman with Gay Bryant. *The Working Woman Report: Succeeding in Business in the Eighties.* New York: Simon and Schuster, 1984.

Endicott, Frank S. *The Endicott Report: Trends in the Employment of College and University Graduates in Business and Industry.* Evanston, Ill.: Northwestern University, various years.

Eppen, Gary D.; Metcalfe, Dennis B.; and Walters, Marjorie E. *The MBA Degree.* Chicago: Chicago Review Press, 1979.

Fader, Shirley Sloan. *From Kitchen to Career: How Any Woman Can Skip Low-level Jobs and Start in the Middle or at the Top.* New York: Stein and Day, 1977.

Fischgrund, Tom, editor. *The Insider's Guide to the Top Ten Business Schools.* Boston: Little, Brown and Co., 1983.

Fogarty, Michael P.; Allen, Isobel; and Walters, Patricia. *Women in Top Jobs 1968-79.* London: Heineman Educational Books, 1981.

Fogarty, Michael P., et al. *Women in Top Jobs: Four Studies in Achievement.* London: George Allen and Unwin, 1971.

Foxworth, Jo. *Wising Up: The Mistakes Women Make in Business and How To Avoid Them.* New York: Delacorte Press, 1980.

Gallese, Liz Roman. *Women Like Us: What Is Happening to the Women of the Harvard Business School, Class of 1975.* New York: William Morrow and Co., 1985.

Ginzberg, Eli, and Yohalem, Alice M. *Corporate Lib: Women's Challenge to Management.* Baltimore and London: Johns Hopkins University Press, 1973.

Glotzer, Arline, and Sheiman, Bruce S. *Lovejoy's Guide to Graduate Business Schools.* New York: Monarch Press, 1983.

Gordon, Francine E., and Strober, Myra H. *Bringing Women into Management.* New York: McGraw-Hill Book Co., 1975.

Grant, W. Vance, and Eiden, Leo J. *Digest of Education Statistics, 1981.* National Center for Education Statistics.

Halcomb, Ruth. *Women Making It: Patterns and Profiles of Success.* New York: Atheneum, 1979.

Harlan, Anne, and Weiss, Carol. *Career Opportunity for Women Managers.* Wellesley, Mass.: Center for Research on Women, Wellesley College, 1979.

Harlan, Ann, and Weiss, Carol. *Moving Up: Women in Managerial Careers Final Report.* Working Paper #86. Wellesley, Mass.: Center for Research on Women, Wellesley College, 1981.

Harlan, Anne, and Weiss, Carol. *Sex Differences in Factors Affecting Managerial Career Ad-*

vancement. Working Paper #56. Wellesley, Mass.: Center for Research on Women, Wellesley College, 1980.

Harragan, Betty Lehan. *Games Mother Never Taught You*. New York: Warner Books, 1978.

Harragan, Betty Lehan. *Knowing the Score: Play-by-play Directions for Women on the Job*. New York: St. Martin's Press, 1980,81,82,83.

Hennig, Margaret, and Jardim, Anne. *The Managerial Woman*. New York: Anchor Press/Doubleday, 1981.

Henry, Fran Worden. *Toughing it Out at Harvard: The Making of a Woman MBA*. New York: G.P. Putnam's Sons, 1983.

Hugstad, Paul. *The Business School in the Eighties: Liberalism vs. Vocationalism*. New York: Praeger Publishers, 1983.

Jelinek, Mariann, and Harlan, Anne. *MBA Goals and Aspirations: Potential Predictors of Later Success Differences between Males and Females*. Working Paper #19, Wellesley, Mass.: Wellesley Center for Research on Women, December 1979.

Jewell, Donald O., editor. *Women and Management: An Expanding Role*. Atlanta, Ga.: Publishing Services Division, School of Business Administration, Georgia State University, 1977.

Josefowitz, Natasha. *Paths to Power: A Woman's Guide from First Job to Top Executive*. Reading, Mass.: Addison-Wesley Publishing Company, 1980.

Kantor, Rosabeth Moss. *Men and Women of the Corporation*. New York: Basic Books, 1977.

Kellogg, Mary Alice. *Fast Track: The Superachievers and How They Made it to Early Success, Status and Power*. New York: McGraw-Hill Book Company, 1978.

Kurst, Charlotte. *The Official Guide to MBA Programs, Admissions and Careers*. Princeton, N.J.: Graduate Management Admissions Council, 1984.

Landau, Suzanne, and Bailey, Geoffrey. *The Landau Strategy: How Working Women Win Top Jobs*. New York: Charkson N. Potter, 1980.

Langer, Steven. *Compensation of MBAs* 2d ed. Park Forest, Ill.: Abbott, Langer and Associates, 1978.

LaRouche, Janice, and Ryan, Regina. *Strategies for Women at Work*. New York: Avon Books, 1984.

Larwood, Laurie, and Wood, Marian M. *Women in Management*. Lexington, Mass.: Lexington Books, 1977.

Leary, Linda F., and Wightman, Lawrence E. *A Demographic Profile of Candidates Taking the Graduate Management Admission Test During 1980-81*. Santa Monica, Calif.: Graduate Management Admission Council, November 1982.

Lee, Nancy. *Targeting the Top*. New York: Doubleday and Co., 1980.

McLane, Helen J. *Selecting, Developing, and Retaining Women Executives*. New York: Van Nostrand Reinhold Co., 1980.

McVicar, Marjorie, and Craig, Julia F. *Minding My Own Business: Entrepreneurial Women Share Their Secrets for Success*. New York: Richard Murek Publishers, 1981.

Manette, Jan. *The Working Girl in a Man's World*. New York: Hawthorn Books, 1966.

Miller, Eugene. *Barron's Guide to Graduate Business Schools*. Woodbury, N.Y.: Barron's Educational Series, 1984.

Missirian, Agnes K. *The Corporate Connection: Why Executive Women Need Mentors To Reach the Top*. Englewood Cliffs, N.J.: Spectrum/PH, 1982.

National Network of Business School Women. Report on 1979 Conference, unpublished.

National Research Council. *Women Scientists in Industry and Government: How Much Progress in the 1970s?* Washington, D.C.: National Academy of Sciences, 1980.

Newton, Derek A. *Think like a Man, Act like a Lady, Work like a Dog*. New York: Doubleday and Co., 1979.

Oran, Daniel, and Shafriz, Jay. *The MBA's Dictionary*. Reston, Va: Reston Publishing Company, Prentice-Hall Company, 1983.

Peskin, Dean B. *Womaning: Overcoming Male Dominance on Executive Row*. Port Washington, N.Y.: Ashley Books, 1982.
Place, Irene, and Plummer, Sylvia. *Women in Management*. Skokie, Ill.: VGM Career Horizons, 1982.
Schlesinger, Phyllis F. *A Study of the Lives of Women Managers at Mid-Career*. Boston, Mass.: Boston University School of Education, 1981.
Scollard, Jeanette Reddish. *No-nonsense Management Tips for Women*. New York: Simon and Schuster, Wallaby Book, 1983.
Seaman, Florence, and Lorimer, Anne. *Winning at Work: A Book for Women*. Philadelphia, Pa.: Running Press, 1979.
Senter, Sylvia; Howe, Marguerite; and Saco, Don. *Women at Work: A Psychologist's Secrets To Getting Ahead in Business*. New York: Coward, McCann and Geoghegan, 1982.
Shaeffer, Ruth Gilberg, and Lynton, Edith F. *Corporate Experiences in Improving Women's Job Opportunities: A Research Report from the Conference Board*. New York: Conference Board, 1979.
Silverstone, Rosalie, and Word, Audrey, editors. *Careers of Professional Women*. London: Croom Helm, 1980.
Stashower, Gloria. *Careers in Management for the New Woman*. New York: Franklin Watts, 1978.
Stead, Bette Ann. *Women in Management*. Englewood Cliffs, N.J.: Prentice-Hall, 1978.
Steele, Addison. *Upward Mobility: How to Win the Rat Race without Becoming a Rat*. New York: Times Books, 1978.
Stern, Barbara B. *Is Networking for You? A Working Woman's Alternative to the Old Boy System*. Englewood Cliffs, N.J.: Prentice-Hall, 1981.
Stolzenberg, Ross M. *The Changing Demand for Graduate Management Education: An Interim Report*. Santa Monica, Calif.: Graduate Management Admissions Council, March 1985.
Stone, Janet, and Bachner, Jane. *Speaking Up: A Book for Every Woman Who Wants To Speak Effectively*. New York: McGraw-Hill Book Co., 1977.
Thompson, Jacqueline. *Image Impact: The Aspiring Woman's Personal Packaging Program*. New York: A & W Publishers, 1981.
Trahey, Jane. *Jane Trahey on Women and Power: Who's Got it, How To Get it*. New York: Rawson Associates Publishers, 1977.
Uris, Auren. *The Executive Breakthrough: 21 Roads to the Top*. Garden City, N.Y.: Doubleday and Co., 1967.
Welch, Mary Scott. *Networking: The Great New Way for Women To Get Ahead*. New York: Harcourt Brace Jovanovich, 1980.
Wheatley, Meg, and Schorr, Marcie Hirsch. *Managing Your Maternity Leave*. Boston, Mass.: Houghton Mifflin, 1983.
Williams, Marcille Gray. *The New Executive Woman*. Radnor, Pa.: Chilton Book Co., 1977.
Williams, Martha, et al. *Women in Management: A Selected Bibliography*. Austin, Texas: University of Texas Center for Social Welfare Research, 1977.
Winter, Maridee Allen. *Mind Your own Business, Be Your own Boss: Every Woman's Guide To Starting a Business and Succeeding*. Englewood Cliffs, N.J.: Prentice-Hall, 1980.

Articles in Periodicals Other than Newspapers

"A Better Crop of B-schools." *Business Week*, 14 September 1981, 111.
Abrahms, Sally. "Future Captains of Industry." *Working Woman*, June 1981, 67–70.
Adkins, Lynn. "Glut Coming in MBA's." *Dun's Review*, March 1980, 104–6.
Allen, Teadra. "The Third Annual Salary Survey." *Working Woman*, January 1982, 51–53.

Alpert, Dee Estelle. "Accepting the Aggressive Female Executive." *MBA* February 1976, 25–28.

"Are MBAs Career Boosters?" *Computer Decisions,* 8 April 1986, 64–65.

"Are MBA's More than Quantitative Robots?" *Business and Society Review,* Winter 1983, 4–12.

"Are You Sure You Want to Go Back for That MBA?" *Business Week,* 11 November 1985, 141–2.

"Babes in the Corporate Woods." *Vogue,* May 1977, 105–6.

Baida, Peter. "M.B.A." *American Scholar,* Winter 1984–85, 23–41.

Banbury-Masland, Brooke, and Brass, Daniel J. "Careers, Marriage, and Children: Are Women Changing Their Minds?" *Business Horizons,* May-June 1985, 81–86.

Bartol, Kathryn M. "The Sex Structuring of Organizations: A Search for Possible Causes." *Academy of Management Review* 3 (October 1978):805–15.

Behrman, Jack N., and Levin, Richard I. "Are Business Schools Doing Their Job?" *Harvard Business Review,* January-February 1984, 140–42.

Bennett, Andrea. "EEOC Data Show Women Gaining at Management Level in Big Banks." *American Banker,* 23 May 1984, 24.

Benson, Gary L. "On the Campus: How Well Do Business Schools Prepare Graduates for the Business World?" *Personnel* 60 (July 1983):61–65.

Berhardt, Marybeth Fidler. "The Female Contribution to Leadership Roles." *American Banker,* 11 September 1984, 21–22.

Berkinow, Louise. "The Paper Tiger." *Savvy,* March 1983, 38–43, 84–85.

Bernstein, Peter W. "Women: The New Stars in Banking." *Fortune,* 12 July 1982, 84–95.

"Best Firms for Female Executives." *Dun's Business Month,* September 1984, 14, 19.

Blotnick, Srully. "Scorn Not the MBA." *Forbes,* October 7, 1985, 180–81.

Bodger, Carole. "Sixth Annual Salary Survey: Who Does What and for How Much." *Working Woman,* January 1985, 65–72.

"Boosting the Careers of B-school Grads." *Business Week,* 11 October 1982, 72.

"The Bottom Line." *Savvy,* July 1985, 18.

Brenner, O.C., and Tomkiewicz, Joseph. "Sex Differences among Business Graduates on Fear of Success and Fear of Appearing Incompetent as Measured by Objective Instruments." *Psychological Reports* 51 (1982):179–82.

Brevetti, Francine C. "Dollars and Sense." *Savvy,* May 1983, 96.

"Bright Forecast for Women and Minority Bank Officials." *ABA Banking Journal* 74 (February 1982):18.

Brose, Michael E. "The Rise of the MBA and the Decline of U.S. Industry." *Marketing News,* 5 August 1983, 13.

Brown, Linda Keller. "Review Essay: Women and Business Management." *Signs* 5 (Winter 1979):266–88.

Brown, Linda Keller, and Kagan, Julia. "The Working Woman Survey: A Survey of Where Corporate Women Are Now and What They Want Next." *Working Woman,* May 1982, 92–96.

"The B-School A-Team." *Forbes,* 28 April 1986, 78–79.

"B-School Grads Are Back in Demand." *Business Week,* 23 May 1983, 52.

"B-Schools Should Think Big." *Business Week,* 24 March 1986, 152.

"B Schools Try to Churn Out Entrepreneurs." *Business Week,* 5 March 1984, 102.

"Bull Market for MBAs." *Time,* 6 August 1973, 65.

Burkhead, Marie. "Under-representation of Women in University-sponsored Management Development Programs." *Journal of Business Education* 48 no. 3 (1972):109–10.

Burns, Cherie. "The Young Turks Are Coming." *Working Woman,* March 1981, 67–69, 118.

Business Week's Guide to Careers. Various editions.

Byrne, John. "Some Thoughts from the Best and the Brightest MBAs." *Forbes*, 3 June 1985, 215–20.

Byrne, John A. "The Battle of the B-Schools Is Getting Bloodier." *Business Week*, 24 March 1986, 61–68.

Campbell, Bebe Moore. "To Be Black, Gifted and Alone." *Savvy*, December 1984, 67–74.

Cancain, Francesca M., "Rapid Social Change: Women Students in Business Schools. *Sociology and Social Research* 66, no. 2 (January 1982):169–83.

"Can You Profit from an MBA?" *In Business*, September–October 1983, 23–25.

Carter, Michael J., and Boslego, Susan. "Women's Recent Progress in the Professions." *Feminist Studies* 7 (Fall 1981):477–504.

"Case for Change: Business Schools." *Economist*, 12 May 1979, 50–51.

Castellano, Joseph F., et al. "The MBA: A Profile of What Business Wants." *Marquette Business Review* 19 (Summer 1975):61–68.

"Chosen Paths: Women in the Professions." *Golden Gate University Magazine*, November 1984, 2–4, 8, 13.

Ciulla, Joanne B. "Do MBA Students Have Ethics Phobia?" *Business and Society Review*, Spring 1985, 52–54.

"Classes for Executives: A Quick Buck for B-Schools." *Business Week*, 11 February 1985, p. 56.

"A Cold Market for New MBAs." *Business Week*, 23 November 1974, 118.

"College Students Get Down to Business." *Money*, December 1985, 137–44.

Crocker, Elizabeth M., and Henry, Ann R. "Factors Affecting Women's Increased Enrollment in Colleges of Business Administration." *Akron Business and Economic Review* 14 (Fall 1981):6–10.

Cronin, Paula. "Women in Business: How Far Have They Come?" *Radcliffe Quarterly*, June 1983, 7–8.

Crosby, Faye. "Selective Vision." *Working Woman*, July 1984, 67–69.

Crow, Graham. "Whither the Mistresses of Business Administration?" *Personnel Management* 13 (September 1981):36–39.

Cuba, Richard; DeCenzo, David; and Anish, Andrea. "Management Practices of Successful Female Business Owners." *American Journal of Small Business*, Fall 1983, 40–46.

Curran, Ann. "Women Directors." *Working Woman*, February 1980, 38–41, 47, 60.

"Degree in Stress." *Glamour*, May 1981, 76.

"Demand Is Soaring for MBA Graduates." *Business Week*, 15 January 1979, 42.

DeMott, John S. "Redefining Executive Education." *Time*, 3 October 1983, 48.

Dentzer, Susan. "Watch Out, Harvard, Here's Florida A&M." *Newsweek*, 24 May 1982, 69.

DeWitt, Karen. "Black Women in Business." *Black Enterprise*, August 1974, 14–20.

Dillon, Tom. "Why So Few Women at the Top?" *Marketing and Media Decisions*, April 1982, 70–71, 118.

Dolecheck, Maynard M., and Dolecheck, Carolyn C. "Sex Discrimination in Company Management." *Louisiana Business Review*, Spring 1983, 18–21.

Donnelly, Robert M. "The Value of an MBA." *Advanced Management Journal* 46 (Spring 1981):59–63.

"A Double Standard for Women Managers' Pay." *Business Week*, 28 November 1977, 61–65.

Drozdowski, Ted E. "Survey Proves Women Are Paid Less than Men." *Purchasing*, 22 December 1983, 14–15.

Dubno, Peter. "Is Corporate Sexism Passé?" *Business and Society Review*, Spring 1985, 59–61.

DuPont, Helen. "The MBA: Ticket to Where the Jobs Are?" *Women's Work*, May/June 1976, 9–11.

"Executive Search Firms: What They Are and Why so Many Companies Use Them." *MBA Executive*, Fall 1982, 5–6.

"Falling off the Fast Track." *Savvy*, August 1986, 32–36, 71.

Feinberg, Phyllis. "Do You Need an MBA?" *Enterprising Woman*, January 1977, 1–2.

Fisher, Maria. "What's an MBA Really Worth?" *Forbes*, 19 December 1983, 176.

Fisk, Jim, and Barron, Robert. "The Rational Publishing Business—the MBA Way." *Publishers Weekly*, July 2, 1982, 26–28.

"Fixing the Blame for MBAs' High Salaries." *Management Review* 70 (November 1981):54.

Flanagan, William. "MBA Degree Magic: Would it Mean Big Earnings for You?" *Vogue*, September 1979, 208.

Flewellen, W.C. Jr., and DeZoort, Frank A. "The Shortage of Women and Members of Minority Groups Enrolled in AACSB Schools, 1973–74." *AACSB Bulletin*, no. 4, Annual Report 1975, 36–42.

Follows, James. "The Case against Credentialism." *Atlantic*, December 1985, 49–67.

Forbes, J. Benjamin, and Piercy, James E. "Rising to the Top: Executive Women in 1983 and Beyond." *Business Horizons*, September-October 1983, 38–47.

Forrester, P.G. "The MBA Mystique." *Management Today*, December 1984, 76–79.

Fortenbaugh, Jennifer. "The Fourth Annual Salary Survey." *Working Woman*, January 1983, 65–68.

Fox, Eugene H. "Business School Survey: Women Outpace Men in Enrollments." *Enterprising Woman*, November 1977, 3, 6.

Fraker, Susan. "Tough Times for MBAs." *Fortune*, 12 December 1983, 64–68, 70–72.

Fraker, Susan. "Why Women Aren't Getting to the Top." *Fortune*, 16 April 1984, 40–45.

Francis, David R. "John H. McArthur: Business School Crisis and Renewal." *Financier*, July 1983, 19–23.

Frank, J. Ingrid, and Robinson, Nina. "Sex: Wharton's Untaught Subject." *Anvil*, Winter 1977, 26–29.

Fraser, Jill Andresky. "You Are Where You Live." *Savvy*, October 1983, 38–48.

Fretz, C.F., and Hayman, Joanne. "Progress for Women: Men Are Still More Equal." *Harvard Business Review* 55 (Winter 1974):133–41.

"Glad Hands Greet MBAs This Spring." *Business Week*, 7 June 1976, 27–28.

Gardner, Janet. "MBA Program for Women Only." *Glamour*, September 1982, 369–70.

Goldstein, Rill Ann. "Can You Profit from an MBA?" *In Business*, September-October 1983, 23–25.

Gorov, Lynda. "Master's of Career and Home: For Most, an MBA Was No Ticket to the Boardroom." *Boston Globe*, 30 October 1984, 41, 56, 58, 59.

Grant, Linda. "Here Come the MBAs." *Working Woman*, September 1977, 18–24.

Greenlaw, Paul S., and Bresee, Catherine. "Woman MBA: A Positive Employment Profile." *Personnel Administrator* 27 (July 1982):55–60.

"Hard Lesson: Trying Times for 1983 MBAs." *Time*, 31 January 1983, 55.

Harrell, Margaret S., et al. "Predicting Compensation among MBA Graduates Five and Ten Years after Graduation." *Journal of Applied Psychology* 62 (October 1977):636–40.

Herbert, T.T. "Investigation into the Nature of the Part-time MBA Student." *Human Relations* 33 (May 1980):279–95.

Herbert, Theordore T. "The MBA and Job Performance." *Akron Business and Economic Review* 8 (Spring 1977):35–40.

Horowitz, Simi. "Is Business School for You?" *Seventeen*, April 1977, 36.

Houston, Jourdan. "Women and the MBA: Fast Track to the Executive Suite?" *Town and Country*, August 1981, 81.

Howard, Cecil G. "Women Bank Managers Rate Their Jobs." *Bankers Magazine*, July-August 1983, 68–72.

"How Executives See Women in Management." *Business Week*, 28 June 1982, 10.

"How to Humanize MBAs." *Fortune,* 31 March 1986, 153–54.

"How to Make the Most of Today's Opportunities." *U.S. News and World Report,* 27 September 1976, 79–82.

"The Hunt Heats up for this Year's MBAs." *Business Week,* 13 February 1978, 29–30.

"In Hotter Pursuit of MBAs." *Business Week,* 7 February 1977, 98.

"Is the MBA Still the Golden Passport?" *Black Enterprise,* February 1981, 43–44.

"It Takes Hard Work for Women to Succeed in the Financial World, but MBAs and Bow-Tied Blouses Help." *American Banker,* 28 March 1985, 24.

Jacobs, Rita. "Corporate Women: Working Together To Get Ahead." *Working Woman,* December 1979, 19–20, 23.

Jaffe, Betsy. "A Forced Fit." *Training and Development Journal* 39 (September 1985):82–83.

Jaffe, Elizabeth Latimer. "Management Women in Transition." Unpublished summary available from the author at Suite 20F, 7 West 14 St., New York, N.Y.

Jenkins, Roger L.: Reizenstein, Richard C.; and Rodgers, F.G. "Report Cards on the MBA." *Harvard Business Review,* September–October 1984, 20–22, 26, 28, 30.

"The Job Market Starts a B-school Stampede." *Business Week,* 2 June 1975, 50–51.

"The Job Market Stays Tight for New MBAs." *Business Week,* 22 December 1975, 14.

"Job Offers Are Chasing the New MBAs Again." *Business Week,* 9 April 1984, 32–33.

Kelly, Kate. "Does an MBA Guarantee Big Money?" *Harper's Bazaar,* October 1979, 14, 94, 96.

Kennedy, Mopsy Strange. "Surviving Ambition and Competition." *Savvy,* May 1980, 32–38.

Kiechel, Walter III. "Beyond Sexist Management." *Fortune,* 15 October 1984, 191–92.

Kiechel, Walter III. "Harvard B-school Restudies Itself." *Fortune,* 18 June 1979, 48–50, 53–54, 57–58.

Kleiman, Carol. "Does Sisterhood Stop at the Top?" *Ms,* March 1981, 100.

Kocolowski, Linda. "Industry Groups Seek Out NAIW Ideas." *National Underwriter: Life and Health Edition,* 3 July 1982, 30.

Kotker, Zane. "Women's Issues: Bosses Recognize Them, Women Resist Them." *Savvy,* November 1980, 44–47.

Krasny, Robin. "Storming Harvard Business School." *Savvy,* June 1981, 32–38.

Kreps, Juanita. "The Hard Road from Access to Ascent: New Problem for Professional Women." *American Banker,* 5 September 1984, 4,6,12–13,23.

Kruse, Thomas M. "Young Women in Business: The Search for Identity." *Supervision,* July 1974, 11–12.

Laczniak, Gene R., and Murphy, Patrick E. "The Role of Business Schools in Educating Future Women Managers." 14 (Fall 1977):21–26.

Lamb, Robert. "A New Crop of MBAs Goes Looking for that 'Fast Track.' " *Fortune,* June 1977, 160–70.

Leviton, Laura C., and Whiteley, Susan E. "Job-seeking Patterns of Female and Male Ph.D. Recipients." *Psychology of Women Quarterly* 5, no. 5 (Supplement 1981):690–701.

Livingston, J.S. "The Myth of the Well-educated Manager." *Harvard Business Review* 49, no. 1 (1971):79–89.

McCain, Nina. "Reflections of the Management Grads." *Boston Globe,* 16 August 1985, 41, 43.

McClenahen, John S. "New Marching Orders for MBAs." *Industry Week,* 8 August 1983, 49, 56.

McGhee, Neil. "Women in Insurance: How Have They Fared?" *National Underwriter: Life and Health Edition,* 28 April 1984, 16–17.

McGrath, Anne. "GMAT Flunks Out at Harvard." *Forbes* 136 (September 23, 1985):199–200.

McMurray, Scott. "Goldman, Sachs Moves to Reassure Stanford Candidates." *Wall Street Journal,* 4 February 1985, 14.

McKendrick, Joseph. "Viewpoint: Men versus Women." 11 (November 1982):11–13.

"Magazine Publishers' Romance with MBAs: Is it Fading?" *Folio,* May 1983, 6–8.

Magill, Barbara A. "Monitoring Trends in the Enrollment of Women in AACSB Schools." AACSB Bulletin 13, no. 1 (October 1976):17–21.

Magnet, Myron. "Baby-boom Executives Are Making it." *Fortune,* 2 September 1985, 22–28.

Mahon, Gigi. "An MBA Is still a Ticket to what those Speedwriting Schools Call 'Mo Pay.' " *Mademoiselle,* May 1980, 66.

"Managing the Woman's Way." *Newsweek,* 17 March 1986, 46–47.

"MBA: The Fast Route to Success?" *Data Management,* June 1986, 34.

"The MBA Glut Is Now Hitting the Top Ten." *Business Week,* 15 March 1982, 30–31.

"MBAs: The New Elite on Campus." *U.S. News and World Report,* 29 October 1979, 86–88.

"MBAs: Where They Work and Where They Are Needed." *Occupational Outlook Quarterly,* Winter 1985, 2–10.

"MBAs in the 1980s: Special Issue." *MBA Executive,* January 1980.

"MBAs Learn a Human Touch." *Newsweek,* 16 June 1986, 48–50.

Mikalachki, Dorothy Martin, and Mikalachki, Alexander. "MBA Women: The New Pioneers." *Business Quarterly,* Spring 1984, 110–14.

Mikalachki, Dorothy Martin, and Mikalachki, Alexander. "Women in Business—Going for Broke." *Business Quarterly,* Summer 1985, 25–32.

Minton, Robert. "B-schools Are Big Business." *Finance,* November 1975, 19–22.

"The Money Chase: Business School Solutions May Be Part of the U. S. Problem." *Time,* 4 May 1981, 58–65.

"More and More, She's the Boss." *Time,* 2 December 1985, 64–66.

Moss, Rose. "What Business Schools Don't Teach." *Women's Review of Books* 2, no. 2 (November 1984):6–7.

Mulholland, Joanna D. "A Comparison of Perceived Career and Educational Influences of Masters of Business Administration (MBA) Graduates for the Purposes of Counseling and Recruiting Women." Contributed Paper to Ninth International Conference, Improving University Teaching, 6–9 July 1983, Dublin, Ireland.

Murray, Jean. "Prosper: Get the Degree that Earns You More Money." *Working Woman,* August 1978, 46–47.

Nelton, Sharon. "Molding Managers for the Tests of Tomorrow." *Nation's Business,* April 1984, 30–31, 34, 36.

"Networking 1981." *Working Woman,* March 1981, 92–104.

"Old Girl Networks: Filling a Vacuum for Business Women." *New England Business,* 3 May 1982, 24.

"One Hundred Top Corporate Women." *Business Week,* 21 June 1976, 56–60.

"On the Campus: How Well Do Business Schools Prepare Graduates for the Business World?" *Personnel,* July 1983, 61–65.

Oster, Sharon M. "Industry Differences in the Level of Discrimination against Women." *Quarterly Journal of Economics* 89 (May 1975):215–29.

O'Toole, Patricia. "The Truth about the Value of an MBA." *Savvy,* July 1981, 14–18.

Perkins, Bernard D. "A Survey of Business Graduates." *South Dakota Business Review* 33 (November 1974):2–9.

Peters, Thomas J., and Austin, Nancy K. "Diamonds in the Rough." *Savvy,* June 1984, 38–46.

Pfeffer, Jeffrey. "Effect of an MBA and Socioeconomic Origins on Business School Graduates' Salaries." *Journal of Applied Psychology* 62 (December 1977):698–705.

Pfeifer, Pat. "Male and Female MBA Candidates: Are There Personality Differences?" *The Business Quarterly* 43 (Spring 1978):77–80.

"A Plan To Rate B Schools by Testing Students." *Business Week,* 19 November 1979, 171, 174.

Price, Margaret. "Networks: Businesswomen Expand Their Horizons." *Industry Week,* 28 June 1982, 56–60.

Priestland, Sue C. "Women Move into Executive Slots but Salaries Lag Behind." *Association Management,* August 1983, 65–67.

Prokesch, Steven. "Classes for Executives: A Quick Buck for B Schools?" *Business Week,* 11 February 1985, 56.

"Recruiting Rites at the Harvard Business School." Institutional Investor, March 1986, 78 ff.

Reha, Rose K. "Preparing Women for Management Roles." *Business Horizons,* April 1979, 68–71.

Rehder, Robert R. "American Business Education: Is it too Late To Change?" *Sloan Management Review* 23 (Winter 1982):63–71.

Rehder, Robert R., and Porter, James C. "The Creative MBA: A New Proposal for Balancing the Science and Art of Management." *Business Horizons,* November-December 1983, 52–54.

Reier, Sharon. "Who Needs an MBA?" *Institutional Investor,* September 1981, 125, 128–29.

"Re-Making the Harvard B-School." *Business Week,* 24 March 1986, 54–58.

Reynolds, Sydney. "Women on the Line." *MBA,* February 1975, 26–30.

Richman, Louis S. "B-school Students' Favorite Professors." *Fortune,* 25 January 1982, 72–79.

Robertson, Wyndham. "Women MBAs, Harvard 1973." *Fortune,* 28 August 1978, 50–54, 60.

Rogan, Helen. "Young Executive Women Advance Farther, Faster than Predecessors." *Wall Street Journal,* 26 October 1984, 33, 36.

Rosen, Benson; Templeton, Mary Ellen; and Kichline, Karen. "The First Few Years on the Job: Women in Management." *Business Horizons* 24 (November-December 1981):26–29.

Rowan, Roy. "How Harvard's Women MBAs Are Managing." *Fortune,* 11 July 1983, 58, 60, 64, 68, 72.

Runde, Robert. "Does an MBA still Pay?" *Money,* June 1982, 126–30.

Runde, Robert. "A Two-tier Market for Lawyers and MBAs." *Money,* May 1980, 80–82.

Sanger, David E. "Harvard Business School at 75: Big Changes Are Resisted," *New York Times,* 5 March 1984, D1, 11.

Schein, Virginia E. "The Relationship between Sex-role Stereotypes and Requisite Management Characteristics." *Journal of Applied Psychology* 60 (1975):340–44.

Schermerhorn, John R., et al. "Women in Management: The MBA Student's Perspective." *Academy of Management Proceedings* 1975, 451–53.

Schultz, Bill. "What Stanford Does Better than Harvard." *Esquire* September 1977, 118, 151–54.

Schwartz, Felice N. "From Getting in to Getting on." *Working Woman,* September 1983, 131–33.

"Sex and Getting Ahead." *Advanced Management Journal* 47 (Summer 1982):53–54.

Shapero, Albert. "Are Business Schools Teaching Business?" *Inc,* January 1982, 13–14.

Shapiro, Ruth. "Will an MBA Make You a VIP?" *Harper's Bazaar,* June 1977, 49, 135–36.

Siegel, Marjorie. "Graduate Business Education: It all Began at Dartmouth College." *Dun's Review,* March 1980, 25–27.

Simmons, Diane. "Women in Bank Management Seen as Alienated, Subject to High Stress." *American Banker,* 28 July 1982, 1, 142–3.

Smith, Adam. "The Half-life of the MBA Mentality." *Esquire,* January 1985, 52–53.

Smith, Lee. "Yale's Business School with a Difference." *Dun's Review,* February 1976, 63–65.

Smolowe, Constance. "Corporations and Women: A Decade of Near-Ms.'s." *MBA,* February 1974, 32–34.

Solomon, Steven. "Whatever Happened to the Class of 76?" *Institutional Investor,* November 1981, 183–84, 189–90.

Stamell, Marcia. "Do 'Making It' Myths Make Sense?" *Mademoiselle,* June 1984, 154–55, 216, 218, 220.

Stautberg, Susan Schiffer. "Bringing Career Skills to Bear on Your Pregnancy." *Wall Street Journal,* 17 June 1985, 20.

Stead, Bette Ann. "Educating Women for Administration." *Business Horizons,* April 1975, 51–56.

Stead, Bette Ann. "Women's Contributions to Management Thought." *Business Horizons,* February 1974, 32–36.

Steele, John E., and Ward, Lewis B. "MBAs: Mobile, Well Situated, Well Paid." *Harvard Business Review* 52 (January-February 1974):99–110.

Steinberg, Rhona, and Shapiro, Stanley. "Sex Differences in Personality Traits of Female and Male MBA Students." *Journal of Applied Psychology* 67, no. 3 (1982):306–10.

Strober, Myra H. "The MBA: Same Passport to Success for Women and Men?" in *Women in the Workplace,* ed. Phyllis A. Wallace (Boston, Mass.: Auburn House Publishing Company, 1982).

Stundza, Patricia. "Bias Still Rules, Study Says." *American Banker* 149 (February 13, 1984):2, 19.

Swartz, Steve. "Business Schools Revise Programs to Meet Firms' Changing Needs." *Wall Street Journal,* 28 March 1985, 35.

"The Swing to Practicality in the B Schools." *Business Week,* 23 July 1979, 190.

Swinyard, Alfred W., and Bond, Floyd A. "Who Gets Promoted?" *Harvard Business Review,* September-October 1980, 6–8, 12–14, 18.

Tait, Grant. "Hard Lessons of an MBA." *Management Today,* July 1983, 60–61.

"Tallahasee's Go-Get-'Em B School." *Fortune,* 28 December 1981, 70–72, 76.

"Talkin' MBA Blues." *Boston Magazine,* December 1985, 132, 134, 136, 138, 140, 141.

Taylor, Alex, III. "Why Women Managers Are Bailing Out." *Fortune,* 18 August 1986, 16–23.

Terborg, J.R. "Women in Management: A Research Review." *Journal of Applied Psychology* 62 (December 1977):647–64.

Terborg, James R., and Ilgen, Daniel R. "A Theoretical Approach to Sex Discrimation in Traditionally Masculine Occupations." *Organizational Behavior and Human Performance* 13 (1975):352–376.

Thackray, John. "The B School Backlash." *Management Today,* August 1981, 58–61.

Thain, Richard J. "Assessing Your Potential for the MBA Degree," in 1984–85 CPC Annual. Bethlehem, Pa: College Placement Council, 1984, 65–67.

Thompson, Jacqueline A. "The Women vs. Chase Manhattan: Diary of a Discrimination Suit." *MBA,* December 1975, 19–29.

"A Time To Recharge." *Management World,* November 1982, 1, 6.

Turbett, Peggy. "It Takes Hard Work for Women To Succeed in the Financial World, but MBAs and Bow-tied Blouses Help." *American Banker,* 28 March 1985, 24.

"Twenty at the Top." *Savvy,* April 1983, 38–47.

"Upswing in the MBA Market." *Nation's Business,* May 1974, 34–35.

"Up the Ladder, Finally." *Business Week,* 24 November 1975.

Veiga, John F., and Nyanouzas, John. "What Women in Management Want: The Ideal Versus the Real." *Academy of Management Journal* 19 Number 1 (1976):137–43.

"Want an MBA? How To Make Business Schools Want You." *Glamour*, December 1983, 256, 258.

Weiner, Andrew. "Why MBAs Fizzle on the Firing Line." *Canadian Business*, February 1981, 108–10, 113.

Weinstein, Alan G., and Srinivasan, V. "Predicting Managerial Success of MBA Graduates." *Journal of Applied Psychology*, April 1974, 207–12.

Weiss, Carol. "Myths about Women and Men Managers." *Radcliffe Quarterly*, June 1983, 4–7.

Weiss, Elaine F. "To B School or not to B School?" *Savvy*, December 1983, 36–41.

Wellemeyer, Marilyn. "The Class the Dollars Fell on." *Fortune*, May 1974, 224–29.

Wellemeyer, Marilyn. "Executives on Campus." *Fortune*, 18 (April 1983): 137–48.

Welsch, Harold P., and Young, Earl C. "Entrepreneurs and Young Executives: An Analysis of Differences along Selected Psychological Dimensions." Presented to the International Council for Small Business, Halifax, N.S., 26–29 June 1983.

Werner, Laurie. "MBA: The Fantasy and the Reality." *Working Woman*, December 1979.

"Wharton Copes with its Identity Crisis." *Business Week*, 23 June 1973, 49–52.

"What Are They Teaching in the B Schools?" *Business Week*, 10 November 1980, 61.

"What's it Like for Women Executives?" *Dun's Review*, December 1975, 58–61.

"What Some Women Dare To Do—and Succeed." *Redbook*, August 1978, 73–74.

"Why Women Need Their own MBA Programs." *Business Week*, 23 February 1974, 102, 107.

Williams, Monci Jo. "The Baby Bust Hits the Job Market." *Fortune*, 27 May 1985, 123–35.

Wills, Kendall J. "Bringing the World into the Classroom." *New York Times*, 20 February 1983.

Windsor, Duane, and Tuggle, Francis D. "Redesigning the MBA Curriculum." *Interfaces* 12 (August 1982): 72–77.

Witten, Mark. "Taking Care of Business." *Saturday Night*, November 1981, 15–16.

"Women Are Entering Management—Slowly." *Chemical Week*, 21 December 1983, 72–77.

"Women Chief Executives Help Each Other with Frank Advice." *Wall Street Journal*, 2 July 1984, 21.

"Women in Business." *Business Today*, Fall 1974, 5–6, 13.

"Women Managers Have Different Styles than Male Managers, a Study Says." *Wall Street Journal*, 12 March 1985, 1.

"Women of the Corporation 1985." *Working Woman*, April 1985, 97–101, 146, 148, 150.

"Women's Plaint: Executive Suite out of Reach." *U.S. News and World Report*, 8 December 1980, 54.

Wood, Marion. "Women in Management: How Is it Working out?" *SAM Advanced Management Journal* 41 (Winter 1976):22–30.

"The Worrisome Boom in Second Rate B-Schools." *Business Week*, 6 March 1978, 82.

Wright, John W. "MBA Salary Survey." *Savvy*, May 1982, 22.

"Your Second Chance at an MBA." *Business Week*, 26 March 1984, 138–41.

"You've Come a Long Way, Baby—But Not as Far as You Thought." *Business Week*, 1 October 1984, 126–28.

Newspaper Articles

This section is arranged chronologically, to give the reader some sense of the trends in newspaper reporting about MBAs. Prior to 1980, for example, here is a range of articles:

"The Rite of Spring: Recruiting of MBAs by Firms Is a Game with Strange Rules." *Wall Street Journal*, 9 April 1974, 1,39.

"Careers: Women MBAs Tell of Discrimination." *New York Times,* 22 June 1977, D13.
"MBA Recipients, Once Eagerly Sought, Now Eagerly Seek Jobs in a Tighter Market." *Wall Street Journal,* 2 November 1979, 48.
"Job Offers Are Lavish in Competition To Hire Business School Graduates." *Wall Street Journal,* 11 February 1980, 1, 25.

By 1981, when the numbers of women had risen enormously, the same flux in supply and demand held true, but there was more attention to concerns about quality of business education. The following is a selection of articles bearing specifically on women MBAs and issues that are of interest to them from 1981–86.

"Starting Salaries up 6-12% for MBAs in Marketing," *Wall Street Journal,* 16 April 1981, 29.
"Status, Security, and Salary Govern Job Choices of Top MBA Candidates," *Wall Street Journal,* 29 April 1981, 31.
"Women MBA Graduates from Some Leading Schools Earn Less than Men," *Wall Street Journal,* 2 June 1981, 1.
"Female Bosses Are Two Times as Accessible to Subordinates as Male Ones," *Wall Street Journal,* 4 August 1981, 1.
"Promotions Grow Few as Baby Boom Group Eyes Managers' Jobs," *Wall Street Journal,* 22 October 1981, 1, 24.
"Women's Networks Come of Age," *New York Times Magazine,* 22 November 1981, 82, 87, 94, 96, 98, 99, 102.
"More Women in Retailing Earning Six Figure Salaries, but Their Proportion in Top Positions Is Still Low," *Women's Wear Daily,* 9 December 1981, 26–7.
"More than 40% of Major Corporations Now Have At Least One Woman Director," *Wall Street Journal,* 23 February 1982, 1.
"An Old Girl Network Renews Ties," *New York Times,* 25 February 1982, sec. II, 13.
"Women's Business School," *New York Times,* 24 March 1982, D1.
"Business Schools Try Harder to Find Jobs for More Demanding, Diverse Graduates," *Wall Street Journal,* 1 April 1982, 52.
"Firms Are Adding Female Directors More Slowly than in the 1970s," *Wall Street Journal,* 7 April 1982, 35.
"Management Gospel Gone Wrong," *New York Times,* 30 May 1982, sec. 3, F1, 21.
"Business Reassesses the MBA," *New York Times,* 30 June 1982, D17.
"Best Managers May Be Women," *Wall Street Journal,* 6 July 1982, 1.
"Business Schools: A Growing Concern," *Women's Wear Daily,* 23 July 1982, 8.
"Are MBAs More Faulty than Flawless on the Job?" *Women's Wear Daily,* 27 July 1982, 16.
"MBA, Ideally: More Basic Analysis," *New York Times,* 31 August 1982, A21.
"Weighing Majors for Cash Value," *New York Times,* 15 September 1982, D21.
"Changing Outlook for Black MBAs," *New York Times,* 11 October 1982, D1, D4.
"Entering Business School," *New York Times,* 8 December 1982, 21.
"Bringing the World into the Classroom," *New York Times,* 20 February 1983, sec. 3, F27.
"Top Business Schools Refocus Curricula," *Christian Science Monitor,* 17 May 1983, 11.
"Giving Managers New Tools," *New York Times,* 20 July 1983, A19.
"Finding Experts and Leaders: A Defense of the MBA," *Wall Street Journal,* 19 December 1983, 24.
"Wage Lag Is Found for White Women," *New York Times,* 16 January 1984, A1.
"Biz Schools Owe Students Better Service," *Wall Street Journal,* 10 February 1984, 26.
"Best Job Chances for Women," *New York Times,* 27 February 1984, B12.
"Small Business: Proposals for Washington, A Quiz, Women's Earnings," *Wall Street Journal,* 23 April 1984, 33.

"Jobless Rate Fell 0.3 Point in May," *New York Times,* 2 June 1984, 1.

"Networks for the Upscale Business Woman Gain Increasing Credibility," *Christian Science Monitor,* 25 June 1984, 15.

"Intensive MBA Programs," *New York Times,* 18 July 1984.

"Women in Their Twenties Form New Career Network," *New York Times,* 30 July 1984, A16.

"Labor Letter: The High Tech MBA," *Wall Street Journal,* 14 August 1984, 1.

"Technology's Dean: Elizabeth E. Bailey, a Computer Whiz at the Helm of Carnegie Mellon." *New York Times,* 26 August 1984, F5.

"Train Up an MBA in a Way He [*sic*] Can Think." *Christian Science Monitor,* 29 August 1984.

"Vive la difference? In Business World: Quelle Difference: Women Are Told to Emulate Men and Shun Provocation such as Open Toed Shoes." *Wall Street Journal,* 5 September 1984, 1.

"A Quicker Route to an MBA." *New York Times,* 16 September 1984, sec. 3, F15.

"Many Women Decide They Want Their Careers rather than Children." *Wall Street Journal,* 10 October 1984, 35.

"Top Women Executives Find Path to Power Is Strewn with Hurdles." *Wall Street Journal,* 25 October 1984, 35.

"Young Executive Women Advance Farther, Faster." *Wall Street Journal,* 26 October 1984, 33.

"Women Executives Feel That men Both Aid and Hinder Their Careers." *Wall Street Journal,* 29 October 1984, 35.

"Executive Women Find It Difficult to Balance Demands of Job, Home." *Wall Street Journal,* 30 October 1984, 33, 35.

"Executive Training Programs." *New York Times,* 14 November 1984, D17.

"Against the Odds: A Woman's Ascent on Wall Street." *New York Times,* 6 January 1985, 16.

"MBAs Shift away from Consulting as Investment-Banking Pay Rises." *Wall Street Journal,* 30 July 1985.

"Older Students See Alternatives to MBA Degree." *Wall Street Journal,* 10 September 1985.

"For Women on the Fast Track, the News Is Heartening." *Boston Globe,* 29 December 1985, 69, 74.

"The MBA: Is It Right for You?" *Worcester Magazine,* 8 January 1986, 19, 21.

"Recruiting Ordeal at Columbia." *New York Times,* 25 January 1986, 33, 42.

"The Corporate Woman: A Special Report." *Wall Street Journal,* 24 March 1986, section 4.

"Giving Up the Dream." *Boston Globe,* 25 March 1986, 43, 52, 53.

"New Action at Banks." *New York Times,* 8 July 1986, D20.

Resources

For basic information about business schools, consult the directories available in public libraries. To determine whether a school is accredited, write the American Assembly of Collegiate Schools of Business, 11500 Olive St., Suite 142, St. Louis, MO 63141 (314-872-8481). For more information about the Graduate Management Admission Test and MBA Forums held throughout the country (where different programs display their wares), write the Graduate Management Admission Council, Box 966, Princeton, NJ 08541. If you need financial aid, write the Graduate and Professional School Financial Aid Service, Box 2614, Princeton, NJ 08541. Some special sources of funding include:

Business and Professional Women's
  Foundation
2012 Massachusetts Ave. NW
Washington, DC 20009
Council for Opportunity in Graduate
  Management Education
675 Massachusetts Ave.
Cambridge, MA 02139

Minority Admissions Recruitment Network
Atlanta University Graduate School of
  Business
Central Office
223 Chestnut St. SW
Atlanta, GA 30314

There is a plethora of women's organizations and networks for women interested in MBAs or who already have MBAs, as well as others in business. Most urban communities have chapters of the Business and Professional Women's Clubs, as well as more specific networks for executive and managerial women. What follows is a small selection; to find what is available in your area, use local resources such as the YWCA, business reporters on the local newspaper, your peers, and national groups which may have local branches or contacts.

Advertising Women of New York
153 E. 57th St.
New York, NY 10022
212-593-1950

Alliance of Female-Owned Businesses
  Involved in Construction
c/o Wayne Equipment
13311 Stark Rd.
Livonia, MI 48150
313-522-9031

American Association of Black Women
  Entrepreneurs
1326 Missouri Ave., Suite 4
Washington, DC 20011
202-231-3751

American Business Women's Association
9100 Ward Parkway
P.O. Box 8728
Kansas City, MO 64114
816-361-6621

American Society of Professional and
   Executive Women
1511 Walnut St.
Philadelphia, PA 19102
215-563-4415

American Society of Women Accountants
35 E. Wacker Dr.
Chicago, IL 60601
312-726-9030

American Woman's Economic
   Development Corporation
60 E. 42d St.
New York, NY 10165
212-692-9100

American Woman's Society of Certified
   Public Accountants
500 N. Michigan Ave., Suite 1400
Chicago, IL 60611
312-661-1700

Association of MBA Executives, Inc.
227 Commerce St.
East Haven, CT 06512
203-467-8870

Catalyst
14 E. 60th St.
New York, NY 10022
212-759-9700

Cosmetic Executive Women
217 E. 85th St., Suite 214
New York, NY 10028
212-535-6177

Financial Women's Association of New
   York
P.O. Box 1605
New York, NY 10185
212-764-6476

International Association for Personnel
   Women
c/o AVIS/Replogle & Associates
5820 Wilshire Blvd.
Los Angeles, CA 90036
213-937-9000

National Association for Female Executives
120 E. 56th St.
1041 3d Ave.
New York, NY 10021
212-371-0740

National Association for Professional Sales
   Women
P.O. Box 255708
Sacramento, CA 25865
916-484-1234

National Association for the Self Employed
2324 Gravel Rd.
Fort Worth, TX 76118
817-589-2475

National Association for Women in Careers
P.O. Box 1383
Arlington Heights, IL 60006
312-870-8991

National Association of Bank Women
500 N. Michigan Ave., Suite 1400
Chicago, IL 60601
312-661-1700

National Association of Black Women
   Entrepreneurs
P.O. Box 1375
Detroit, MI 48231
313-341-7400

National Association of Insurance Women
P.O. Box 4410
1847 E. 15th
Tulsa, OK 74159
918-744-5195

National Association of Minority Women
   in Business
906 Grand Ave., Suite 500
Kansas City, MO 64116
816-421-3335

National Association of Women Business
   Owners
600 S. Federal St., Suite 400
Chicago, IL 60605
312-346-2330

National Black MBA Association
111 E. Wacker Dr.
Suite 600
Chicago, IL 60601
312-644-6610

National Forum for Executive Women
1101 15th St. NW, Suite 400
Washington, DC 20005
202-857-3100

National Network of Graduate Business
   School Women
University of Tennessee
Graduate Business Programs
527 Stokeley Management Center
Knoxville, TN 37996

National Network of Women in Sales
P.O. Box 578442
Chicago, IL 60657
312-577-1944

National Women's Economic Alliance
605 14th St. NW, Suite 900
Washington, DC 20005
202-393-5257

Professional Women in Construction
26 Easton Ave.
White Plains, NY 10605
914-328-9059

Section for Women in Public
  Administration
c/o Georgia Lyn Brown
6865 Newland St.
Arvada, CO 80003
303-825-7141

Women Entrepreneurs
1390 Market St., Suite 908
San Francisco, CA 94102
415-929-0129

Women in Data Processing
P.O. Box 22818
San Diego, CA 92122
619-569-5615

Women in Management
P.O. Box 11268
Chicago, IL 60611
312-963-0134

Women in Management Division
Academy of Management
c/o Dr. Marsha Katz
Loyola University of Chicago
Department of Management
820 N. Michigan Avenue
Chicago, IL 60611
312-670-2895

Women in Sales Association
Eight Madison Ave.
Valhalla, NY 10595
914-946-3802

Women Life Underwriters Conference
1922 F St. NW
Washington, DC 20006
202-331-6008